Be Lucky

Be Lucky

The story of George Martin
The Casual Comedian

Mike Martin

Copyright © 2012 Mike Martin.
All rights reserved.

No part of this publication may be reproduced, stored in a retrieval system, or transmitted, in any form or by any means, electronic, mechanical, photocopying, recording, or otherwise, without written permission of the author.

ISBN 978-0-9571967-0-4

Published by
MGM9 PUBLISHING
c/o GOWR
328 Grays Inn Rd.
London
WC1X 8BZ

Printed and bound by CPI Group (UK) Ltd, Croydon, CR0 4YY

For my sons, Laurie and Chris … so that they can
understand something about their grandfather,
who they never really knew.

And for my sister, Sue, and brother, Ray, in memory of our Dad,
who we did know… a bit.

*"Your dad was a really nice guy … probably too
nice for show-business …"*

(Sir Bruce Forsyth)

Contents

Foreword	viii
Introduction	xi
Acknowledgements	xiii
King Rat	1
The Little Shirt me Muvver Made for Me	4
Aldershot: Gateway to the World	11
War Under the Spotlight	18
One Stage at a Time	34
Into the Mill	42
A Star is Born	54
Variety	64
It's All in Black and White	79
Family Man?	94
Performer to Publican	108
Changing Times	115
Typing for the Taxman	126
Basil to the Rescue	133
David and Basil	139
A Double Life	149
Family Juggling	159
All Change	177
Decline	189
Salad Days Over	194
Swansong	203
The Final Curtain	209
Reflections	217
Index of Names	231

Foreword
by ROY HUDD OBE

As the author, Mike Martin, writes, "This book is a labour of love."

It's true. Mike's love for his dad, George, comes through on every page.

To those of us who only knew George as a fellow toiler in the field of comicking, he was very easy to love. He was an avuncular, gentle, witty, full of bonhomie, always ready for a party, topical joke writing, supremely professional performer.

Mike has captured all this in his diligently researched and detailed chronicle of "The Casual Comedian."

In Mike's own words, "Is his story worth telling? A forgotten comedian from over half a century ago?"

I say "Yes." George's story is an invaluable close up of the show business scene of the 1940's, 50s, 60s and 70s – a most important, yet invariably neglected, period of our show business heritage.

Mike is a dyed in the wool professional performer himself and so doesn't see the story through rose coloured spectacles.

He has tried, so very hard, to be objective about his Dad. He's tried to strike a balance between all the success, the rave notices, the worship of friends, the time spent raising money for charity and the other side. He's tried, with warts and all, to tell stories of a father who, through the pressures of the job he was doing, didn't spend as much time with his children as most other Dads did. But he still can't hide his pride in, and his love for, his all too scarcely seen father.

I must just quote, hidden away amongst anecdotes of George and his cronies late night carousing, one poignant little gem. A present from his Dad that Mike has never forgotten. A shoebox with a viewing hole cut in the end. It was a peepshow. He looked through the hole into a haunted house where a terrified figure in a four poster bed was assailed by floating ghosts and demons from a grandfather clock while bats fluttered at the ceiling. "All of it fashioned from pieces of card and thin wire." Who wouldn't love a Dad who'd make something like that? Or one who, when his son lay sobbing in bed dreading a dental appointment to replace a broken tooth, comforted him with wise words and made him laugh with some stories he'd never heard before. I bet Mike wrote them down!

Mike wants to know, and so do I, why isn't George remembered as well as so many of his contemporaries? He was certainly up there with all the big names. Just look at the list at the end of the book. He succeeded and became a top of the bill in variety, cabaret, pantomime (he was perhaps the best *Buttons* in *Cinderella* I've ever seen), radio and television. When he stopped performing regularly he took to writing. Perhaps this is the reason he isn't as well remembered. People still seem to think comics make it up as they go along. He became a writer of songs and parodies and, of course, of all his own highly topical material.

He then had a huge and lasting success. He created, with Ivan Owen, the personality of the unforgettable *Basil Brush*. He wrote Basil's shows and stage routines for years. The story of their parting is a sad one I'm afraid. Like Hancock with Galton and Simpson, Ivan thought he could do it without George.

Eventually, things couldn't have been worse for the loveable raconteur. He was confined to a hospital bed, unable to speak. What a fate for a man whose words, spoken or written, had earned him a living nearly all his life.

This celebration of that life has all the ingredients of a classic show business biography. It's packed with anecdotes, classic stories of comedians, singers and speciality acts - the famous and infamous.

Mike has woven a beautiful, affectionate and truthful picture of a talented enigma, something nearly all people who make us laugh are.

George was an original - as so many comics of yester-year were. I doubt if we'll ever see performers like him again. He belonged to a time when funny men were gentle souls. They didn't rush all over the stage shouting and swearing at the audience. They were, relaxed, laid back, and yes, casual. They let their audience come to them. Their intimate, "bloke telling you a story in a pub" characters have all but disappeared from the show business scene.

No more Max Millers, Jack Bennys, Robb Wiltons, Max Bygraves or , alas, George Martins.

Introduction

I am the youngest son of George Martin. At least, I *think* I am. He was so full of surprises (*some* of which are related in these pages) that I have come to the conclusion that his complete story will never be known.

I have done my best to tell the tale of a man who made his mark in show-business, even though he is largely forgotten now. The reasons for this are complicated. He had his moment of national fame and yet it disappeared with almost uncanny abruptness. The visual record of his performing career is virtually non-existent, and for years it seemed to me that his name was almost always omitted from any account of the era in which he was prominent. It was like a conspiracy.

And yet one does not have to delve very far into this book to find the proof of how significant he was. These pages are filled with glowing praise from numerous colleagues and friends, but I have striven to ensure that the compliments and respect are balanced with other available material to paint a definitive picture.

His catch phrase was "Be Lucky", and, in many ways, he certainly was... for most of his life anyway, although his last years were tinged with sadness and struggle.

From a working class background, he forged a career which took him into a world formerly unknown to his family, planting the seeds of a performing dynasty. From a "Boy Baritone", he developed into a first class artiste who played all the top venues in the land, became a star of radio and television, then a prolific scriptwriter for numerous high profile performers. Eventually he was as comfortable "hob-knobbing" at top society functions with Royalty as he was having a drink in the pub with his Aunt Queenie!

Like my sister and brother, I did not enjoy a typical father/child relationship with him. The nature of his profession did not allow that luxury. As we grew up, he was often absent; in fact it was an *event* when he was actually at home... and he was never around for long.

And yet we adored him.

Did he deserve it? That hardly matters. Whatever anyone thinks, he will always be on a pedestal for me, although there have been times when that pedestal got a little shaky.

The writing of this book has been a labour of love. Therapeutic too, because it has allowed me to lay many ghosts to rest. Some have said, or intimated, "Who cares?" but that is irrelevant too. A forgotten comedian from over half a century ago? Is his story worth telling?

The answer is a resounding "Yes". The saga of George Martin, The Casual Comedian, *does* matter, in its own right, because he earned his place in the history of British show-business and was much more than just an "also ran". As will be seen, his original style was an inspiration to many, a contribution which has previously been unjustly overlooked by the wider world. And his work as a writer deserves recognition too. My intention is to redress this balance and, hopefully, help his name find a place amongst the more familiar stars of post war entertainment.

But not only that. His story is interesting enough to be worthy of being heard anyway.

Bless you, Dad. I hope I have done you justice.

Acknowledgements

Apart from a lifetime of memories, so many sources contributed to the research for this book I do not think I will be able to list them all.

However, I would like to express my eternal thanks to all those who furnished me with material which locked itself into my brain long before I ever considered committing it all to paper. And then to those who specifically responded to my requests, a big thank you.

They are...

Liz Adams, Tom Anderson, Joe Baker, David Berglas, The Beverley Sisters (Joy, Babs and Teddy), Michael Black, Bryan Burdon, Kenny Cantor, Pat Church, Dec Cluskey, Paul Daniels, Freddie Davies, Roger de Courcey, Bill Egan, John Fisher, Bruce Forsyth, Derek Fowlds, Keith Harris, Roy Hudd, Mark Lewisohn, Matthew Lloyd, Joan Martin, Ray Martin, Sue Martin, Johnny Mans, Rocky Mason, Bill Maynard, Royston Mayoh, Chas McDevitt, Alan McGowan, Joyce McGowan, Vivienne Nixon, John O'Neill, Nicholas Parsons, Bill Pertwee, Jimmy Perry, Tom Plummer, Maurice Poole, Bob Potter, Mike Redway, Ed Stewart, Clive Stock, Ronnie Stringer, John Wade, Bert Weedon, Mike Winters, Bryn Williams, Chris Woodward and Cy Young.

Also much gratitude for the kind assistance of Jeff Walden at the B.B.C. Written Archives Centre (Caversham) and help from the staff of the British Film Institute and Archival Television Audio Incorporated.

And thank you Doug McKenzie for the use of several of your photographs, and Marjorie Regan for the cover design and her technical expertise.

Every effort has been made to identify the source of all the images in this book and they have been credited, with thanks, where possible.

Chapter 1

KING RAT

Sunday November 28th. 1971
The Great Room, Grosvenor House Hotel, Park Lane, London, W1.

The annual ball of the Grand Order of Water Rats. Opulence and grandeur in Great Britain's biggest banqueting room, with over 1,200 diners present for this revered event in the show-business calendar.

The King Rat of the Order surveyed his surroundings proudly. His year in office had been an eventful one. Looking up from his position at the centre of the top table, his gaze drifted across the names of Past King Rats, emblazoned on individual blue and gold banners draped from the surrounding balconies. Legendary stars of the entertainment profession such as Frankie Vaughan, Arthur Haynes, Ted Ray, Tommy Trinder, Robb Wilton, Bud Flanagan, "Wee" Georgie Wood and Will Hay; in fact going right back to the likes of Victorian Music Hall hero Dan Leno.

As King Rat for 1971, a new name would now be joining them for posterity. His own banner. A warm glow for a night to remember...

The Water Rats; long renowned as an exclusive club, a show-business brotherhood with charitable aims. Throughout the year so much had happened; fund raising shows and events, promotional visits and auctions, presentations to Royalty.

Much to be proud of indeed. And so much fun too. All those fortnightly meetings with Brother Rats in their private lodge room at the Eccentric Club in St. James'. Bonhomie and laughter. A unique place where pros gathered to swap anecdotes and plunge into a pit of nostalgia.

Speeches, presentations, cabaret… special words from the guest of honour, actor Edward Woodward. Fancy food, fine wines and drinks at outrageous prices, but who's counting on a night like this?

King Rat was wearing his well known benevolent smile and he turned it towards his lady, Maggie. She too was basking in the sheer joy of the occasion. Beaming like a Royal, she always excelled in situations such as this. A social asset, you might say. Larger than life, stunningly dressed, Maggie could always be counted upon to rise to the required social niceties. Only to be expected when one considered her past career as a leading light of the D'Oyly Carte opera company. Deep in conversation with actor Roger Moore, who was seated beside her, Maggie responded to her King Rat with a knowing nod.

All around them the magnificent room was buzzing with lively conversation, laughter and the tinkle of glasses. A sea of distinguished looking men in black dinner jackets, puffing on quality cigars and quaffing brandy, their ladies drifting between the tables of white linen, resplendent in their glittering ball gowns.

Swinging to the infectious rhythm of Edmundo Ros and his Latin American Orchestra, the dance floor was filled with grandly clad bodies and wherever one's eyes fell, a famous face could be seen. Henry Cooper, Les Dawson, Vera Lynn, Mantovani, Dickie Henderson, Sandie Shaw, Hughie Green and Rolf Harris, to name but a few on the guest list … like a "who's who" of the entertainment profession.

Just below the top table, well within the eye line of King Rat, sat his special guests. In a circle like King Arthur's knights, but on a round table which groaned under the weight of myriad bottles and decoration, this was reserved for family and close friends. King Rat's sister Joyce and her husband Bob, who at one time had shared the stage with his brother-in-law for some of his earliest professional appearances. Also their son Alan, and King Rat's younger brother Bill, another stalwart of the profession. He and Bob probably knew more about King Rat's colourful past than anybody.

Billy and Annie McComb were there too, Billy being a silver tongued Irish magician whose career mirrored that of his host.

And then there was King Rat's daughter, Sue.

At 25 years old, Sue was a belle of the ball. Immensely proud of her dad, there had been some typical teenage problems, but deep down she was aware of the closeness she shared with him. As a child she had adored the glamour and magic of show-business. From Christmas parties at the Windmill Theatre and the backstage atmosphere of variety halls, through to the pantomimes which she could never see too much of. She loved to dance and sing, and knew all the words of the songs her dad wrote for these shows.

With children of her own now, Sue could not help but feel a little special as she made her entrance down the sweeping staircase, escorted by Eric Morecambe and Ernie Wise, one on either arm.

As for King Rat, he was making the most of his night. It was the pinnacle of a varied career, one which had seen many ups and downs, but tonight belonged to him. With the plaudits of his colleagues, Brother Rats and scores of others ringing in his ears, he could take pride in the fact that regardless of anything else, he had been placed at the top of the tree. This really meant something. Voted here by his peers, a symbol of the depth of affection and respect he had won in a business not renowned for fair play.

A long road and a tale which involves the many aspects of the post war entertainment profession, a business both ruthless and enchanting.

The story of George Martin, the Casual Comedian.

Chapter 2

THE LITTLE SHIRT ME MUVVER MADE FOR ME

George Martin's ancestry bears no relation to the entertainment pedigree which would eventually dominate his family.

His grandfather, Fred Martin, was an unremarkable chap it seems. Born in 1864 in Suffolk, the eldest of the eleven children produced by Benjamin Martin and his wife Eliza, Fred followed a long family tradition by becoming an agricultural labourer. Ben's father William had worked the land too, likewise *his* father, (also a William) and they all sired many children. Not a lot else to do in 19th. century East Anglia, I guess!

Victorian England not being a land of great opportunity for average individuals, it is little wonder that so many young men chose to take the Queen's shilling and join the army. When Fred enrolled in the Norfolk Militia at Great Yarmouth in 1884, it was at a time when the British Empire was at its peak. It was said that the sun never set on the Queen's world wide dominions, and, as one of her red coated soldiers, naïve youths might well get the chance to see some of it.

Of course, that also meant the odds were fairly high that one might be plunged into great danger facing enemies such as fierce Zulus or bloodthirsty Afghan tribesmen, but, depending upon survival, it would all result in good storytelling for the grandchildren.

However, Fred was not destined to play a role in any of history's memorable conflicts. And judging by his military records he did not quite possess the physical attributes of a warrior hero. With scars on his torso and standing less than 5ft 6in in height, he weighed a little over 9 stone, with a chest measurement of 32 inches; not exactly a man mountain. Then, having undergone 56 day's training at the depot and several month's service as a militia man, he enlisted in the 4th. Norfolk Regiment's 1st. Battalion in January 1885. By this time his chest had apparently expanded by one and three quarter inches, so it seems that army life was good for him. He also attained a Certificate of Education (*4th*. Class!) in the same year.

Fred is described as having a fresh complexion with light brown hair and blue eyes, his religion being recorded as Wesleyan. He served in Gibraltar, India and Rangoon but there is no record of anything notable having occurred, except for his marriage to 17 year old Alice Charlesworth in 1887. As one of the "Holy Boys", presumably he was an able enough soldier because that same year he was granted an extra penny Good Conduct Pay to add to his weekly shilling, and this was increased by a further penny 4 years later. (The Norfolks were known as the "Holy Boys" because of their cap badge insignia which represented Brittania. In the 18th. century Spanish soldiers had mistakenly thought this to be the Virgin Mary.)

Completing his service in January 1893, Fred was transferred to the Army Reserve List and worked at several jobs in civilian life including becoming a bricklayer's labourer, plus a spell toiling in the laundry at Sandhurst Military Academy. He did, however, follow the family tradition of producing numerous children (8, in fact) and it is interesting to note that the eldest, Kate, was born just 3 months after his wedding. Either the shortest gestation period in history or he and Alice had been careless whilst indulging in an age old activity. And this at a time when such situations could be socially disastrous.

Stationed for a time in the garrison town of Aldershot, Hampshire, the young couple had been wed in the nearby hamlet of Frimley, Surrey; presumably the district where they had met. Coming out of the army, Fred and his family decided to settle in the Aldershot area, and although he was recalled to the military at the outbreak of the Boer War in 1899, once again the records are hazy and it is not certain if he actually went back into action. What *is* known is that he died of heart failure in 1902, at the young age of 37, and was buried in Hawley, Hampshire.

Fred and Alice's 4th. child, a son named William, was born in 1896. He grew up to be quite a slight fellow, like his father, but he apparently had a good head for figures. Placid by nature, he was also musical and took up the round backed mandolin. When the First World War broke out in 1914, he joined the Royal Navy.

As a midshipman on H.M.S. Opportune he experienced his share of seaborne action, wherein the roar of the gigantic guns left him with a lifelong hearing impediment. When the war ended in 1918, he left the Navy and enrolled on an accountant's course during which time he met his future wife.

Lil Vinden was not outwardly a perfect match for Bill Martin. She was a large woman, not so much in build but in personality, and it seemed she somehow dwarfed him at times. Her family were big and brash, bred from Romany stock. Lil had seven sisters and two brothers, although one, George, had died as a toddler.

The parents were George Vinden and Emily Ayres, both colourful characters whose families did not fit any conventional mould. The Vindens were independent traders and the Ayres had fairground connections; painted horse-drawn caravans, the lot.

Old George sold all kinds of things from the back of his cart. Often it was fish which he would take to Ascot, then, usually inebriated, he would sleep it off on the ride home and let his well schooled horse take the lead. The only stop would be to dump the unsold merchandise into the canal.

They lived at Upper Hale, near Aldershot, but their first child, Mary Ann (known as Polly), is a bit of a mystery because her birth records state "father unknown" and she is registered as Ayres. The plot thickens because she was apparently rather sweet and demure by nature whereas the rest of the family, were, (and I quote those who knew them) somewhat "rough and ready"!

So, after Polly came Alice, Edie, Lil, Gertie, Ivy, Queenie, ill fated George, Doris and a boy named Stan.

As this rowdy bunch made its mark around the area, mainly in the local pubs, Lil grew up favouring bar work. Being a garrison town, Aldershot's hostelries were mostly frequented by troops and

Lil soon learned how to deal with drunken men, although she was actually working as a waitress at the Angel Hotel in nearby Guildford when she met Bill Martin.

This unlikely couple obviously connected because, regardless of surface differences, they remained together for the rest of their long lives. With ups and downs, of course, but perhaps it helped when Lil would nag Bill in her fiery way and he was able to escape by switching off his hearing aid!

The newly married couple took rooms in Pavilion Road, Aldershot, and it was there that their first child was born on February 26th. 1922; a boy whom they named George Frederick after both their fathers.

Hard to imagine then that this wrinkled bundle would one day become the Casual Comedian.

It was not long before siblings arrived to join George…Joyce (1924) and Bill (1927).

The senior Bill was working for the Borough Council now, reading and emptying meters, although he supplemented his income by selling Walls ice cream from an adapted bicycle. He had to stop paying visits to his family's road however, because it was becoming too obvious that free samples were depleting his supply.

The children were happy, indulging themselves in the simple fun which abounded between the world wars. Not well off, but comfortable enough, they made plenty of friends locally when attending the East End infant's school, and later Newport Road school. Young George was a popular lad who took to all manner of sports with great enthusiasm. Very much "one of the boys", he also delighted in pranks, especially if it involved affectionately tormenting his sister. Joyce would regularly be terrified by her elder brother locking her in the outside toilet and continuously pulling the chain. He would also make her a special drink of vinegar, mashed bread and pickled onions which she would be "persuaded" to consume. Regardless of all this, she thought the world of him!

Aldershot in those days would be habitually visited by travelling entertainers, one of whom was a hard bitten adventurer with a wooden leg who called himself Dare Devil Peggy. His speciality involved diving from a high board into a flaming pool, a spectacle which enthralled the local populace.

Keen to emulate this showmanship, George would take a penny from Joyce's pocket money every Friday to buy paraffin and a little cellophane doll. He would then stage his own version of Dare Devil Peggy's routine. Unlike Peggy, the doll never survived.

Apart from this, George showcased his early stage desires in many ways. He loved to sing, and his grandad would stand him on the table and reward him with a penny for warbling *The Little Shirt Me Muvver Made For Me*. Ronnie, the son of Aunt Alice, recalled sometimes dancing with his cousin for the old man. "And George always come up best", he smiled, along with memories of rides on the cart, with boozy grandad asleep, as the horse "saw us home".

Aldershot had it's own variety theatre too; the Hippodrome, so young George and the other local children would have plenty of opportunity to "star spot" the big names of the day. By hanging around the stage door, they would catch fleeting glimpses of the likes of Arthur Askey and the Western Brothers. And then there was the "tuppeny rush" at the cinema, when for the grand sum of two pennies, kids could run amok rushing for the front seats to view the latest big films from Hollywood, a world so far away, it might as well have been another planet. Great value for money in those days. Two big features starring idols such as Douglas Fairbanks, along with the comedies of Laurel and Hardy. All this with an orange thrown in for free!

It was not until 1931 that another child came along to complete the Martin family; a sister, Rita, whom everyone doted upon. For practical reasons, another move was necessary and so a three bed-roomed house was found in Chetwode Place near the public lido.

Along with being a keen cricketer, footballer, runner and hurdler, George was also an accomplished swimmer and he spent a lot of time in the pool. As soon as he could, he got a job there as a lifeguard. Physically, he did not take after his dad, and although slim, was actually quite well built, eventually growing to a height of approximately 5 feet 11 inches.

Although Lil's sisters gradually dispersed to other areas of the country, notably London, they were a close knit family who loved nothing better than a good booze up and sing-song. Granny Vinden (nee Ayres) enjoyed her Guinness and at gatherings would always end up singing "Hif hoi had moi way, hoi would neffer grow oolldd …"

As for the lone, surviving son, Stan, who, as the baby of the family was totally adored and beyond reproach, he developed his own methods of making ends meet.

Red haired and ruddy faced, Stan followed his Romany roots, never settling as he battled his way through life. Wheeling and dealing, he could turn his hand to anything and often did. Outwardly charming, Stan had an instantly likeable personality, but he was also devious with an eye for any opportunity going. A lovable rogue who possessed a natural antagonism towards any kind of officialdom. Consequently, he was forever pulling strokes which would get him into all kinds of trouble, very often implicating friends and family who would inevitably forgive him anything. Visits to his council house would unveil such sights as coal in the bath, a goat tied to a tree in the garden, and, apparently a horse in the front room! He was as hard as nails too and was never reluctant to settle disputes with his fists. On one occasion, a man in a pub made the mistake of insulting one of his sisters and Stan put things right by punching the man from one end of the bar to the other.

George, Joyce, Bill and Rita were much favoured by their gregarious relatives and they grew up in an atmosphere of good time partying. Pub people through and through.

Like virtually all youngsters of his generation, George was smoking heavily, a social necessity in those days, without any health concerns. Frequenting the pubs and local clubs with his mates as soon as he could, George became a well known local face, taking any opportunity he could to show off his fine deep singing voice. He soon went under the name of The Boy Baritone.

The term "teenager" was unknown then. Young people did not have their own style of dress and an average 16 year old would just resemble a fresh faced version of their parents; a young man donning a dull jacket, tie and baggy trousers. However, the spirit of the young burned as brightly as any generation before or since, and this particular generation would soon be caught up in events which would not only upend their lives but also the organization and outlook of the entire world.

A sporting youth. George, as a boy, sitting in the middle, second from the left.

As a nattily dressed 17 year old.

Chapter 3

ALDERSHOT: GATEWAY TO THE WORLD

On leaving school, George gained employment as an office boy at the Mid-Southern Utility Company where he became close friends with a lad in the same situation, one Bill Egan. They shared many interests, not least of all a passion for music and the numerous dance bands which were so popular in the late 1930s. Bill recalled George's considerable artistic talent and of how he would produce colourful illustrations with appropriate captions, such as a dancing gas cooker and a pale blue flame character with the name "Mr. Therm". It seems that some of George's ideas were used commercially, ("Brilliantly conceived," said Bill) but he never received any financial reward for his efforts.

The atmosphere at Mid-Southern, despite the japes of George, Bill and co., was rather Dickensian. The boy's department was supervised by a dour figure named Mr. West who would sit on a high stool at his desk, overlooking his minions like Ebenezer Scrooge. Mr. West possessed a pedestal telephone which had an ear-piece extended on a line which attached to the main instrument.

George decided that it would be a laugh to press this earpiece onto an inkpad and then wait for Mr. West to receive a call. Inevitably, when the much anticipated call came, the office was in uproar when the long faced supervisor ended up with a black ear, stained with an indelible substance which could not be removed for days!

It seems this cost George his job, but he probably considered the resulting hilarity worth it. From here he became a meter reader, like his father had been, and there are endless stories of the various impish stunts he and his friends carried out to get them through the routine days of work.

Once he was ordered to move a huge pile of box files from one floor to the floor below and he decided that it would save time and effort to lower them down, tied with string, from the outside window. Unfortunately, the string broke and dozens of neatly filed documents blew chaotically up the street.

On another occasion, George and his gang were made aware of a new product called Ex-Lax, a strong laxative which, to the eye and taste, resembled chocolate. Acquiring some, they first of all offered it around to the unsuspecting office girls, and then a considerable amount was eaten by the manager. He was a big fellow with a huge walrus moustache. At first all seemed normal until suddenly the manager could be seen running desperately towards the lavatory, shedding articles of clothing. "I've never seen a man wear so many waistcoats," said George, many years later. Unfortunately for this manager, the effects of the Ex-Lax were far reaching because when he was riding his bicycle up-hill on his way home that evening, the effort of pedalling brought about the full effect!

George also had an excellent ear for music and it was natural that he would gravitate towards playing an instrument. His early attempts at playing his dad's mandolin were unsuccessful because he could not manoeuvre his large, club ended fingers around the narrow neck and frets. He always remained frustrated by his clubbed fingers which prevented him from playing stringed instruments. However, he took much more easily to the piano accordion which his dad had also acquired.

This bulky instrument seemed made for George and he would spend hours finding his way around the keys and bellows, picking out tunes and accompanying his vocals. The first tune he mastered to his satisfaction was *Pennies from Heaven*, and he would proudly play this party-piece to pub audiences whenever the opportunity arose. This brief display of talent was satisfactory until one evening he found himself cornered by a burly drunken Irishman who demanded that he play some tunes from the "awld country". George's protests that he could only play the one tune did not impress this unreasonable Fenian, and it was only when a large clenched fist was held threateningly under George's nose that he suddenly found his repertoire expanding to include something which resembled jigs and reels! They still sounded suspiciously like *Pennies from Heaven* though!

Teaching himself was fine, but his ability took great leaps of progress when he found someone to show him more advanced techniques.

Regularly frequenting the local drinking establishments and halls of entertainment had put him in close proximity to musicians who played in the many bands working the circuit. He became well known to them, especially as he would get on stage to sing or lark about as often as he could. One of the band leaders, a pianist named Jack Marshall, became fond of George and was impressed by his enthusiasm and budding talent. Jack soon took George under his wing, starting by showing him a few tricks to improve his accordion playing but soon progressing to regular piano lessons at his house. An accomplished musician himself, Jack found a

The Tango Trio – Jack, Jim and George.

willing pupil in George who quickly took on board the rudiments of music theory. Before long George had become part of The Tango Trio with Jack on piano and a lad named Jim on double bass. One of their early, prestigious gigs involved playing at the opening of the swish new Ritz Cinema in Victoria Road, a dominating edifice which George's uncle, Stan Vinden, had helped to construct.

In early 1939, with snow on the ground, 17 year old George found himself spending one Saturday night at the Parish Church Hall in Church Lane. This was not really a regular haunt of his, but for some reason he was at one of the hall's weekly socials; another excuse to listen to music, have a drink and a laugh and maybe a few dances with the local girls. Of course, he knew most of the people in attendance, at least by sight, and soon the evening was filled with laughter and the swish of dancing feet.

The band was in full swing as they called everyone onto the floor for the party events. A big circle was formed and the crowd were told that they had to pick a partner. It was then that George found himself in the company of a pretty girl with long, wavy dark hair who grabbed him by the hand .

He knew her vaguely, although it is doubtful that they had ever really spoken up to this point. However, he knew her brother, Doug Hewitt, who worked at the Mid-Southern with him. Right now though, she was smiling and egging him on and he responded willingly, even though she had the advantage of being 5 months older than him. (A big gap when you are 17!)

Her name was Joan and they were soon connecting like a house on fire, going through the animated moves of *Underneath the Spreading Chestnut Tree*, swaying back and forth, with arms in the air as they simulated the bending branches of the said tree. Simple fun, but a great hoot in 1939!

By the end of the evening, George and Joan were still together and he offered to walk her home. She explained that she was with her brother who was standing away from them. Casting a few dark looks in their direction, Doug, a couple of years older than Joan, had been entrusted by their parents to look after his sister that evening, a chore he was reluctantly carrying out. The Hewitts lived at the top of the town in Frederick Street, completely in the opposite direction to George whose family had recently moved to Boxalls Lane, but this was no deterrent for the smitten youth.

And so they walked together to her front gate. It took about thirty minutes but must have seemed longer with Doug striding watchfully ahead of them. George suggested that they meet the following day and Joan accepted.

When he knocked at the door on Sunday afternoon, Joan came out to greet him and asked, "What are we going to do?"

"I thought we might go and visit my granny," suggested George.

This was a great disappointment to Joan who thought she might be getting treated to the cinema. Forthright by nature, she looked him straight in the eye and asked, "What would I want to visit your granny for?"

George was undeterred, ushering her along , by foot, towards Granny's house. Not mean by nature, but a little embarrassed, George declined to tell her that he had only "thruppence" to his name. This was because on the previous night he had accidentally knocked over a tray of drinks and this had cost him most of his wages.

Unaware of this, Joan was not very impressed by her first date with George Martin. By the time they had left the company of Granny Vinden and George had escorted Joan home, she had made up her mind that she was not over keen to see him again.

As it happened, fate would not keep them apart for long.

Joan worked as a cashier at Thomas Whites' store and George suddenly began making regular appearances to read the meter. Her desk was at the top of the stairs where the meter was located and she soon got used to him turning up. Also, it seemed that the meter at her home needed reading more than anyone else's, because George became a familiar face there too, especially when Joan's mum, Florrie, welcomed him with cups of tea.

Joan also used to see him at other social occasions, so it was only a short time before she and her friend Joan Evans were going around as a foursome with George and Bill Egan. One night, early in their courtship, at a dance at Badshot Lea Scout Hut, Jack Marshall's band were playing and Jack called George up onto the stage.

Unaware of George's talent at this time, Joan cringed and thought,

"Oh gawd, what's this going to be like?" but she was pleasantly surprised, in fact impressed, by his confident rendition of *Lords of the Air*.

From then on, Joan got used to seeing George's regular stage appearances as his accordion playing improved and he began gigging around the area.

As the youth of Aldershot enjoyed itself with uncomplicated pursuits, getting on with their jobs and making the most of their limited leisure time, world events were taking a much darker turn.

Great Britain's conservative government was in turmoil over the activities of Germany's *Reich Fuhrer* Adolf Hitler. Prime Minister Neville Chamberlain, a mild mannered fellow, was wary of confrontation but he knew that matters were reaching the point where something had to be done. How much more appeasement could the nations of Europe tolerate as the Aryan dictator pursued his policy of swallowing up the continent?

Austria, the Czechoslovakian Sudetenland, Czechoslovakia itself, and now Poland facing invasion. Under great pressure, Chamberlain reluctantly decided to act. German armed forces had swept into Poland, and the British government, supported by France and other countries, issued an ultimatum. If Germany did not agree to withdraw their assault by 11am. on the morning of September 3rd. 1939, then war would be declared.

It was a Sunday and Joan had set off in the morning for George's home with a kitten for his sister Joyce. By 11am. the whole family were seated around the wireless set waiting for the Prime Minister's promised broadcast. 15 minutes later Chamberlain came on air to utter those immortal words, "… no such undertaking has been received".

Bill Martin senior gave a sigh and muttered, "Not again", his mind doubtless thrown back to the horrors of the first world war. For the youngsters, it was all a bit of a lark and quite exciting. George and Joan decided to go out for a walk and as they strolled up Cranmore Lane, they both noticed a strangely still atmosphere. No one seemed to be around. For a while they sat on the summit of a hill, staring at the sky and expecting to see German bombers come sweeping in.

Nothing happened, however, and so they made their way to Joan's house for lunch where Joan's dad, Jack, was quietly reflective about the news. He had every right to be, having won the Military Medal as a Tommy fighting on the Somme in 1915.

That afternoon, George and Joan went out again and found themselves at the bottom of Redan Hill at the Drill Hall, which was the headquarters for the Territorial Army. There, behind the fence, along with many other local lads, was their friend Bill Egan, already in uniform. As a member of the T.A., no time had been wasted in calling in the army reserve. Passing drinks to Bill through the wire, they all began to realise that this might be a serious business after all. They were not to meet again for years.

Chapter 4

WAR UNDER THE SPOTLIGHT

George was keen to enlist, but at 17, and not being a member of the T.A., he would have to wait until his birthday in February. Not wishing to waste any time, like so many others, he immediately enrolled in the local Home Guard and did his bit marching about with a broom handle over his shoulder. No guns for "Dad's Army" at this stage of the war.

Joan was now working at the department store Park and Sparkles, a job she disliked because of the dowdy atmosphere. The wages were terrible and she was tired of the miserable "fogeys" she worked with, one of whom was an old spinster who heartily disapproved of Joan meeting her boyfriend after work. Part of Joan's job was to put loose change into a metal chamber which was whizzed around the store's ceiling on a wire. One day this chamber was not attached properly, and as it passed over Mr. Sparkles (who was up a ladder), it dislodged, dropped through the air and hit him on the head.

About as amused as Mr. West had been by the inking of his ear, Joan's irate boss accused her of doing it on purpose.

Defiant to the end, Joan replied, "On purpose? If I was that clever, I wouldn't be working here, would I?"

That was her cue to leave, and when she turned 18, later that month, she was taken on as a trainee operator at the military telephone exchange.

George spent a few frustrating months kicking his heels, watching many of his friends go into the forces, but finally, on his 18th.

birthday, he was able to join them. He had already decided that the army was not for him. Too predictable in Aldershot. Also, the blue uniform of the Royal Air Force was much nicer than khaki. Something more glamorous about the R.A.F. as well.

The thought of zooming around the skies engaging in chivalrous combat with the Luftwaffe seemed to be an appealing way to fight a war, and so, with a couple of his mates, he tried to enlist. They decided that they wanted to be gunners, but this was early in the hostilities when manpower was not in short supply. Entry restrictions for air crew were particularly conditional and George failed his medical owing to a childhood bout of rheumatic fever which, technically, had left him with a weak heart. Deeply disappointed, George said goodbye to his mates, both of whom were accepted. Within a few months, news came through that they had both been killed in action.

George was able to enlist as ground crew, however, initially going into the R.A.F. Regiment whose role was similar to infantry in that they were to guard airfields.

His basic training took place in Blackpool, the furthest he had ever been away from home at this time. It was a baptism of fire, but such was the case for many thousands of youngsters who found themselves in the same situation. They were all in it together, of course, and a general feeling of camaraderie soon prevailed. One northern lad named Alwyn Brightmore, who met George at the time, recalled indulging in such frivolous activities as urinating in one another's boots!

George quickly made new friends in the billet, and his entertaining skills made him especially popular. Not with literally everyone, though. One corporal decided to abuse his position and began to make a habit of coming down hard on the new recruits. A bully to the core, this character was making his presence felt by casting a dark cloud over the otherwise "chummy" atmosphere. One evening, as the men relaxed in their hut, this corporal began throwing his weight around, as usual, shouting and even taking swipes at various individuals.

George was sitting on his bunk cleaning his rifle. Aware of what was happening, he decided that something would have to be done to nip this in the bud. As the corporal reached him and started to open his mouth, George swung around and pointed the rifle straight at the astonished bully's face.

"I'm telling you now, "said George flatly, "if you come at me, I shall smash this rifle over your head. If that doesn't stop you, I shall clip the bayonet on and stab you, and if *that* doesn't stop you, I shall put a bullet in the breech and shoot you. Alright?"

The corporal swallowed heavily and nodded. He got the point and never bothered George again.

The night sky was completely clear. Black as coal and illuminated by the bright twinkling of countless stars.

AC2 (Aircraftsman 2nd. Class) George Martin, hunched in his R.A.F. issue greatcoat and, cradling his .303 rifle, took in the spectacle with a sense of wonderment. He was all alone at his gun post, in the middle of the night, passing the monotony of the dragging hours by indulging in a spot of philosophy.

With nothing else to do, he was able to devote a lot of thought to the concept of infinity, even though the very idea of it was making his mind spin. How far away were those stars? What lay beyond them? How could something never end?

Aircraftsman George Martin

Pondering on such matters was not usually on the agenda for the average working class lad from Hampshire, but young George's life had been through many changes over the last few weeks. Service life, new friends and experiences, education, opportunity and travel. From Blackpool, his first posting had been across the sea to Northern Ireland; to the station at R.A.F. Aldergrove where he now sat on yet another all night guard duty.

There had been grim experiences too. Once, as he sat at his post at the end of the runway, an aircraft sped towards him, gathering speed as it prepared to take off. Instead of soaring into the air, as expected, George was stunned to witness what appeared to be some kind of explosion from somewhere on board. Instinctively ducking as the faltering aeroplane roared over his head, its propellers almost clipping his cap, George turned and watched in horror as it dipped towards a nearby barrack room which he knew was filled with young airmen getting ready for the evening.

The moment seemed to take on a slow motion quality as the helpless George saw the stricken machine plough relentlessly into the building, exploding as it did so and engulfing the whole area in a fireball. Any human screams were hidden by the deafening booms of multiple explosions as whistling debris flew through the air.

It took a long time before any rescue teams could get anywhere near the inferno, but when they finally did, it was a sickening sight.

George was involved in the clean-up operation; by far the worst task he had ever had to undertake in his short life. There was not much left to see which resembled the hut full of laughing youngsters, who one moment had been so vibrant before being swamped by fire and shrapnel. Instead, their place had been taken by a blackened, twisted mass of smoking wreckage, wreathed in the nauseating stench of burned flesh.

George had known these men. He kicked a smouldering boot aside, only to see that it contained a section of severed foot. Elsewhere a large charred stump was recognized as the shape of an airman roasted into position as he shaved, his razor still in his hand.

This had not even been the result of enemy action. Rumour soon spread that this was sabotage, the work of the I.R.A. who would do anything to exploit their desire to remove British rule from Ireland. Eire had already declared its neutrality in the war.

All in all though, George enjoyed his time in the "Mob", as it was affectionately called. Unlike many, he had a lucky war. Following on from his civilian trade where he had begun training as an electrician, he eventually qualified under R.A.F. guidance and started fitting bombers with their wiring.

He still kept in regular touch with Joan and saw her whenever he could get home on leave. Although Joan was in what was known as a "reserved occupation" at the military telephone exchange (which meant that she was exempt from conscription), she decided to volunteer anyway and in early 1942 she also joined the air force. This was the W.A.A.F., of course, the Women's Auxiliary Air Force, where she was employed using her skills as a telephone operator. Before long she was sent to a remote area of Southern Scotland, R.A.F. Wigtown, while George was stationed at the other end of the country at a base near Cambridge.

Even so, regardless of the distance, they decided to get married and this they did at St. Michael's Parish Church, Aldershot, on May 16th. 1942, during a few snatched days leave.

It was a fun filled family wedding during which two worlds collided. Joan's family were quiet people, straight laced and home loving, whereas George's relations, as usual, used the occasion as another excuse for a boozy "knees-up". The sisters came out in force, (most of them having relocated back to the area to escape the Blitz) dancing, singing, drinking and bickering, but it was all in the spirit of one hell of a good time! Never had the Badshot Lea Working Men's Club seen more action, all to the strains of Jack Marshall's excellent little band. George got up to perform with them for old time's sake.

Uncle Stan was there too, up to one of his scams, naturally. He was working as a cab driver, for a firm belonging to a family friend, Cyril Parlane. Cyril had supplied a free cab service to the happy couple as a wedding present and Stan was doing his bit. One of Joan's sober and naïve aunts had remarked on the nice young man who had picked her up at the station; so nice, in fact, that she had given him a handsome tip on top of the fare. Fare? These cabs were supposed to be free! Stan was the driver in question.

Being a strapping, fit looking chap, Stan, in his trilby hat, seemed rather out of place around the town where just about every single able bodied man was in uniform. The reason for this was medical, apparently, but he was often confronted by soldiers who wanted to know how he had managed to escape being called up. It was particularly an issue for the Canadian squaddies, it seems, who were a dominating force around Aldershot at this time, frustrated and far from home. If they got too confrontational with their questions, Uncle Stan would respond in the time honoured fashion and it is a family legend which claims that he put more Canadian soldiers in hospital than the German Army did!

Enjoyable wedding and reception aside, there was a war on, so no honeymoon. The newlyweds spent that night back at Joan's parent's house. Celebrations continued, however, and Joan recalled an occasion when the two of them, both in uniform, were trying to get home after another party when George collapsed unconscious in a hedge. If a jeep full of Canadians had not come by and offered assistance, he probably would have stayed there until the morning!

Before long, George and Joan were separated again and had to return to their respective bases. And then came the bombshell.

George was going to be stationed abroad.

This was a huge concern. Newly married, it was bad enough

May 16th. 1942. Bill and Lil, younger brother Bill, sister Joyce, sister Rita, George, Joan, Julie Stonehouse, "Pip" Toomer (Joan's cousin), Florrie and Jack (Joan's parents).

being separated in the United Kingdom without the added stress of being continents apart. Joan remembered how her brother Doug, fresh in the Army in early 1940, had been on his way to France when the country had capitulated and he had been re-routed to the Middle East. That had been more than 2 years ago and the family had not seen him since. (In fact, he was not to return until after the war; another 3 years.)

Speculation grew as to where George might be sent. There were so many dangerous theatres of conflict; the battlegrounds of the middle eastern deserts, the horrors of warfare against the Japanese in the jungles of the Far East…

But George's luck was to hold. He got sent to Canada.

As far as postings went, Canada was probably just about the most desired of all.

It did mean being a long way from home for an extended period, but where the war was concerned, it could hardly be safer.

Surrounded by prairies and wide open skies, with the Atlantic Ocean on one side and the Pacific on the other, one would be well out of range of enemy fire. The R.A.F. had established several bases there, where air crew could be trained in safety, and George found himself first of all at Swiftcurrent, close to the North American border. Later he would be transferred to the exotically named Moosejaw in Saskatchewan.

By now he was 20 years old, a seasoned airman who knew all the tricks. (No longer an "Erk", as novice airmen were known.) Almost immediately he was snapped up by the base's concert party and was soon well involved in shows for the entertainment hungry servicemen. This put him in a privileged position and enabled him to have quite a "cushy" time.

On a personal level, these must have been great days for the young men fortunate enough to be placed in such a dreamlike location. They had only ever experienced surroundings like this in the cowboy movies they had seen before the war, never imagining that they would one day be sent there at the government's expense.

George made the most of it and had a whale of a time. Amongst his many new pals, his closest affinity evolved with a tall, broad shouldered Scotsman from Edinburgh, named Bob McGowan. Bob was a handsome devil, with a fashionable pencil thin moustache. Quietly spoken but sharing George's wicked sense of humour, the pair quickly became firm friends. Bob also had a hankering for the stage, a passion which was hugely helped by him being blessed with a fine singing voice. A smooth, baritone crooner of the first degree; the kind of vocal which was very much in vogue in the 1940s. "Frank Sinatra with muscles," is how George used to introduce him.

It did not take them long to start performing together and they honed a polished act; Martin & McGowan. This review from a local newspaper of just one of the shows they did conjures up an impression of what they must have been like; *"... George Martin and Bob McGowan, entertainers de-luxe! George and his piano-accordion and lovely voice and smile, and Bob's soothing singing just took them by storm, and they kept encoring them so long the boys were near exhaustion. They put up a swell show, the two of them, and Pennant won't forget even if they have to put on a special chicken dinner for them again"*!!!

Pals: George and Bob

There were good times a-plenty, and being so close to the border, they were able to travel regularly down into the United States itself, to cities such as Chicago, where, in their R.A.F. blue, they were welcomed like war heroes. British accents were a real novelty to Americans in those days and, it seems, the girls adored them.

Bob used to speak wistfully of the time they hi-jacked an ambulance for transport. Engrossed in an intimate party with some young ladies in the back of the vehicle, they failed to notice the handbrake slipping. Suddenly realising that they were slopping about in water, they awoke to the fact that they had rolled down the slope into a river!

George and Bob were so close that George would entrust his friend with his wages every week, because they both knew that he would blow it all immediately if he had the chance. This was an attitude to finance that George would retain throughout his entire life.

Alongside his love for music and entertainment, George also kept his sporting instincts. He took up boxing for a while and became fairly proficient. That was until a bout with a huge sailor wherein he took such a beating that he thought, "Why am I doing this?"

This was around the same time when, in the street outside a bar one night, he decided to go to the rescue of a woman who was being knocked about by her partner. Attempting to intervene by confronting the "wife beater", George was stunned to receive heavy blows from behind as the woman set about him with her handbag crying out, "Leave him alone!" So much for gallantry!

There were often darker sides to the Canadian experience. Local tearaways in zoot suits were terrorising the town. For quite a while, the airmen at the base tolerated the activities of these hoodlums as they caused trouble in the bars and clubs. It was *their* country, after all. But the final straw was reached when an old man was severely beaten up by the gang.

Deciding to teach them a lesson, a large contingent of airmen formed themselves into a vigilante group. Improvised weapons were made in the service workshops. George fashioned a short piece of flexible metal in a rubber tube, an effective club which could still be found in his office many years later.

With the base commander's unofficial blessing, the men went to town in trucks and, with military precision, set about giving the *zoot-suiters* a taste of their own medicine. There was a lot less trouble after that.

Another disturbing incident occurred, involving George when he was walking back to the base alone one night. Bundled up in his greatcoat, he trudged along through heavy snow, the deeply drifting kind which only appears in places like Canada. Reaching a bridge, he spotted a figure walking towards him.

Thinking they would just pass one another, George was shocked when the man suddenly launched an attack on him. Defending himself, George struggled to keep his assailant at bay. They pushed and scuffled until George was able, after considerable effort, to force the man back onto the wall of the bridge. With blows raining down upon him, George finally managed to get the upper hand and, with a desperate shove, caught his opponent off balance, tipping him over the edge.

As the mystery man slipped out of sight, into the gloom, George turned, anxious to hurry away, but as he did so he heard a muffled splash as the body connected with deep water.

This was a harrowing experience and George simply did not know what to do for the best. The man had attacked him and he was just defending himself. Was it a robbery, or some kind of vendetta, or just a violent lunatic? And now this man might be at the bottom of the river. Or maybe he had managed to clamber out, soaked, frozen and having got his just desserts… or dead.

George shuddered at the thought and it troubled him greatly. He decided to keep quiet about it and wait and see if there was any follow up. After a worrying few days, he heard nothing, but the image of that man disappearing over the edge of that bridge was to haunt him for years.

Even though the reality of war was thousands of miles away, tangible things still cropped up to remind the Canadian castaways that they were part of the conflict, doing their bit, albeit at a distance. German soldiers, sailors and airmen who were taken prisoner were sometimes sent to internment camps in Canada. Some of these men found themselves under the armed guard of, by now *AC1*, George Martin, huddled below deck on a pitching, flat bottomed boat. George struggled to decide what troubled him most; his seasickness or the fact that he was alone, guarding the enemy with an unloaded rifle!

Generally, however, life was pretty good. It is easy to picture the bonhomie of these young men, pushing the boat out and making the most of their time away from what could often be the monotony of the home country. True, they were in the service, doing their jobs and subject to discipline, but, all in all, they had fallen on their feet.

George and Bob were in their element, honing their performing skills in numerous shows and playing impromptu wherever yet another party might arise. Photographs exist of them, and their pals, larking about with six-guns, dressed in ten gallon hats and *chapaderos* or even done up in full Royal Canadian Mountie uniform. Geographically, they were able to learn many new songs and tunes which would rarely, or never, be heard back home. Consequently, their repertoire expanded to include such gems as *Cow-Cow Boogie* and *Ragtime Cowboy Joe*. In later years, they would often speak of such scenarios as travelling down into the States by train, watching glorious sunsets over the mountains and forests from the comfort of the observation car. Here they would position themselves, George on his accordion and Bob singing requests, as their fellow travellers kept the drink and cigarettes flowing.

But it could not last forever. Bob was stationed back to England.

Back in the U.K., George's new bride had made the most of the separation from her husband. Joan actually remained at her posting in Scotland for an extended period where, like George, she was safe from the ravages of war. The remote Galloway coast was not exactly a priority target for German bombers and so she was able to relax, enjoying the dances and indulging in the forbidden, yet common, W.A.A.F. activity of discarding her compulsory gas mask so that she could use the case to carry her make-up!

When George had first been sent abroad, Joan had made enquiries as to whether it would be possible to transfer for a posting to join him, but her request was denied. Instead she concentrated on new friends, making do with the regular letters which would pass between her and George. On one occasion, she miscalculated his reaction to some photographs she sent him which showed her and another W.A.A.F. enjoying an outing with a couple of R.A.F. men. Joan maintained this was all innocent fun, but George's response

On the razzle on the prairie.

was quite indignant, demanding to know if she had given any consideration to how he might feel, stuck so far away and having to view pictures of his wife in the company of strange men.

Joan thought his attitude ridiculous, although some would say he might have had a point. That said, it was not as if he was living the life of a monk in Canada. Far from it! (He just never sent any photographic evidence.)

Joan would make the journey

south to Aldershot whenever her leaves were long enough to warrant the trip. Eventually she was re-posted, ferried around to such places as Torquay and Tangmere where she had a brief, but memorable, confrontation with a legendary war hero.

Squadron Leader Douglas Bader, the legless air combat ace, and veteran of the Battle of Britain, had recently returned from a well publicized stint as a prisoner-of-war. Now stationed at Tangmere, Bader was renowned for his grouchy, no nonsense approach, an attitude which many admired.

Manning the station's telephone console, LACW Joan Martin reacted as quickly as she could to the impatient clicking and flashing on the switchboard.

"What the hell took you so long, woman?" snapped the familiar, clipped tones of her superior officer, "Put your bloody knitting down and put me through!"

Resisting the temptation to respond in the way she would have liked (and thereby getting herself undoubtedly put on a serious charge!), Joan re-routed his call. Forever more, whenever people spoke of Bader's heroic exploits and achievements, Joan would just say, "Huh, that miserable, rude bastard"!

On one of Joan's leaves, something strangely synchronistic was to occur.

She was on London's Waterloo station, waiting to catch a train to Aldershot. The concourse was packed with people, most of them garbed in the uniforms of many services and nations, as was the way during the war. In uniform herself, Joan was idling away her time, not paying much attention to her surroundings, until a certain group of men caught her eye.

They were in R.A.F. blue, but there was something a bit different about their uniforms, a nicer issue than normal. They were, in her words, "making a jolly row", and, noting the insignia on their shoulder tabs, she thought to herself, "I bet they've just got back from Canada".

Listening to the men's banter for a while, she was soon able to confirm her hunch. There was something very familiar about one of

George and Buddy

them. Tall and handsome with a soft, deep Scottish accent; just like the close pal George had told her about in his letters.

Joan took a chance and approached him.

"Excuse me," she ventured, "my husband is in Canada ... are you Bob McGowan, by any chance?"

Bob did a double take as realisation swept over him. "Are you George's wife?"

It was an incredible meeting; a million to one chance which must have been fated. Without it, the lives of many in the Martin family would have taken a very different course.

Bob was on his way to his new posting at R.A.F. Hartford Bridge at Blackbushe which, amazingly, was just a few miles from

Aldershot. Because of the close link with George, Joan immediately arranged for Bob to meet the Martin clan, and the big, amiable Scotsman was welcomed warmly by all of them. He had many stories about his friend, of course, and answered their questions willingly, but I think it can be assumed that certain things were not mentioned!

They were all taken in by Bob's gentle charm, especially George's sister Joyce who was quickly smitten. She was, at this time, actually going out with a Canadian staff sergeant named Dickie, but, after Joyce had fallen for Bob and his dancing skills, Dickie got his marching orders.

George remained in Canada for quite a while after Bob left and he got a new partner for his double act, one Buddy Logan, the brother of Jimmy Logan who was later to become a well known Scottish comedian and actor. But, with the war coming to an end, George was also eventually sent home, having been away for over two years.

It must have been an emotional reunion for them all, and George was over the moon about the incredible coincidence which had introduced Bob to his family.

1945, and the war was virtually over, but the process of "de-mob" for the millions of servicemen and women was going to be long and drawn out. VE Day (Victory Over Europe) came in May and VJ (Victory over Japan) came in August.

George and Joan, as a married couple, were permitted to live off camp (from Tangmere) in lodgings, and, well before the end of the year, Joan was expecting their first child.

Everything appeared to be working out fine. Bob and Joyce just married, George and Joan about to produce a baby, peace in our time, and all that… prospects seemed good. Nobody expected the tragedy which loomed around the corner…

George's young brother, Bill, now well in his teens, was about to be called up for national service and he chose the R.A.F., naturally. He was also keen to get into the entertainment business and was already displaying the family trait of musical ability. Unlike George, he could get his fingers around stringed instruments and, alongside his piano playing, Joan actually bought him his first guitar.

Rita, the baby sister, was 14 years old now. Blonde, pretty, and somewhat precocious, she was a girl of considerable spirit who knew what she wanted and usually got it. Very much a Martin, she was a singer too, her favourite party pieces to perform being *Watch the Birdie* and *Sailor with the Navy Blue Eyes*. She got on very well with Joan.

Completely out of the blue, she fell ill and rapidly declined, so much so that she was isolated in hospital. It was diphtheria, a dreadfully serious malady of the era. The family rallied around, George rushed home on compassionate leave, but it was hopeless. Rita died.

It was a huge shock. Rita, so young and full of life. Bill senior was so distraught at the loss of his youngest daughter he sought comfort by attending spiritualist meetings. Although he never spoke about the intense interest he developed in spiritualism, he was involved for years until one day when he abruptly stopped attending. All he would say on the subject was, "I've found out what I wanted to know".

Martin & McGowan – "worth a chicken dinner!"

Chapter 5

ONE STAGE AT A TIME

Heavily pregnant, Joan came out of the W.A.A.F. and she and George moved into her parent's house. With tragedy still weighing heavily upon the family, the birth of their baby in April 1946 was welcome good news. A daughter who they named Susan Rita in honour of the auntie she would never meet.

George was finally "demobbed" from the R.A.F. that year, having attained the rank of corporal. Now he would have to find another way of earning a living for his young family, but as a qualified electrician this was not too much of a problem.

And he could go back to gigging too. A much more seasoned performer than he had been before the war, he and Bob revived Martin & McGowan and started clinching some respectable engagements locally. He would certainly need the money, because in September 1947 another baby came along, a boy this time; Raymond.

Money was tight. Many fine quality instruments had been impounded from the military bands of the defeated German Army and George managed to get his hands on an excellent trumpet. He felt guilty about this, as it was technically theft, of course, but he eased his conscience with the thought that it was payback time against the forces which had dropped bombs on his aunties.

Not being a brass player, he thought he might be able to glean a few easy pounds by selling it on. Presenting himself at a music shop well outside of his local area, George was relieved to find the owner to be interested in buying this trumpet. With a good price agreed between them, George, hoping to be anonymous, was dismayed when the buyer started filling in some paperwork and asking for identification.

Thinking quickly, George said the first name which came into his head. For no known reason it was "Da Costa".

"Ah," exclaimed the shop owner, looking up excitedly, "you must be one of the Bracknell Da Costas…"

With sweat breaking out on his forehead, George gulped and smiled nervously, "Well, distantly…" he mumbled, and got out of the shop, cash in hand, as quickly as he could!

George also had his eye on solo bookings. Whilst still in the R.A.F., he had grasped every opportunity to add to his stage experience. His early appearances had been mainly musical but when he auditioned as a straight singer at the sergeant's mess and found himself up against Leonard Osborne, a well known baritone from the D'Oyly Carte opera company, he rapidly changed his act to include a few jokes. Although this was quite a primitive effort, using pretty desperate material he had gleaned from tuppeny comics, it went down well enough for him to be encouraged to go further down the route of comedy.

Towards the end of his service, he also appeared in a major talent show in which he was placed second. The winner was another young airman who was struggling to make a name for himself as a singing comedian; Max Bygraves.

As early as June 1945, George applied to the B.B.C. under the billing George "Ay! Ay!" Martin, the R.A.F. "Cheeky Chappy! (A blatant loan from the famous funny man Max Miller.) This title emblazoned the top of his specially headed publicity, (produced at great expense!) alongside a picture of him grinning and waving a straw boater with a rakish scarf around his neck. Underneath his name came the boast; "Comedian, Vocal Raconteur, Compere, Singing Accordianist. Heard on the air in Canada, the U.S.A. and through the medium of the B.B.C."

This resulted in a contract to appear on the Carrol Levis new discoveries radio show. Still stationed at Tangmere, George caught the train from Chichester to London, presenting himself at the Paris

Cinema in Regent Street for the broadcast. For this he received a fee of 8 guineas (8 pounds, 8 shillings and 0 pence in the currency of the day), plus return rail fare at the service rate of 10 shillings and a further £1 subsistence. Compared to the average working wage at the time, it was quite a handsome sum; enough to make any aspiring performer weigh up the advantages of a possible show-business career.

Competition was stiff, however. Although the variety scene was still quite healthy immediately after the war, with hundreds of theatres countrywide presenting hundreds of acts, the business was more overcrowded than it had ever been. Many de-mobbed service personnel with entertainment aspirations, just like George, had earned their spurs performing in concert parties. Now they were emerging into a new world which looked like it would be facing a few bleak years as it rebuilt itself. For "Joe Public", it would be grim, but for a favoured few, if they had the talent, there was a silver lining to be grabbed upon the stage. People would always need entertaining, to be cheered up in these austere times. Radio was the really big medium at the time, where stars were created, but television, after a shaky start, was just beginning to be taken seriously.

George's broadcast had gone down well enough, but not so much as to change his life. For now, it was back to R.A.F. life, eventual discharge, a shared home with his in-laws and that young family to support.

Working as an electrician and doing his gigs, George, always a social animal, did not stick to a routine. Never the greatest timekeeper in the world, his erratic schedule did not go down well with Joan's parents who, traditional in their outlook and seeking a quiet life, were somewhat fazed by his coming and going. Before long, this created tension in the Hewitt household and George decided that the time had come to move on.

One day George turned up at the house in a van driven by a friend.

"Come on," he said to Joan, "We're going."

They moved into George's parent's house in Boxalls Lane. This proved to be a crowded environment but one much more suited to George's lifestyle. Joan, along with her new baby, was happy to go along with it.

Apart from Bill senior and Lil, Joyce and Bob were living there too, along with young Bill whenever he came home on leave from the air force. Bill and Lil were delighted to have the extra company, which no doubt helped to ease the grief of their recent loss. The Martin family were pulling together.

It must have been a chaotic but essentially happy period for them all. When Bill had served his time in the R.A.F., he joined George and Bob and they formed a close harmony trio called, (what else?) The Martin Brothers. With George on accordion and Bill playing a fine, chunky guitar accompaniment, Bob took up the double bass. Practising every day, they developed a strong, tight sound with smooth harmonies, their set list including many of the songs which George and Bob had brought back from Canada. *Ragtime Cowboy Joe*, of course, and other such character ditties as *Sioux City Sue*, *The Woody Woodpecker Song* and *Quantralagusta*. Bob would then bring things back to a more stable level, making the girls swoon with his crooning renditions of ballads such as *My Ideal*.

Home life, with these boys around, was a lot of fun. Parties, music, drinking and horseplay. When not rehearsing, The Martin Brothers liked to amuse themselves with such delightful pursuits as farting competitions. Staggering home from gigs or visits to the pub, the tipsy trio would take forever getting to bed ... challenging each other as to who could reach the top of the stairs first by allowing one step per fart.

Bill senior, now working as an accountant, had an exciting moment. Religiously doing his football pools every week, his quiet demeanour evaporated one day when he shouted out that he had won. The family was rich! For a brief period the celebrations resounded around Boxalls Lane and the old man even threw his tie on the open fire saying he could now buy lots of new ones! The excitement was short lived, unfortunately, when the authorities informed him that, owing to some technicality, they would not accept his perm.

But things were going really well for The Martin Brothers and they were a great hit at the local venues. The three of them were all doing day jobs at the R.E.M.E. but it was starting to look like they might be serious contenders for a professional show-business career.

They were far from discouraged by their audition at the Aldershot Hippodrome when hard nosed Jewish producer Philip Hindin had told them, "You'll never get anywhere".

George's mind must have been uncertain about which route to take.

His brother and brother-in-law were keen on the trio and yet George himself obviously felt that he could make it alone.

This is evident from the application which he sent to the B.B.C. for a *Variety Bandbox* audition in April 1948. Producer Dennis Main Wilson (a top man at the corporation who was destined to produce and pioneer *The Goon Show*, *Hancock* and many other hit shows) wrote back, adding him to the waiting list. As it happened, an audition date came up quickly and George did his stuff on Friday May 28th. in Studio 2 at The Aeolian Hall, New Bond Street, W1.

The attending producers who sat in judgement arrived at the following verdicts;

"Weak material but a nice style of delivery. Good singing voice." (Eric Spear)

"As a solo audience comic with new, better material, yes." (Max Kester)

"A pleasant personality but seems to have no original material. I suggest he is heard again, but must bring some new gags with him." (Charles Maxwell)

Quite encouraging, but what exactly happened here is a little confusing. Going by the existing archives, the impression is given that George auditioned as a solo act, yet there is a contradictory internal memo from Frank Hooper, the B.B.C.'s Variety Bookings Manager, dated just 3 days after the audition. In this memo, Hooper states his feeling that The Martin Brothers are not suitable but that George on his own is wanted for a further audition in front of senior producers. A suggestion was made that Dennis Main Wilson should help George by talking over the finer points of his act.

Were The Martin Brothers seen at the same time, or did George take the opportunity to push the trio verbally during his own audition? Whatever, it seems that George grew impatient over the next few months, hearing nothing more, until he chased it up with a letter in November. This resulted in a further audition for George, on his own, on January 25th. 1949.

This time the verdict was not quite so positive. Three different producers were not over enthusiastic, although they did say, between them, that his patter might go better with a full audience and that he should be tried out on a "First Time Here" programme.

Strangely, all three said that he should not sing. Perhaps he was having an off day vocally, because up to this point his voice had always been considered an asset.

In the meantime, The Martin Brothers were doing the rounds of agents and auditions, getting themselves bookings but not really progressing. That was until they managed to get themselves a date to appear before Vivian Van Damm himself at the Windmill Theatre in the heart of Soho.

The Windmill is a legend now in showbiz circles. It was where so many post war comedians took their first steps to stardom. Peter Sellers, Jimmy Edwards, Bruce Forsyth, Harry Secombe, Tommy Cooper, Dick Emery… the list seems endless. Kenneth More, the 1950s film star, was even employed there as a stage hand.

The unique thing about the place was that it staged nude revue. All very tastefully done, girls would pose naked in various tableaux depicting artistic scenes or stylized episodes from history. The important element, which kept it all strictly legal in the eyes of the Lord Chancellor, was that the girls remained rigidly still as they posed. To move a muscle would render the entire production liable to obscenity laws.

There were six shows a day, six days a week, and although the audience was made up almost entirely of men who were mainly there for the rare sight of female flesh, acts were employed to try and keep the momentum going as the next scene was set. In this atmosphere, it was very difficult for comics to get any attention from the audience, let alone laughs. Between shows there would be a rush for the front seats, binoculars were strictly forbidden and it was a common sight for comics to see men sitting in the audience reading newspapers during their acts. When the girls came on, these newspapers would be transferred to the men's laps, often with hands underneath, moving!

Van Damm was the owner/manager and he ran a very tight ship with strict rules, especially regarding the moral behaviour of his girls. He conducted all auditions personally and it was in front of him that The Martin Brothers went through their paces on Wednesday March 16th. 1949. The Old Man or VD (as he was known) was always ruthlessly honest and many an auditionee had their act cut short with a resounding, "Next". Benny Hill was but one future star who failed to impress Van Damm.

But VD liked the trio, although he did not employ them immediately. It was different for comedian Arthur English who also auditioned that same morning. He was back on stage, in the show, that very afternoon! Arthur was well known to the Martin boys because, like them, he was an Aldershot lad. He had a short lived variety career as the "Spiv", an image which would quickly date because it characterized the "wide boys" of the war years. With drawn on moustache, floppy trilby hat and a ridiculously oversized, floral tie, Arthur became a name for a while. Following this, he was actually to create a new, successful career for himself as a straight actor.

The Martin Brothers had to wait a couple of months before they actually appeared in a Windmill show, but they finally got there for their debut on May 30th. in the edition of Revudeville number 222, booked for a six week run; their first proper professional engagement.

Their day jobs abandoned, this was the plunge they had been longing to take.

The Martin Brothers – Bill, Bob and George

Chapter 6

INTO THE MILL

In many ways, the Windmill was a baptism of fire for these young men. Of course, they were all ex-servicemen and had been around a bit (especially George and Bob), but, even so, their red blood must have been truly fired up as they found themselves surrounded by a bevy of naked beauties every day of their working lives.

To the girls themselves it meant nothing to have to squeeze hurriedly past these rampant entertainers as they hurried back and forth to their dressing rooms between scenes. The crush must have got especially close on the stone steps backstage. Such terrible conditions for these innocent novices, as their eyes protruded on stalks from their sweating brows!

They shared the bill with Arthur English, who was well established by now; also a young Jewish comedian named Bernard Spear. Long days which began in the morning and stretched through until they caught their late train home close to midnight. Indeed, six shows every day; a packed schedule, but as an act it made them even tighter. By the end of the run they were as sharp as a razor… confident and ready to take on the world.

In April, while they were waiting for their Windmill season to begin, George wrote to the B.B.C. again, specifically pushing The Martin Brothers for *Variety Bandbox*. Regardless of his solo ambitions, this must have meant that his heart was still very much with the trio but the corporation were determined to have George on his own. In July they offered him a solo spot on the prestigious radio show *Stars

In Scotland admiring one of the loves of his life... whisky!

of Tomorrow, but he turned it down owing to a "prior engagement".

This engagement must have been The Martin Brothers' next booking which took them to Scotland for shows in Glasgow and Edinburgh. They shared the bill with a very youthful Lionel Blair who was doing a dancing act with his sister Joyce. Also in the show was an act called Chic & Mandi, half of which was to evolve into the wonderfully droll solo comedian, Chic Murray.

I think it must have been at the beginning of this run that the trio had a mishap which they often laughed about in future years. Following an early show, as they took their bows, they were told that they had to exit the stage quickly to the left. This they did, facing the front and grinning widely, only to all smash into each other as they ploughed into a bricked up wall! Bill damaged his guitar.

Bob was fortunate in that he was able to stay with his parents; in fact his wife Joyce travelled up to join him, bringing with her their new baby son, Alan.

Bill was a free spirit, but George had to ensure that he sent a large chunk of his earnings home every week to support Joan and their two small children, Sue and Ray. George also spent a lot of time honing the act. He wrote the patter and scored the arrangements but always took an equal share of the money, a situation which Joan questioned, to no avail.

But The Martin Brothers were really establishing themselves now as a marketable act and from Scotland they were engaged almost immediately to join a touring show called *Buttons and Bows*. Along with acts such as Ken Roberts, Reg Lloyd and Peggy & Bobby, they set off for Germany to do the rounds of the many allied military bases which had been established in the newly occupied country.

This tour was another landmark in the education of the trio and they learned a lot about life on the road. Mainly it was fun, but with regular reminders of the horrors of the war which had so recently been fought; especially when they worked at Belsen. The newly destroyed concentration camp was still very much in evidence, with its pall of misery and death hanging in the air. Generally, the country was in ruins, although the surviving populace were already working industriously to rebuild their nation.

One night, at a party in a hotel after the show, George was playing the piano, leading a sing-song for the revellers. As he finished a number, he stood up to take a "cod" bow, somehow twisted his foot on the polished floor and took a heavy tumble. The resulting laughs he got were short lived as he lay there writhing in pain. Landing awkwardly, he had managed to break his leg.

So much for the rest of the tour. Abruptly having to leave the show, The Martin Brothers travelled home to England and George was laid up with his leg in plaster.

By now, George, Joan and the children had their own home, a modest affair at 63 Moreland Road, Aldershot. It had one big room on the ground floor and two bedrooms upstairs. Water had to be manually pumped up to the bathroom from the lower level.

Without the security of a full time job, George knew he could not afford to be an invalid for long. Bob and Bill had been forced to go back to their former employment, but George wasted no time in trying to find something for himself in the entertainment profession. On October 10th. 1949, he wrote to the B.B.C.'s Variety Booking Department to remind them of the offer he had turned down in the summer. Although admitting to his accident, he added, "I get around very well and am quite capable of doing a broadcast".

It worked and he did *Variety Bandbox* in November. Not long after this he secured a booking for *Stars of Tomorrow*, the show he had previously declined. A recording actually exists of this show and it is enlightening to hear the young George Martin, long before he became the "Casual Comedian", working at anything but a casual pace. His delivery is rapid and his voice high pitched, although maybe nerves played a part in this. One has to listen to it with an understanding of the era in which it was done. Tastes have changed, of course, and these were more innocent times, but it is a confident performance, full of energy.

Introduced by compere Jerry Desmonde (who would later become the straight man in so many classic Norman Wisdom films), George bounces up to the microphone to the cacophony of a full orchestra. He blurts out that he is going to perform an excerpt from his latest film, "My *only* film… Confessions of a Dope Addict…" etc., and goes on to speak of policemen at the door, "Six feet tall;

An early show. What it was is anyone's guess, but it looks like fun! George is in the middle, between the two ladies.

two Yard men, you see…" Dramatic music accompanies his manic description of grabbing a knife and a gun… "I shot up one street and cut up another… keep still or I'll drill ya… hup' two, three, four, left roit, left roit…"

All this gets huge laughs, believe it or not! He goes on to say, "That's the trouble with Hollywood; they shoot too many films and not enough actors!"

Well, I guess you had to be there, although I did like the bizarre "off the wall" quality of lines like, "My father thinks he's a chicken. We would have him cured but we need the eggs"!

In time honoured music hall style he finishes with a song, one he wrote himself; "*Knocking On The Door Came Love*", and a fine number it is too.

The Martin Brothers had officially come to an end and George was faced with a decision. Could he make it on his own?

Joan encouraged him to go back to the Windmill, where he was already known to Van Damm.

"Audition on your own," she reasoned, "and get it out of your system. If he doesn't take you, you can always go back to being an electrician."

This was true. He had his trade to fall back on, so there was nothing to lose.

Gathering together the best aspects of an act which he thought should appeal to the Old Man, he was received at the theatre like a newcomer. Coming to the end of his audition spot, V.D. called him aside and said, "What you are doing is no good, but you've got *something*. Go away and work on it and come back tomorrow… and finish with a comic song!"

A bit bewildered by this, George decided to stay in London that night to concentrate on improving his act. Finding a cheap room, and under the light of a dim, bare bulb, George thought it through and came up with some new ideas.

The next morning, back at the Windmill, he went through his paces again, bearing in mind what he had been told. It did the trick and Van Damm liked what he saw.

And so began a record run for a resident comedian at the Windmill "We Never Closed" Theatre.

Somewhere with Jessie Matthews

George Martin commenced his solo career in earnest at the Windmill on June 5th. 1950, in Revudeville number 231.

The promotional photograph for this production, sent out as a press release by P.R. Kenneth Bandy, showed a life-sized, grinning, cartoon horse leaning on the batwing doors of a saloon. George is standing a little uncertainly in front of these doors dressed in a cowboy outfit and holding his accordion, accompanied by the blurb, *"Music! Music! Music! says the horse, and guest artist GEORGE MARTIN supplies the answer …"*

George actually took over from Arthur English as resident comedian. It was a fairly easy transition as George was already familiar with the schedule of continuous shows, but he quickly learned to adapt his style to suit the venue's unique audience.

Regular faces would appear in the front rows and these were the main culprits who read their newspapers during the acts as they waited for the girls to come back. George decided to slow the pace of his delivery, thinking to himself, "If they're not bothering, I'll take it easy too."

He developed an image very much his own. Instead of the suit and bow tie look, and maybe a comical hat, favoured by so many funny men of the time, George took to the stage in slacks and an open neck shirt. Wandering nonchalantly onto the Mill's mirrored stage, he would carry a newspaper, just like those men in the audience, as if he was joining them. Turning the pages he would make comments on the day's news, creating gags out of any situation.

It was a fresh approach, original and attention grabbing, and his musical ability helped too. An early review in The Stage newspaper (August 31st. 1950) sums it up; *"There are some first class variety acts in the new Revudeville 233, presented here by Vivian Van Damm on Monday. One of them is George Martin, an excellent comedian with a style entirely his own. His humour is of the diffident, inconsequent style, and during his sojourn of the stage, which is punctuated with laughter, he sings and plays the piano-accordion extremely well"*.

A year later, the same publication's review for edition 242 (August 30th. 1951) was saying; *"… George Martin, who is rapidly and deservedly making himself a favourite here. His quiet, confidential style and his numerous new gags represent comedy at its best, and that he succeeds in making Windmill audiences laugh is evidence of his ability"*.

That is how the Casual Comedian evolved.

It was a hectic schedule during and between the shows, with much rushing about, but friendships were forged in an atmosphere of camaraderie which was unique to the show-business scene in those days.

Working as a chorus boy was a keen young performer who

proved to be an asset as a dancer, singer, musician and light comedian. Bruce Forsyth.

Bruce and George became friends and they spent a lot of time chatting between shows, either in the theatre's upstairs canteen or in a café close by. Over numerous cups of tea, they would discuss their aspirations and George, forever coming up with topical material for his act, would try his gags out on Bruce.

"He had such a quick brain," recalled Bruce, "and he would use me as an audience. If I laughed, then the gag would be in the next show!"

Although Bruce was not a drinker, as such, George certainly was, so when not with Bruce, George would spend a lot of time across the road in "Pop" Allen's club. "Pops" was a regular haunt for those cast members who liked something a bit stronger than tea in their leisure time and it became a cosy retreat from the routine of the shows. Pop welcomed the show-business fraternity warmly, but his premises always smelled of boiled ham because of the meats his wife cured to sell.

Just across the road from the Windmill was Archer Street which housed the headquarters of the Musician's Union. Every Monday scores of musicians would gather in the street outside the office, creating a chaotic free-for-all as they hustled for engagements. It was quite a battle to fight your way through the crowd, but George already knew a few of them and would get to know many more as his career progressed and he played other venues around the country.

Happy with George's approach, Van Damm continued to re-employ him from edition to edition, every 6 weeks like clockwork. A lot of the other artistes would come and go but George remained, as if on the inventory. As a result, this was where he initially forged many of the friendships with fellow performers which he would retain throughout his life. Every night he would catch the late train back home to Aldershot, then be back on it again to return in the morning.

Although V.D. frowned on any serious fraternization between his girls and the acts, inevitably relationships did come to fruition. For instance, Bruce Forsyth and dancer Penny Calvert became an item and got married, going on to work as a double act after they left the Windmill. Likewise, John Law, another chorus boy, got married to Windmill girl Margaret Cooper. George and Joan were invited to the wedding and their children, Sue and Ray, were bridesmaid and page boy at the ceremony.

Each Christmas, the management would throw a party for the children of the cast, hosted by the Windmill girls.

"What are most people's memories of Christmas parties?" asked Ray, "Mine are of beautiful showgirls in scanty costumes serving orange squash, holding my hand and pushing me around on tin toys. Sounds like a male fantasy? Well, it's all true and I have seen the photographs that prove it!"

Indeed, the girls made a great fuss of the children, although they did wear a bit more for these parties than they wore on stage. Ray remembers when, aged about four, the top of one of the girl's costumes gave way and he called out, happily, "Oh look, one of Auntie Jean's bosoms has come out!"

Five year old Sue was in awe of the theatre, a fascination which was never to leave her.

Positioned in the heart of Soho, the streets surrounding the Windmill were not the kind of place to take your grandmother after dark. To say they were frequented by "ladies of the night" might be an understatement. One night after the last show, Joan had come up to town because she and George were going on somewhere. As she waited for him at the stage door, wrapped up in a big fur coat, she was suddenly propositioned by a man in the shadows. This man actually reached forward and grabbed her shoulders from behind, but she stepped out of the coat leaving him holding it. He beat a hasty retreat as George appeared.

Maybe that evening they were going on to Quaglino's; a nearby nightclub where George began appearing nightly in cabaret when the Windmill shut up shop.

Surrounded by showgirls every working day would be a temptation to any red blooded male, and it seems that George succumbed to the charms of at least one. How and when this began must remain the secret of those involved but it was to lead to grief, as we shall see.

In the meantime, George's name was becoming well known

throughout the business and good reports of his work were filtering through to the powers that be. He had already caught the attention of the biggest and most powerful Entertainment Agency in the country, the Grade Organization. Run by three Jewish brothers, Lew and Leslie Grade and Bernard Delfont, they had just about everyone who mattered signed to their books. Lew was particularly dominant, an ex-performer himself who had once been a Charleston dance champion. Later he would go on to spearhead independent television and move into film production. As soon as they were made aware of the fresh young talent known as The Casual Comedian, they wanted him.

The B.B.C. were showing a renewed interest too. Producer Dennis Main Wilson, always a shrewd talent spotter, had kept an eye on George's progress since those first auditions. In February 1952 he sent a memo to the Variety Bookings Manager which said, "As you requested, I went down to the Windmill Theatre last week to see George Martin. Your observations about his work are fully justified. His material is good; a lot of it old stuff but adapted with new twists. He has great repose on stage and a very warm, sympathetic personality. Besides his own role of a very "chummy" raconteur, his character voices sounded quite good. I feel that he has great potential as a solo performer, and would like to audition him for production work as well. Incidentally, he is a very good looking young man, moves easily, never staying stationary for long, and I am sure he would be useful to T.V. In conclusion, may I add that he is one of the few comics I have known to make an all male audience at the Windmill roar with laughter".

Praise indeed from the very top. This memo instigated a mini flood of visits to the Windmill by various production executives and although their opinions were a rather mixed bag, the overall view was that the Casual Comedian would certainly be worth using. A point was made that much of the act depended upon the way George moved on stage, a feature which would obviously be lost on radio. It was also mentioned that the majority of the material he used at the Windmill would be too suggestive for broadcast, but generally it was felt that his "refreshingly different approach" was a find.

George had now been resident at the Windmill for almost two

years and, although he had been happy there, he was anxious to spread his wings in other areas of the profession. The Grades wanted him for their Moss Empire variety circuit and the B.B.C. were beginning to offer him regular radio work. With another *Variety Bandbox* show under his belt in June 1952, for the grand sum of 15 guineas, it looked like there would definitely be full time employment for him on stage away from the security of Revudeville.

A domestic drama seems to have been the final straw.

Joan somehow found out about an affair George was having with one of the Windmill girls. Never one to handle such matters with subtlety, Joan reacted with her characteristic fire and went straight to Lil, George's mother, with the news. Although she adored "her George", Lil thought it outrageous that her son was behaving like this with a young family in tow. Without delay, the pair of enraged women caught a train to London and went to see Van Damm himself at the Windmill.

The Old Man was appalled. He was of the "old school" and could not condone such immorality. Obtaining the girl's address, Joan and Lil went by tube to her flat where, by all accounts, they made quite a scene. The poor girl made herself scarce and would not answer the door but she had to suffer the ruckus of a drama unfolding in the street outside as Lil shouted abuse up to her window.

George was unaware of what was going on at this time. He was actually preparing to do a live radio broadcast and Joan, feeling malicious, decided to wait until an opportune moment to break the news to him.

Knowing that he was going on air at a certain hour, she left it until the last moment to call the production, just as he was about to step before the microphone, saying that she needed to speak to him urgently.

As he came to the phone, Joan let him have it. The tirade must have been quite a shock to him, but, professional to the core, he carried on to do his act as planned.

Joan was listening, mischievously hoping that she had spoiled his day, but she was surprised, and grudgingly in admiration, of the fact that he did one of the best shows she had ever heard him do! Obviously, he could work well under pressure.

The whole incident certainly threw a spanner in the works. Joan believed that the girl had been sacked from the show, as she disappeared from the cast, and George was read the V.D. riot act. Although he carried on for a while, it was time to move on. When he left the Windmill, he had completed 2,275 performances.

Joan did not exactly forgive him, but it seems that she and George were able to address the matter and put it into perspective. I guess he must have promised to be a "good boy" in the future as he promised to concentrate on his budding career.

Chapter 7

A STAR IS BORN

Things were looking good for George on the professional horizon.

As soon as he was free, the Grades began booking him into their theatres, usually for week long stints on variety bills around the country. The B.B.C. also began using him regularly, and over the next few months he made many radio appearances on shows such as *Henry Hall's Guest Night*, *One Minute Please*, *Variety Fanfare* (from Manchester), *The Spice of Life* (from Bradford) and *Variety Ahoy!* (from Glasgow). There was also *Worker's Playtime*, a live show which went out from various work places around the country, often from factory canteens to boost the morale of the workers.

Also, as recommended by Dennis Main Wilson, the new medium of television beckoned him, but this proved to be a bit of a hiccup in his early career. It appears his first T.V. spot had been in March 1952; a show called *Top Hat Rendezvous* from Lime Grove studios. (The producer was Richard Afton who became notorious in the 1970s as an acerbic newspaper columnist in the Evening News.) But George was actually given his own T.V. series, *The George Martin Show*, that same year.

It was all very exciting. The producer was Gordon Crier and the scriptwriter one Talbot Rothwell, who later went on to script the *Carry On* films. New to the medium, George allowed himself to be manipulated, feeling that those in power must know best, but he was uncomfortable with the way he was being presented.

Having made his name for being "casual", he quickly realized that something was not quite right about the format of his show. He was put into sketches and situations which portrayed him as a bit of a buffoon. Slapstick scenarios like trying to eat soup on a moving train were not really his forte. As had been noted by those who had seen him at The Windmill, his act needed an air of sophistication.

To make matters worse, top executives were not amused. Cecil McGivern, the Controller of Television Programmes, wrote to the Head of Television Light Entertainment, Ronald Waldman, saying he found the shows "… unfunny, unclever and with completely pedestrian production", going on to call what he had seen, "puerile and rather offensive nonsense…" and demanding, " Let me have, a.s.a.p., any reason why I should not cancel the rest of the series?"

Ouch! Strong stuff, and quite a blow to the budding new star, even though he was receiving a fee of 42 guineas per show. But Waldman was diplomatically defensive and hit back gently in a memo dated July 7th., "*The George Martin Show* is not what I want it to be… not yet…"

Heads were put together and there was a rapid re-vamp of the format. Although the rest of the series was far from satisfactory, it improved and moved at least partly in the right direction. By September Waldman was able to write to the Grades with the news that he was delighted to see that figures for the show were "rocketing up" since the format change. Appreciation index figures showed that, for comparison, *The Jewell and Warris Show* had risen 15 points in 4 programmes but *The George Martin Show* had zoomed by 23 points in just 2 programmes.

Regardless of the *kudos* of his own television series, the experience did not do him any favours. A couple of years later, a similar thing happened to that great comedy duo Morecambe & Wise in their first T.V. series, *Running Wild*. Widely experienced in live theatre performance, they were out of their depth and badly directed on screen, and were heavily panned. Ironic then, that they went on to later become the most loved and successful act on British television. As for George, he decided that in the future he would insist upon writing all his own material.

Never-the-less, his star continued to shine and during that same year he made guest appearances on several other T.V. shows, including *Garrison Theatre*, *Well You Asked For It*, *Sugar and Spice* and *The Daily Mail Awards Show*.

Things were also happening for him on the stage too and he scooped some great engagements, notably his first appearance at the London Palladium, the dream booking for any variety performer. This was a two week run to do a first half support spot for American recording star Guy Mitchell, of *She Wears Red Feathers and a Huli-Huli Skirt* fame, backed by the George Mitchell Singers. Also on the bill were an acrobatic comical duo called Medlock & Marlowe, comedian Archie Robbins, Eva & Nick (adagio dancing), Olga Varona (swinging gracefully upside down from a rope!) the Pauline Grant Ballet (featuring Gillian Lynne), the entire Billy Cotton Band and the Tiller Girls. As you can see, punters really got value for money when they went to a show back then. This time, The Stage had this to say; *"George Martin, also for the first time here, is a comedian with an admirably casual and impromptu manner, and with material that is well linked and full of subtle and telling satire"*.

It was on this show that George forged a long friendship with Billy Cotton's novelty vocalist, Alan Breeze, a man whose ability to eat a whole one pound slab of Cheddar cheese in one hit became a party piece when out for dinner with him.

Joan and the children went backstage several times during the run and it seems that Sue was particularly in her element. George had taken Ray to see the pre-war cowboy film star Tex Ritter in a Western show at one of the London stadiums and Ray says, "I don't remember much about the show… I think that Dad, who before the war had played the accordion at Saturday Morning Pictures where they showed all the cowboy films, was more of a fan than I was". Ray had been taken backstage to meet Tex and was given a red box which contained a pair of matching silver toy six guns in leather holsters. Back at the Palladium, when Ray showed Guy Mitchell these guns, the singer got really excited and, taking a gun each, he and Ray stalked one another around the dressing room sofa until somebody rushed in to remind him that he was due on stage.

In February 1953, George was back at the Palladium as part of a big show called *Rat's Revels*, along with Medlock & Marlowe (again), Herbie Marks, Jon Pertwee, Hetty King, Albert Whelan, Frederick Ferrari, Nat Mills & Bobbie, Rob Murray, Charlie Chester, Wilbur Evans, Bertha Wilmott, Jewell & Warris, Harry Lester and his Hayseeds, Clarkson Rose, The Ebonaires, Winifred Attwell, Bob Monkhouse, George Elrick, David Hughes, The Bogino Troupe, Fred Russell, Cyril Dowler, Woolf Phillips and Jimmy "Aye, aye, that's yer lot!" Wheeler.

Good grief, *what* a bill!

That winter he had also been offered his first pantomime; *Mother Goose* at the Opera House Leicester, with Bill Fraser in the titular role and George playing Jack. This would have been a first class production, panto being a real feather in the cap for a variety performer, and proof yet again that he was much in demand.

However, maybe George was a little nervous of anything outside of his comfort zone, following the negative response to his T.V. series. Even though posters had already been printed, he had a meeting with his agent and the producer and said that he felt he was not yet ready to play pantomime.

The bookers were aghast and told him everything would be alright and that he must do it, but George was adamant. As the argument wore on, the agent became exasperated and blurted out, "If you don't do it, I shall have to throw myself out of that window!"

Without hesitation, George went to the window and lifted the latch. "Here," he answered, defiantly, "I'll open it for you…"

Surprisingly, George got his way, which says something about his confidence, and, some would say, "bloody minded-ness", but the fact that the bookers gave in proves that they must have valued him.

In fact, with the Grades behind him and a growing reputation, he went from strength to strength and was in great demand.

Working regularly, George was also sent for meetings with various industry V.I.P.s.. On one such occasion, he found himself on his best behaviour in a top West End of London restaurant for lunch with some particularly important executives. An important move for his budding career, he knew that he needed to impress these moguls with charm and sophistication, underlining the casual characteristics upon which he had built his name.

All went well, and though nervous, George had acquitted himself stylishly during the main meal. When the coffee arrived and big cigars were lit, he was in full flow, confidently selling his ability as he poured cream into his cup.

Getting laughs and with all eyes on him, he took a sip of his coffee and nearly gagged. The taste was totally unexpected and really foul. Managing to suppress his expression, he looked into his cup and saw big globules of white coagulation swirling around on the surface of the dark coffee. Stirring vigorously, these globules were going nowhere, and it was then that he realised that he had used mayonnaise instead of cream! Too embarrassed to draw attention to his error, he gulped it down.

George was now a regular fixture on the number one variety circuit, playing Moss Empires and other prestigious venues the length and breadth of the country. Anywhere from Glasgow to Plymouth and from Swansea across to Norwich, George travelled, as was the norm for any book-able performer during the golden period of variety. The whole scene was conducive to the special camaraderie which arose between these artistes, the unique closeness and understanding of shared experience in an unreal world.

===== PROGRAMME—continued =====

10 "ANCHORS AWEIGH"   THE VARGA MODELS

11 MORECAMBE & WISE ... ...   More Fun

12   "DEGA'S BALLET"
   PHYLLIS DIXEY and Girls

13 GEORGE MARTIN ... ...   The New Comedian

14 EDDIE GORDON ...   The Silent Humorist
   assisted by NANCY

15   "THE BALLET EGYPTIAN"
   PHYLLIS DIXEY and Girls

16 "SNUFFY" JACK TRACY

17   "THE BRIDE'S DREAM"
   PHYLLIS DIXEY and The Girls
   with The Entire Company

The Management reserves the right to refuse admission to the Theatre, and to change, vary or omit, without previous notice, any item of the programme

THIS THEATRE IS DISINFECTED THROUGHOUT WITH JEYES' FLUID

In accordance with the requirements of the Licensing Justices :
(a) The public may leave at the end of the performance by all exits and entrances other than those used as queue waiting-rooms, and the doors of such exits and entrances shall at the time be open. (b) All gangways, passages and staircases shall be kept entirely free from chairs or any other obstructions. (c) Persons shall not be permitted to stand or sit in any of the intersecting gangways. (d) The fireproof curtain shall at all times be maintained in working order and shall be lowered at the beginning of and during the time of every performance.

PLEASE NOTE—PHOTOGRAPHING IN THE THEATRE IS FORBIDDEN
Productions and Variety Acts, being the copyright of the Theatre Proprietors or Variety Artistes, the unauthorised photographing of scenes and acts is illegal

An early variety bill for George; "The Phyllis Dixey Show". (Note that the theatre is disinfected throughout with Jeyes fluid!)

Crewe railway terminus became an infamous meeting point for these nomadic performers as they criss-crossed the nation, swapping stories as they boarded their train connections to take them onwards to their next engagement. Typically a variety booking would be for a week, involving maybe 10 acts on a bill. Two shows nightly, first house 6.00pm., second house 8.15pm.. From the moment they began to arrive at the theatre on a Monday morning for the band call, through to what would often be a party after the last show on Saturday, the performers would bond like a family.

A band call was when the newly arrived acts would gather in the empty theatre's stalls, in front of the orchestra pit, to take their turn with their band parts (music and stage cues) for perusal and run through by the musical director and his musicians. These leather bound parts were like gold dust to an act, and they were lined up along the edge of the pit in strict order of arrival. Often the acts would be booked into the same theatrical "digs", and this is where so many hilarious landlady stories originated.

The acts were incredibly varied with amazing names and bill matter. For example... Shek Ben Ali (*Nobody inside, nobody outside*), The Two Pirates (*Oh yes there is – Oh no, there isn't!*), Gay and Barry, Deveen and his New York Blondes, Bob Nelson (*Almost a Sailor!*), Reggie Redcliffe and his rumba xylophone, Walter's Comedy Dogs and a Monkey, "Checker" Wheel (*The man with the educated feet*), Eva May Wong, and, my special favourite... The Three Aberdonians, who boasted they were "*Too mean to tell you what they do*"!

Many of these "turns" were of mysterious origin, especially the circus type speciality acts ("speshes") who had found their way to Great Britain from all parts of the globe. Some of them were as tough as old boots, hardened by years of experience on the road, or perhaps by traumatic experiences in occupied Europe during the still recent war. They were not to be messed with.

One eastern European refugee performed an act with a large brown bear. Not exactly politically correct in today's enlightened times, but back then it was acceptable, and this man and his bear seemed to have an understanding. He treated the animal well and spent a lot of time rehearsing and taking it through its paces and tricks.

George was on the bill with them at some coastal town. When not performing, the bear was kept in a cage in the theatre's backyard and, one afternoon, George heard a commotion. Investigating, he found the bear being tormented by a pair of laughing American sailors who were poking a broom through the bars of the cage. The bear was very distressed, roaring in pain and swiping its big claws helplessly at the sailors as they jabbed the broom into its face.

As George moved to intervene, the sailors hurried away, still chuckling, and entered the pub across the road. Immediately, George went off to find the bear's owner who did not say a word as he comforted the animal, calming it down and pulling the hard bristles from its snout and teeth.

At last, his face dark with suppressed fury, the bear man asked, "Where are zay?"

George indicated the pub and the man stalked purposefully towards it. Within moments the pub was echoing to the sounds of a terrible fight. The bear man emerged soon afterwards looking much more content, leaving behind on the floor of the bar two badly beaten sailors.

Glasgow Empire was renowned as the toughest gig on the circuit. The hard bitten, working class crowd there seemed to particularly detest southern comedians who tried to work in an American style. Apparently Des O'Connor was one young comic who suffered badly from the *"ky-ike"* as it was known, when those on stage would be subjected to a barrage of catcalls and abuse. It got so bad one night that it is said Des actually fainted on stage.

Another who experienced the Glaswegian wrath was Jimmy Edwards, he of the handlebar moustache and "Whacko" catchphrase. Jim's act involved him sitting on a trunk, punctuating his trombone playing with gags delivered in a loud upper class accent. He had actually had a distinguished war career, flying dangerous missions as a pilot in the R.A.F.. His bravery had won him the D.F.C. but maybe that had been a safer option than Glasgow!

In the middle of his act, a rough looking fellow stood up in the stalls and shouted, in broad Glaswegian, what sounded like, "I thunk yoor veery goot!", which actually translates as "I think you're very good".

Unaware of this and assuming that it was another customary insult, Jim decided he had had enough. Glaring into the crowd, he tiredly responded with, "Oh, why don't you piss off?"

It nearly caused a riot and the war hero was lucky to get out of the theatre in one piece.

The next morning, the outraged theatre manager contacted the head booker for Moss Empires, Ms. Cissie Williams.

"Last night," he fumed, "that Jimmy Edwards told my audience to piss off!"

"Really?" replied Ms. Williams, "Well, its about time somebody did."

George's own Glasgow experiences as a performer were pretty painless. He seemed to get away with it and the rough crowd took to him for some reason. However, one weekend night as he was leaving the stage door, he heard an approaching ruckus.

A group of drunks were rolling along the street making one hell of a row. As they passed a parked car, one of them, for no reason what-so-ever, put his fist through the side window. This was in full, blatant view of a policeman who just watched them pass by.

Incredulous, George asked, "Aren't you going to do anything about that?"

"Och, no," muttered the policeman, ruefully, "Ye dinna go near 'em on a Saturday neet."

Commencing at Chiswick Empire on Monday March 16th. 1953, George went on tour with the show *Mr.Pastry Comes to Town*, featuring the well known comic actor Richard Hearne. Hearne's Mr.Pastry character was a much loved rendition of a bumbling old man, complete with walrus moustache and bowler hat. His slapstick skills were first rate and this tour was very much a family show involving lively sketches and Hearne's legendary performance of the Lancers, an inventive solo dance routine. Scene One, called Mr. Pastry's Pie, involved George (playing 'Worcester Sauce') as well as an unknown actor named Warren Mitchell. One day Mitchell would become T.V.'s monstrously brilliant comic creation, Alf Garnett, but at that time he liked to amuse himself with practical jokes like placing little rolled up pieces of wet brown paper on beds in the digs so that the cast would think the cat had misbehaved!

Also in the show were acrobats The Volantes, adagio act Boyer & Ravel, magician Ali Bey and vocal harmony singers The Tanner Sisters, all supported by Betty Hobbs Globe Girls. By April, this happy production had reached the Granada Cinema Woolwich, then George went back to more radio broadcasts, including another *Henry Hall's Guest Night*, this time alongside budding young comedian Tony Hancock.

MANCHESTER HIPPODROME
ARDWICK GREEN

6-25   EASTER WEEK - APRIL 6th, 1953   8-40
Matinees Easter Monday & Saturday at 2-30

"MR. PASTRY COMES TO TOWN"

WITH

RICHARD HEARNE

Mr. Hearne is nationally celebrated on Television as "MR. PASTRY" particularly on Children's Television. This lovable eccentric character is also famous for his "One Man Lancers" and for his acrobatic prowess.

★

| TANNER SISTERS | ★ | ALI BEY | ★ | GEORGE MARTIN |

THE VOLANTES ★ BOYER & RAVEL

BETTY HOBBS GLOBE GIRLS

Chapter 8

VARIETY

The Grade Organization, ever ambitious, were pursuing all kinds of avenues to ensure that their theatres stayed full. With the characteristic vision which was to eventually create Lew's international empire of entertainment, they looked much further than most other British impresarios. Already they could see the ultimate threat which hung over live theatre performances... television. Although still in its infancy, and with most of the nation still without the luxury of owning a set, Lew recognized that it was only a matter of time before the new medium became affordable for all. Why then would people bother to go out for their entertainment when they could enjoy it from the comfort of their own homes?

Radio was still King, and for some years now the theatre bill toppers had been the radio stars. Arthur *"Hello Playmates!"* Askey, Tommy *"You Lucky People"* Trinder, Ted *"Ray's a Laugh"* Ray, Sandy *"Can you 'ear me Mother?"* Powell, Max *"'ere's a funny thing"* Miller and ventriloquist Peter Brough with his "naughty boy" dummy, *Archie Andrews.* Brough's radio show *Educating Archie* was hugely popular for years and amongst those who became stars directly as a result of weekly appearances on the show as Archie's foils were Max Bygraves, Tony Hancock, Hattie Jacques and even Julie Andrews. Of course, the idea of ventriloquism on the radio was, in essence, quite absurd but the show certainly worked. Live performances were not quite so successful, however, as Brough was not exactly the world's greatest "vent" and spent most of the act trying to hide the movements of his mouth!

And then there were The Goons, whose anarchic and completely original humour had taken the world of radio by storm. The main players in the bizarre world they created were Peter Sellers, Spike Milligan, Harry Secombe and Michael Bentine. All ex-servicemen who were part of the new wave of comedians to emerge from the war, these four had all "cut their teeth" in variety before pooling their resources to create radio legend *The Goon Show*. They all had original individual acts which were not always understood by simplistic post-war audiences. Sellers was an excellent impressionist who once played gramophone records on stage at the Windmill, telling the audience, "You may not want to listen to me, so how about me playing you some of my favourite records?" Secombe performed a unique act in which he demonstrated the comical way different men shaved. (At least he had his fine operatic singing voice to fall back on!) Bentine, a brilliant man who had worked in military intelligence, would dash madly onto the stage sporting a wild black wig and a false beard. These he would remove to reveal a genuine long, bushy hair style and a beard of his own!

As for Milligan, he was in another world. His variety act was years ahead of its time and hard for the average punter to appreciate. He was always experimental, sometimes making his entrance pointing aimlessly into the air.

"Look at that," he would say in his crazy "Eccles" voice, then, slowly lowering his extended hand, would add, "A finger!"

Working with the Goons, George was in the middle of his act one night when one of his gags got a much bigger laugh than usual. As the laugh rolled on, George turned around to see Spike walking across the stage behind him leading a horse!

Milligan would also use recorded noises playing off stage, often of a baby crying.

"Shut that bloomin' baby up!" he would cry, then he would produce a paper bag from his pocket and offer it into the wings.

"There you go, little feller, have a sweetie…" he would coo, then he would draw a revolver and fire a shot through the bag. Pretty outrageous stuff, even by modern standards!

*The
Casual
Comedian
in action*

During the performance, the gun misfired and exploded in his hand injuring him quite badly. Bearing in mind the illusionist Kardoma, who often put an advertisement in The Performer magazine stating, "*Kardoma; fills the stage with flags!*", Spike put his own ad in the following week saying, "*Milligan; fills the stage with blood!*"

Ray recalls, "My mother (Joan) was embarrassed by Harry Secombe walking alongside her through the streets with his jumper pulled up over his head making insane laughing noises at passers-by".

Michael Bentine (who billed himself as The Missing Link) took Ray and Sue out to the countryside to collect blackberries. Suddenly realising that they did not have anything to store their harvest in, Bentine, in Ray's words, "… went to a sweet shop and bought two ounces of about twenty different kinds of sweets, tipped them out on the back seat of the car and used the bags for the blackberries".

Punters liked to visit the theatre to put a face to the voices they knew so well on the air. The natural extension to this, and a much more exciting one, was to put well known faces from movies on the stage. The British ones were first; Will Hay, George Formby with his ukulele, the Crazy Gang, Gracie Fields, Norman Wisdom, etc., although they were all already seasoned theatre performers in their own right. British films had that cosy, home spun feeling about them, but Hollywood movies were in another league of exoticism. The Grades figured that if they could entice leading film stars over from America to play variety dates, it could bring a new lease of life to the genre.

Naturally, that would be very expensive, but full theatres and prestige would ease the blow, so it was an enormous coup for Lew, Leslie and Bernard when they started putting on big productions starring the likes of Danny Kaye, Mickey Rooney, Bob Hope, Judy Garland and the double act Martin and Lewis (Dean and Jerry, that is…)

Big selling recording stars fell into the same remit. That was how George had been booked to appear with Guy Mitchell. In June 1953,

PROGRAM

1. **BILLY TERNENT**
   AND HIS
   BROADCASTING ORCHESTRA
   featuring
   EVA BEYNON & JOHNNY WEBB

2. **GEORGE MARTIN**
   The Casual Comedian
   from his own T.V. Show

   ★ INTERVAL

3. **BILLY TERNENT**
   AND HIS
   BROADCASTING ORCHESTRA

4. # FRANK SINATRA
   with BILL MILLER at the piano

1. The public may leave at the end of the performance or exhibition by all exit doors and such doors must at that time be open. 2. All gangways, corridors, staircases and external passage-ways intended for exit shall be kept entirely free from obstructions whether permanent or temporary. 3. Persons shall not be permitted to stand in any of the gangways intersecting the seating, or to sit in any of the other gangways. If standing be permitted in the gangways at the sides and rear of the seating it shall be limited to the number indicated in the notices exhibited in those positions. 4. Safety Curtain must be lowered and raised in the presence of the audience.

★ WALLS ICE CREAM, SCHWEPPES MINERALS, CONFECTIONERY & CIGARETTES ON SALE IN THE FOYERS DURING THE INTERVAL

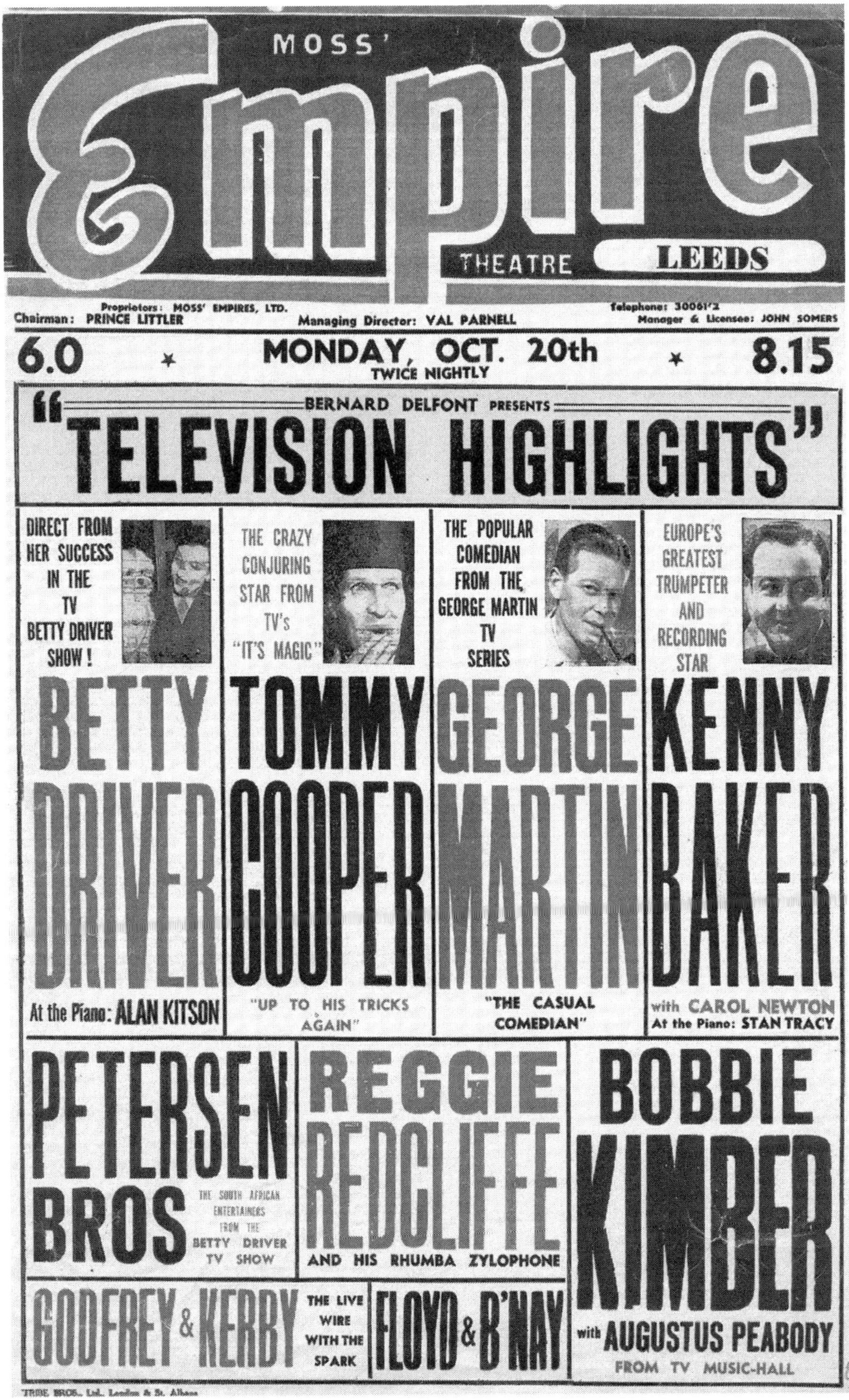

MOSS' Empire THEATRE LEEDS

Proprietors: MOSS' EMPIRES, LTD.
Chairman: PRINCE LITTLER Managing Director: VAL PARNELL
Telephone: 30061-2
Manager & Licensee: JOHN SOMERS

6.0 ✱ **MONDAY, OCT. 20th** ✱ **8.15**
TWICE NIGHTLY

BERNARD DELFONT PRESENTS
"TELEVISION HIGHLIGHTS"

DIRECT FROM HER SUCCESS IN THE TV BETTY DRIVER SHOW!
BETTY DRIVER
At the Piano: ALAN KITSON

THE CRAZY CONJURING STAR FROM TV's "IT'S MAGIC"
TOMMY COOPER
"UP TO HIS TRICKS AGAIN"

THE POPULAR COMEDIAN FROM THE GEORGE MARTIN TV SERIES
GEORGE MARTIN
"THE CASUAL COMEDIAN"

EUROPE'S GREATEST TRUMPETER AND RECORDING STAR
KENNY BAKER
with CAROL NEWTON
At the Piano: STAN TRACY

PETERSEN BROS
THE SOUTH AFRICAN ENTERTAINERS FROM THE BETTY DRIVER TV SHOW

REGGIE REDCLIFFE
AND HIS RHUMBA ZYLOPHONE

BOBBIE KIMBER
with AUGUSTUS PEABODY
FROM TV MUSIC-HALL

GODFREY & KERBY THE LIVE WIRE WITH THE SPARK **FLOYD & B'NAY**

TRIBE BROS., Ltd., London & St. Albans

he was support comic for Frank Sinatra at the Granada in Tooting, South London. He played several other dates with Sinatra, including the notorious Glasgow Empire, and Joan remembers Ol'Blue Eyes standing in the wings watching George's act, laughing heartily and commenting, "This guy is *good*". This was at the time when Sinatra's career was just about to undergo an enormous re-birth of success following his impressive role in the film *From Here to Eternity*.

Laurel and Hardy's film careers had more or less ground to a halt by this stage, but they were still big enough draws to fill theatres on two different tours they did in Great Britain during the early 1950s. I cannot track down exactly where it was, but I remember George speaking of at least one appearance he made with them somewhere.

As he got busier and the travelling became a real consideration, George bought his first car; a black, second hand Ford Pilot. Sue and Ray loved that car because it had running boards along the sides, just like the ones in gangster films. It also had a wide sun hatch, so the children could have a whale of a time, standing on the back seat with their heads sticking out of the roof as their Dad sped along en-route to his next appearance.

By now George, Joan and the children had moved to a council house in Friend Avenue, on an estate just on the outskirts of Aldershot. Now that Sue and Ray were attending school, they were not able to spend so much time accompanying their dad on the road, so he decided to find some company by buying a dog. This was Sally, a small black cocker spaniel which travelled with him for a brief period before contracting distemper. Sadly, she had to be put down.

Now that television was taking a hold on the nation and more and more people were purchasing T.V. sets, variety bills started to push those artistes who were making regular appearances on the box.

Bernard Delfont put out a touring production called *Television Highlights* featuring singer Betty Driver, comedy magician Tommy Cooper and George. All three were prominent on T.V., having had their own shows, so they took it in turns to top the bill. Betty Driver, who used to serenade her pet poodle on stage, was destined to become an even bigger star, thanks to her portrayal of Betty the barmaid from *Coronation Street*. Tommy Cooper, of course, became one of the icons of British comedy.

Tommy and George got on very well and they began sharing each other's cars on tour. They were together one day, with Tommy driving, when they found themselves proceeding the wrong way up a one way street.

Flagged down by a policeman, the loony conjuror was told, "I'm sorry sir, I'm afraid I shall have to book you."

"Well," responded Tommy, "you can only do that through the Grade Organization."

Sharing digs together, they were settling down to their evening meal when the landlady suddenly announced, "I used to be a turn myself, you know."

Curious, the two comics asked her what her particular talent had been. Dancer? Singer? Acrobat, perhaps?

"Animal impressions," she mumbled, hesitantly.

Intrigued, and stifling their chuckles, Tommy was the first to speak. "Can you do one for us, please?"

The landlady blushed and said, "Oh no, I couldn't possibly do it in front of anyone anymore."

"What a shame…" said George.

"Pity…" echoed Tommy, as their hostess hurried out of the room.

Moments later, from the refuge of the kitchen, they heard a resounding, "Moo-oo-oo…"

George and Tommy were stunned into silence, biting their lips to contain their laughter. Soon the lady was back into the dining room to serve them their main course.

"That was marvellous," gushed Tommy, "A cow, wasn't it? Do another one."

"Not in front of people," she insisted, as she scurried back to the kitchen.

Barely a moment passed before they heard a frantic, "Quack, quack, quack…"

And so it went on… "Woof, woof!", "Baaaa…", "Cock-a-doodle dooooo!" for the rest of the week!

Some of the cast of the Television Highlights tour. Kenny Baker, Betty Driver, "Augustus Peabody" (the vent doll of Bobbie Kimber) and George.

(Y.E.news photo Leeds)

By this time, George had honed his act into a fine art. He was very self assured on stage now and had the "casual" image nailed to perfection.

His originality was a real bonus and his ability to come up with what seemed like endless reams of topical material was much admired. Each day he would comb the newspapers, making notes and extracting funny ideas from the latest world or home events. Very often he would come up with a totally fresh comic slant on a story, but even when that proved difficult, an old gag could always be twisted to fit.

Consequently, his live lunchtime broadcasts on shows like *Worker's Playtime* were impressive because he was making jokes already about news which had only broken that very morning.

Likewise in his weekly theatre stints when his act would often

Second spot as the Sergeant Major.

alter from night to night as he adapted to the day's events.

His image had come a long way since the R.A.F.'s "Cheeky Chappy". Now he would stroll nonchalantly on stage, instantly putting the audience at ease with his benign smile and easy manner. It was all very relaxed but he was also watch-able, commanding attention with his comments about politicians and the state of the country. Sometimes he would use character voices, but usually he just relied on his observational line of chat.

He still dressed casually; the open necked shirt or maybe a thin cardigan, always clutching a newspaper which he would constantly refer to. In addition, he used a pipe as a prop, the stem of which he would prod at the pages for emphasis. He was not actually a pipe smoker (Players cigarettes were his choice), but in the early days of his career he would light the pipe on stage to add a bit of tastefully smoky atmosphere. That was until one performance when he unthinkingly put the pipe into his trouser pocket. The material actually caught fire and so he never lit it again after that!

Although it was this image that made his name, he quickly realised that it would benefit him to come up with an alternative, totally different act. This was because he was often required to do a second spot on a show. The idea he found could not have been more of a contrast to the Casual Comedian. In full uniform, complete with false, waxed moustache and swagger stick, he undertook the persona of a British Army Sergeant Major. *"Well calculated to bring a chill of recollection to many a manly chest"* said one review. Too true when one considered how many men in those days had been subjected to parade ground dressings down, not only during the war but carrying on with the government's policy of National Service. Although the Sergeant Major was something of a hate figure, complete with George's yelling, he somehow made it a symbol of fun and the character was well received.

Every comedian had their own signature tune and George adopted an old 1920s song. This was *Spread a Little Happiness* by the English musical comedy composer Vivian Ellis. Nowadays it is much better known as a single released by the pop star Sting from his 1980s film *Brimstone and Treacle,* but in the 1950s, the general public knew that its opening bars meant an appearance by George Martin. He also came up with his own catchphrase which he would always use to sign off his act… "Be lucky".

Ellis had written the song in 1929 for his musical *Mr. Cinders*, which was an inversion of the fairy tale, *Cinderella*, but with the gender roles reversed.

So, it was significant that the first pantomime George actually agreed to do was *Cinderella*, in the winter of 1953. It was at the Brixton Empress Theatre and he was cast as Buttons, a role he was undoubtedly born to play.

In the title role was 23 year old Shirley Abicair, recently arrived from Australia to seek her fortune. Her pretty face and talent for playing the zither were quickly spotted and she was being promoted heavily.

George excelled in his role as the "matey" servant and a review which describes the *"delightful quaintness of the kitchen scene"* goes on to say that he, *"… excels in his blending of light humour, topical wit and pathos."*

At the time, Max Bygraves had enjoyed a big hit with his recording of a novelty song called, *Big 'ead*, and George put his own

EMPRESS BRIXTON

A V.T.C. THEATRE
BOX OFFICE OPEN FROM 10 a.m.
TELEPHONE: BRI. 2201

CHAIRMAN: REGINALD C. BROMHEAD   MANAGING DIRECTOR: GERARD HEATH   MANAGER: DOYLE CROSSLEY

6.30   Commencing **BOXING DAY, 26th DECEMBER**   **8.45**
MATINEE EVERY DAY AT 2.30
THREE SHOWS DAILY   —   FOR TWO WEEKS ONLY

HINGE'S PRODUCTIONS LTD. present   THE GRAND CHRISTMAS PANTOMIME

CINDERELLA

THE TELEVISION STARS

SHIRLEY ABICAIR
AS "CINDERELLA"

GEORGE MARTIN
AS "BUTTONS"

HILDA CAMPBELL-RUSSELL AS "PRINCE CHARMING"

SAM KERN and **ROY DE YONG** AS "THE UGLY SISTERS"

ELSIE DUNN AS "DANDINI"   **BILLY GRANT** AS "BARON"

PETER KENT AS "SMASHEM"   **LESLIE WALLIS** AS "BARONESS"

PATRICIA ELLIOT AS "FAIRY"   MAGNIFICENT CRYSTAL COACH AND REAL LIVE PONIES   **AL CLIFFORD** AS "GRABBEM"

ADELAIDE ELLIOT'S FAMOUS **DANCING STARLETS**   TWELVE GLORIOUS SCENES AND A HUGE ALL STAR COMPANY   FULL LONDON CHORUS & BALLET Choreography by **MERRIE JANISS**

BOOK NOW! ★ A WEST END PANTOMIME AT USUAL PRICES ★ BOOK NOW!

TAYLORS, PRINTERS, WOMBWELL, YORKS.

stamp on this by turning it into a rousing chorus number which encouraged loud audience participation. The show actually transferred to the Metropolitan Theatre Edgware Road halfway through the run, and Shirley Abicair, for reasons which are somewhat obscure, dropped out. Her place was taken by the Fairy Queen, Patricia Elliott.

1953 had been another eventful year for George. Apart from a hectic schedule on the work front, he had also attended his brother's wedding in February. (Bill's new bride was actually the winner of the Miss Aldershot competition, one Cynthia Middleton.)

When The Martin Brother's split up, Bill and Bob were both briefly at a loose end. Bill quickly found work with another act, The Joe Daniels Trio, and Bob started his own band which became Mac and his Music. However, music alone was not enough for Bob, Joyce and their baby, so they bought into a dry cleaning business which eventually did very well.

As for Bill, he decided to follow his big brother onto the stage as a solo comic. He did reasonably well, securing a season back at the Windmill, touring the halls and playing in pantomime. So that there would be no confusion, he billed himself as the guitar playing comedian; Bill Vinden, his mother's maiden name.

Bill had become a fine musician, not only as a solid, jazz style guitarist, but notably as a strong pianist with a huge repertoire and an ability to busk along with anything.

But, like Bob, Bill was not convinced that show-business alone was enough to pay the bills. Also, it was inevitable that he was a bit in the shadow of his more famous brother. Perhaps under pressure from his new wife, he became landlord of a pub; The Angler's Rest, in the Ash Vale area just outside of Aldershot.

Bill and Cynthia would produce their only child in 1954, a son named Trevor.

On March 23rd. of the same year, Joan gave birth again, another boy; Michael George... yours truly, the author of this book.

Buttons

Following the troubles resulting from George's affair with the Windmill girl, he and Joan had patched things up and, it seems, Michael was the result of their reconciliation.

Just two days before the birth, George was in Cardiff doing a B.B.C. radio broadcast called *Saturday Starlight*. On the night of the birth itself, Joan had been at a dance, so Michael was a rather inconvenient arrival in the early hours of the morning.

1954 was also the centenary of the founding of Aldershot's Military Garrison in the Crimean War. Celebrations were in order, so a televised show was put on at the Garrison Theatre starring George (aptly doing his Sergeant Major act, of course), Cicely Courtenidge, Cyril Fletcher and full supporting cast.

In May George went on a long tour with his old friend Guy Mitchell who was over from the U.S.A. again to play the countrywide Moss Empires. Comedian Joe Church was also on this tour and it was the beginning of a life long, close friendship for the two comics. They would often travel and share digs together. Joe recalled that George was always fun to be with. Although Joe was two years older than George, which Joe did not realise at the time, he somehow always regarded his friend like a big brother. "I think it was because he always got bigger billing than me!" said Joe.

This led to a general feeling around the profession that George and Joe really were related. When working on his own, Joe would turn up at a theatre for his band call on a Monday and the stage doorman would often say, "Your brother was here last week" and Joe would answer, "If you mean George Martin, he's not my brother, he's my mate!"

A bit later George and Joe would also tour together in the Al Martino Show.

Chapter 9

IT'S ALL IN BLACK AND WHITE

The variety period was a golden age for all of those who experienced it first hand. It seems that anyone who lived through it looks back on those days fondly, if not just for the fact that it was a time when there was plenty of work for entertainers.

George stayed busy and remained in demand for numerous requests. Live appearances, radio, T.V., charity shows and all kinds of social invitations.

On the road, there were plenty of opportunities to catch up with past acquaintances who may have dispersed to various parts of the country. For instance, his cousin Ronnie said, "No one clapped louder than me when The Casual Comedian came to Blackpool". Following a separation of several years, George was delighted to be visited backstage at the Palladium by his old Aldershot workmate Bill Egan.

At another theatre one night after the show, George got a message from the stage door to say that an old service friend from the war was anxious to see him. It was not unusual for this to happen as many men he had served with would come and say hello when he was working in their town.

"What's his name?" asked George, only to be told, "He wants to surprise you."

Intrigued, George agreed to see him, but when the man turned up in his dressing room, with a couple of others, George did not recognize any of them.

"Hello George!" beamed this stranger, throwing his arms around him and pumping his hand vigorously. "Just been out front. Great show!" Turning to his companions, he added, "I always knew he'd get somewhere. So good to see you, mate!"

George was perplexed. He was pretty certain that he had never seen this man before in his life, but, taking it slowly, he smiled and said, "Now you're going to have to remind me..."

The man's expression dimmed just a little and he looked slightly deflated, but he persisted, "Ha, ha, George, always the joker. Don't tell me you don't remember me?"

"Well, I must be honest..."

"Ha, ha, ha..." The man was starting to lose face now. "Come on, mate. Don't you remember when we were in the army together... in Cairo?"

George nodded, knowingly. "I'm sorry, my friend. You've got the wrong man. I was in the Air Force in Canada."

The stranger looked horrified. "Don't be daft. Course you weren't. You were with me in the army, in Cairo."

George shook his head. "No, really. R.A.F. in Canada."

"Oh, come on," said the increasingly disappointed man, "Think *back*!"

It was at this point that George saw the complete absurdity of the situation. He tried to remain amiable with this complete stranger but the man was now getting quite hostile. Flouncing out of the room, he barked at his bewildered companions, "Huh, that's the trouble when they get famous... they get all big headed and don't want to know you!"

A similar situation also arose when someone insisted that he had known George during his childhood in Leicester.

"No," sighed George, "I'm from Aldershot."

At least, on this occasion, the mistake could probably be explained by confusion with fellow comedian, Bill Maynard, *The Sweater Boy*, who had been born in Farnham, near Aldershot, but had moved to Leicester as a child.

In the winter of '54, George was engaged for his second pantomime; *Jack and the Beanstalk*, this time at Wimbledon Theatre. George played Jack's brother, Georgie, much to the delight of his

The Sergeant Major with Arthur Haynes.

children, who would cheer him on as he indulged in various stunts which included climbing all over the giant's furniture. Even at such a young age, Ray was puzzled by the perspective of the giant's image. He could never quite understand how the giant's first appearance involved a huge hand emerging from the wings, which was at least the size of a full grown adult. Yet, in the second half of the show, when the giant finally made a complete entry, he stomped across the stage as a figure only about 10 feet high with an oversized head!

Joan Mann played Jack in this show (following in the long established panto tradition of females playing the lead male part) and George's 8 year old daughter Sue enjoyed regular treats in Miss Mann's dressing room eating crumpets with cream cheese and celery. Sue thought this to be the height of sophistication, the best "tea" ever!

1955 brought further progress with George's basic B.B.C. broadcasting fee being raised from 21 to 25 guineas. This meant, along with all his other potential income, he was actually earning very well, enough for some of the Martin family's neighbours in Friend Avenue to begin questioning why a celebrity was still occupying a council house. This was not helped when George employed a publicity agent who told the press that his client was earning a fortune, actually quoting a figure which was well in excess of the truth.

When George queried this highly paid PR's motive, he was told, "Its good for your image."

"That's all very well," said George, "but now the neighbours won't talk to us!"

This did plant a seed with him and Joan that maybe they should start looking for somewhere else to live.

But it was still a hectic time with lots of distraction. The Grades negotiated a long term B.B.C. television contract for him which began on September 5th. 1955 for an initial two year period. (Clause 3 in the paperwork exercised an option to extend the contract if required.) It guaranteed financial reward of £400 for the first year, rising to £450 for the second year, with the promise of a minimum six programmes annually. Programmes in excess of six were to be paid at the rate of £50 per show. Any repeats would incur a further fee of £50 per showing. This money was to be paid to George on a regular quarterly basis.

And so George's television career really took off as he embarked on a round of guest spots. *It's a Great Life*, *Face the Music*, *Variety Parade*, *First House*, *Monday Melody*, *The Jimmy Wheeler Show* and *Those Beverley Sisters*, to mention but a few. The Beverley Sisters were at the peak of their popularity. Joy and her twin sisters, Babs and Teddy, had become big stars at a young age, on stage, screen, radio and record. George struck a chord with them straightaway, worked regularly on the same bills and found a musical compatibility too.

Jimmy Wheeler was a "larger than life" character comedian whose capacity for "stopping gin going bad" was legendary. He and George would often match each other, drink for drink. Jimmy's hilarious performances never seemed to be adversely affected by his drinking habits although there was one memorable occasion when he made his entrance and fell straight into the orchestra pit, accompanying himself with his familiar catchphrase, "Aye, aye, that's yer lot!"

The world of television was full of colourful characters, not all

Working with the Beverley Sisters.

of them with variety backgrounds. Gilbert Harding was a stern faced personality who looked like a bank manager, although he made his name on the panel game *What's My Line?*, alongside David Nixon, Lady Isobel Barnett and Barbara Kelly. He was notorious for his brusque manner, cutting comments and manners which stopped just short of being plain rude. Largely, it was a gimmick for him, in much the same way as personalities on T.V. panels grew to promote themselves in shows many years later. George actually got on socially with him very well and spent a lot of time in his company. Harding certainly had a more sensitive side although George was deeply shocked when he witnessed his friend's darker traits.

One night in a hotel bar, as the barmaid came around to collect the glasses, Harding was at his worst. His reaction to her polite request to "drink up" because the bar was closing was, "Fuck off you festering bitch"!

By way of complete contrast to this behaviour, Kenneth Horne, who also came to prominence around this time, was a total gentleman. Mild mannered, amiable, witty and, all in all, the archetypal Englishman. He is mostly remembered for his long running radio programme *Round the Horne* with Kenneth Williams, but in May 1957 he and George embarked on a seven part television series together.

It was called *Pleasure Boat* and it was transmitted live fortnightly on Friday evenings at 8.00pm.. The idea was a kind of mini variety show aboard a small pleasure cruiser, making its way along various waterways, including the Solent, the Norfolk Broads, the Scottish lochs and even a cruise in Holland. The format was informal with Horne playing the vessel's Commander and George as a kind of bosun figure. George would interact with his surroundings, telling a few topical gags and introducing the likes of crew members such as crooner Michael Holliday, all supported by the charms of five "Crew Girls" who, according to the Radio Times, could be depended upon to, "look decorative and show a leg"!

The first show took place on the Thames aboard the good ship Mapledurham. It was a jolly little series and typical of the easy going entertainment of the era. Strangely enough, George's passport does not bear a stamp for Holland during this period. Perhaps such a formality was more easily overlooked under the circumstances back then, but it is interesting to note that the document does bear a Dutch stamp from February 11th until the 23rd. 1955. I do not know of any

Radio Times.

reason why he would have been in the Netherlands at that time, but maybe there were engagements for the military again.

Also relevant to this is the story of a very nice watch he owned which had been a gift. One day when he was shaving, Joan had noticed that the back of this watch lying beside the sink was engraved with a personal message to "My darling George..."

Challenging him over this, Joan was somewhat taken aback by his reaction which was one of total denial. Apparently, when the offending watch had been thrust under his nose, he had calmly looked at it and shrugged.

"What message?" he asked, innocently.

"There!" snapped Joan, pointing out the words.

"I can't see anything." replied George as he carried on shaving.

Incredulous, Joan persisted in challenging him, but he just continued to deny that there was anything written on the watch! In the end, she gave up, but it cannot have exactly helped their relationship.

"That was always the trouble with him," said Joan, years later, "like an ostrich with his head in the sand. If he didn't want to face something he would ignore it. I think he was trying to drive me mad, like that bloke with the woman in the film *Gaslight*!"

Whilst not condoning his methods, I must say I have always grudgingly respected the sheer nerve he must have had in carrying out such tactics!

Ironically, this same watch was to feature in a dramatic little incident during the transmission of a *Pleasure Boat* show. Live on air, as the boat chugged along the waterway, George was describing something on the far shore. To make his point, he threw out his arm quite forcefully and the watch flew off of his wrist, disappearing forever into the current with a plop. Very symbolic, some might say...

Joan made a television appearance herself, courtesy of her husband. In December 1956, she appeared in a programme called *Lets Make a Date*, which was a kind of interview/variety show in which celebrity's spouses spoke about their other halves. She was interviewed by Brian Reece, the actor who played the title role in the popular radio series *The Adventures of P.C. 49*, and George came on in person to perform a spot. Produced by Barney Colehan (of *The Good Old Days* fame), this show also included the television debuts of some contrasting famous faces. Firstly, the puppet pigs Pinky and Perky, who would go on to much greater things, and also a very inexperienced and raw 19 year old girl called Shirley Bassey. Bassey's first single had been released earlier that year. It was entitled *Burn My Candle at Both Ends* and it had been banned by the B.B.C. for suggestive lyrics!

Other T.V. shows George featured in that year included something called *Tess and Jim*, as well as *We Are Your Servants*, in which he played the role of a floor manager, engaging in some banter with Terry-Thomas.

On February 4th. 1957, the Windmill Theatre celebrated its 25th. Anniversary in style with a glittering, multi-layered event. The birthday show took place at the theatre itself, but there was also a special radio show, reams of newspaper coverage and a television broadcast from the Trocadero where numerous stars paid a cabaret tribute to Van Damm. The film star Kenneth More opened the theatre show in overalls, sweeping the stage whilst uttering the single line, "You've got to start somewhere". Jimmy Edwards appeared too, seated on a beer crate, saying, "I devised this so that I could get from the stage to the boozer in three minutes flat!" Bruce Forsyth was in cracking form, apparently, and The Stage reported that, *"George Martin looked happy doing his casual comedy, leaning on the piano and sucking his pipe as he did when a Mill regular"*.

When the show was over, everything moved up the road to the

Trocadero where the fun resumed until the small hours. It was a black tie occasion and even the B.B.C. cameramen were in evening dress, amidst *"gaily bedecked festive raiment"*. This part of the evening was compered by Richard Murdoch and he presented such turns as Benny Hill and Bob Monkhouse who sang a duet about their rejection from Windmill auditions, which amused Van Damm no end. Harry Secombe performed some opera and Peter Sellers came on in disguise as the stage doorman to be interviewed by George. The Stage described this sketch as an *"hilarious interlude"*. The audience was filled with V.I.P.s, including B.B.C. top executives Cecil Madden and Ronnie Waldman, as well as impresario Emile Littler.

George's young brother, Bill, was still youthful enough to be greatly impressed by the wall to wall celebrities. Emerging excitedly from the gent's toilet, he rushed up to George and gushed, "Hey, guess what? I've just had a piss with Kenneth More!"

Although George was doing well and making many friends in show business, incidents were beginning to occur which, it seems, were to ultimately harm his career. Laid back by nature, he possessed an attitude which translated, basically, as "live for the moment". He had a reputation for being generous, with his money, time and favours, but unfortunately his priorities did not always gel with everyone else's agenda. This could often be summed up in the phrase "out of sight, out of mind", a general rule of thumb which he stuck to throughout his life. He could be warm, thoughtful, charming and helpful. A terrific party guest, he was also entertaining and usually the first to buy a big round at the bar, but these traits only seemed to be apparent if he was actually present. Sadly, there was also a highly unreliable side to him, and he was hopeless with his finances.

Strewn throughout the record of his success, there are numerous examples of this. In October 1956, a strong letter of complaint was sent to the Grades by the B.B.C.'s Variety Booking Manager about George's lackadaisical behaviour. This referred to a particular incident when he had been booked to appear on a *Midday Music Hall* broadcast and had not presented himself to the producer, who was ranting with worry. George was eventually found calmly sitting in his dressing room making adjustments to the script. No contract had been returned either. This was not the last time the Grades had to apologise on his behalf.

It was not uncommon for Joan to answer a telephone call around lunchtime with some concerned voice on the end of the line asking for George. Joan had learned early on to always ask who was speaking before she gave out any information. Inevitably it would be someone like Burton Brown, his main contact at the Grade's office, or perhaps a worried T.V. or radio employee wanting to know where he was. Often they would be saying, "He is supposed to be here now", and Joan would cover for the fact that he was still upstairs in bed with the lie, "Well, he left ages ago".

Once when he missed a band call on a variety booking, he was not unduly worried because he knew the band and felt confident that it would not matter. However, a lesson seems to have been in order because when he collected his money from the theatre manager at the end of the week's run, a hefty chunk of cash was missing. When he queried it, he was told that on the instructions of Ms. Cissie Williams, he had been fined as a punishment.

Feeling sure that she had no right to authorise an unofficial fine, he went to his representative union, the Variety Artistes

Federation, to complain only to be told, "Oh no, we can't fight Moss Empires... they're too big."

George was so annoyed by this that when the V.A.F. man came around to collect his annual subscription, George refused to pay it saying, "You lot weren't there to help when I needed you. You're no good to me."

Consequently, George was not represented by a union for many years to come, until he joined Equity much later in life. (By this time, the V.A.F. had merged with Equity.)

Another complication arose which was not specifically George's fault. A memo from the B.B.C.'s Tom Sloan blamed the Grades for dishonouring the terms of George's long term T.V. agreement by putting him into pantomime in the winter of 1955 when he should have been "guesting" on the *Vera Lynn Show*. (The panto in question was, I think, *Robinson Crusoe*, with Avril Angers in Folkestone.)

There is no way of knowing for sure, but this kind of thing was probably instrumental in the decision the B.B.C. made towards the end of his two year T.V. contract. They decided to not exercise the option in Clause 3, meaning that they would not be interested in extending it for a further year. The same memo also states that they were also not interested in similar terms for Dennis Spicer and Edna Savage, although they were yet to decide about Petula Clark.

This must have been quite a blow at the time, as George was at the peak of his popularity. Work was still coming in, and he continued to perform in television, but losing the security of a solid commitment was quite significant. However, it did leave him free to be able to make appearances on the brand new independent T.V. channel which Lew Grade had been hugely instrumental in setting up to rival the B.B.C..

Variety dates were still rolling in but there were already strong indications that the entire scene was on borrowed time. As previously stated, the growing popularity of television was beginning to noticeably affect theatre attendances, and venues were becoming increasingly desperate to find attractions which could be guaranteed to "put bums on seats".

Audiences were changing too. This had first been noticed in the early 50s when American singing star Johnnie Ray had topped at the Palladium. It was quite a novelty at the time to see young girls actually standing up and screaming from the stalls, but this kind of thing would become the norm as more stars of this calibre were booked to tour the halls.

Rock 'n' Roll had crashed into the British public's sensibility with the release of the film *Rock Around the Clock*, and when the star of the movie, Bill Haley, came over to do a variety tour with his Comets, homespun youth went wild.

As a precursor to the real onset of Rock n' Roll, Britain underwent the short, but influential, skiffle craze. Spearheaded by Lonnie Donegan, but followed by other emerging skiffle stars such as Chas McDevitt, this phenomenon was a huge hit with teenagers. At last they had found an outlet for their simmering post war frustrations. The music was simple but infectious, based on old American blues and country material, and anyone could play it. Countless bands featuring cheap guitars, tea chest basses and washboards sprang up all over the place. (Two chords were all that were generally needed, although some of the more advanced combos might learn three, or even four!)

As skiffle gave way to the more sophisticated complexities of Rock n' Roll, George found himself supporting more and more artistes who specifically appealed to the younger generation. Bills headlined by the likes of Frankie Lymon and the Teenagers, for instance. Consequently, the family element of variety shows began to dwindle as the mums and dads would not come out to see these performers. And yet the young stars would still be supported by the type of acts who had always appeared... jugglers, acrobatic dancers, magicians, animal specialities and conventional comedians; the kind of fare which did not really go down too well with teenagers who had turned up to rock the night away. It was a paradox and dilemma of epic proportions which spelled the end of variety.

And yet, by the same token, when old school variety acts began to bemoan the fact that television and rock music was killing their living, it had to be acknowledged that these two things were just what was keeping variety's head above the water in those last few years.

But, in the mid to late 50s, there was still a spark remaining in the scene. In May 1956 George returned to his home town to appear for a week headlining his own show at the Hippodrome, where he had witnessed his first taste of variety as a child.

A great "All Star" Holiday Attraction featuring Aldershot's own Star Radio and Television Comedian – First Time Here! GEORGE MARTIN, The Casual Comedian – in A W(H)IT AND GLAMOUR PARADE.

This production was another sign of times to come, because although the support acts included traditional turns like Canadian dancers Chic & Candy Ross, "Laugh Tonic" Len Howe & Audrey and Shek-Ben-Ali, second on the bill was Denise Vane, "the Navy's own pin-up lovely and Olympic model". Within a few years this sort of attraction had degenerated into outright nude revue shows as the theatres fought a losing battle to bring people in, albeit a very different kind of audience to the one attracted by the likes of Gracie Fields.

For some reason, George was always haunted by the feeling that he had not done very well in the Aldershot show. Too close to home, perhaps.

As the 50s progressed, Britain began to produce more home grown talent to rival the youthful American stars. The country's answer to Elvis Presley had initially been chirpy Tommy Steele, but his popularity was quite quickly usurped by a much more smouldering singer, one Cliff Richard, backed by The Shadows. George appeared with them all and he, like all variety performers, was seeing the "writing on the wall".

Skiffle star Chas McDevitt (of *Freight Train* fame) recalled a memorable week's variety with George at the Granada in Shrewsbury, a show topped by "Queen of the Keyboard" Winifred Atwell. Chas spoke of some pretty wild parties taking place, when the local butcher's wife performed striptease on a table and rubber necked comedian Nat Jackley did his infamous impression of a bulldog by crawling around naked on all fours with his testicles crammed between his legs! Nat and George made an arrangement with a local brewery whereby they would find an excuse to mention the beer during every performance. As a reward, a crate of the brew would be delivered to the stage door every day.

Some of the shows during this time could be classed as a

compromise, because rather than always being straight Rock n' Roll, the youngsters also screamed for some of the more conventional singers, like Dickie Valentine. Struggling to make himself heard whilst performing his act immediately before Valentine's appearance on stage, George became exasperated by hundreds of girls chanting, "We want Dick! We want Dick!"

Rolling his eyes, George merely made the dry comment, "I'll bet you do", but he found himself carpeted by the venue's manager who indignantly scolded him with the words, "I will not have that kind of filth in my theatre"!

Goodness, how times have changed...

HIPPODROME - ALDERSHOT

Lessees: Milstead Productions Ltd. Gen. Man. & Lic. Newman Maurice
Man. Dir. J. Rowland Sales F.V.I. Tel. Box Office, Aldershot 2304

6-0 ★ MONDAY, MAY 21st 1956 ★ 8-10

The Management take Pleasure in Presenting
A GREAT "ALL STAR" HOLIDAY ATTRACTION
—— FEATURING ——
Aldershot's own Star Radio and Television Comedian

FIRST TIME HERE!

GEORGE MARTIN

THE CASUAL COMEDIAN—in

A W(H)IT AND GLAMOUR PARADE

DENISE VANE

THE NAVY'S OWN PIN-UP LOVELY AND OLYMPIC GAMES MODEL

Almost a Sailor **BOB NELSON**	HERE'S ANOTHER LAUGH TONIC **LEN HOWE**	**KITTY GILLOW**
Canadian Dancers **CHIC & CANDY ROSS**	**AND AUDREY**	THE PERSONALITY MALE

PAKISTAN'S FAMOUS COMEDY MAGICIAN
NOBODY INSIDE
NOBODY OUTSIDE **SHEK-BEN-ALI**

Richard Whewell (Bolton) Limited.

Chapter 10

FAMILY MAN?

So what of George Martin the character? I have already given an indication of the complexities of his personality, as in his ability to show a cavalier attitude to his work. Of course, everyone is complicated, but George often seemed to show traits which were a trifle confusing to those who knew him well.

He had enjoyed a fairly smooth journey from struggling artiste to successful celebrity, but unlike most in his position, he did not seem very interested in promoting himself. Courting publicity appeared alien to him and he just happily coasted along, taking the offers that came to him, doing the jobs and enjoying the perks along the way. For instance, if he was recognised in public (a common occurrence), instead of basking in the adulation and compliments, he would quite often say something like, "No, that's not me. That's my brother". George just would not play the publicity game, which must have been enormously frustrating to those who were trying to direct his career. By contrast, his fellow Aldershot comedian friend, Arthur English, actively sought out any opportunity to get his name into the newspapers, but George was the total opposite. He loved the "business", as it were, but he did not condone a lot of the territory which went with it.

A letter I received from The Beverley Sisters bears this out.

"George simply was unique and without doubt one of the most special people we have ever known. He was unquestionably a brilliant artist and a brilliant friend. Unusually kind and gentle, with that exquisite sense of humour.

He worked hard, and happily had enormous success, but we three always felt he was far too modest, with a lack of ego to promote himself. George created an entirely new and original style for his comedy, unlike any other comedian.

Of course, we also adored his singing voice and his completely self taught musicality. He wrote a beautiful song for us, A Small Shepherd Boy, which we recorded on Columbia, Christmas 1961.

Everyone loved George, he was simply a one off, a truly lovely and massively talented man."

Indeed, his popularity was without question, but when it came to the actual *business* of show-business he really did not seem to care.

Also, although he was well loved by his friends and appreciated socially, he did not suffer fools gladly. Generally calm by nature, if he saw an injustice or was backed into a corner, he was capable of fighting back with considerable force, examples of which we shall see as this book progresses.

He had a habit of going through phases, whereby he would take to something enthusiastically for a short time before dropping it abruptly. For example, he once decided that he was going to the pub too often, so he started spending his leisure time building intricate models of buildings, laboriously concentrating on the smallest detail. Characteristically, the one I particularly remember was of a pub!

He was actually very creative and good with his hands. I vividly recall a mini-masterpiece he made for me as a child. It was just a shoebox with a viewing hole cut in the end, but when I looked inside, a whole new world emerged. By manipulating little controllers on the outside of the box, I was looking into a haunted house. Doors would open beneath a gothic sign which warned, "Abandon Hope All Ye Who Enter Here". In a spooky, panelled room, a terrified figure shook with fright in a four poster bed as ghosts and demons floated by, wraiths materialised from a grandfather clock and bats fluttered at the ceiling. All of it fashioned from pieces of card and thin wire.

Once he bought a tent, the idea being to save himself money on digs when on the road. This brain wave was short lived however, the final straw being when he pitched it late one night in the fog and woke the next morning to find himself camped on a grass verge next to a footpath with hordes of commuters trudging past him!

I was about 3 years old when we finally moved from our council house. Pressure from the local authority had been growing and George and Joan decided to buy a large, 5 bed-roomed detached house a couple of miles from Aldershot. The address was 64 Osborne Rd., Farnborough, Hampshire, and we kids loved that house. It was like a child's fantasy, with a big garden full of nooks and crannies. French windows opened onto a long lawn which led to a fish pond and a heavily vegetated sloped rockery. Stone steps wound up to an elevated greenhouse, beneath which was a World War 2 vintage air raid shelter. There was also a shed containing rabbit hutches and a chicken run.

The potential of this garden for imaginary scenarios was endless. The rockery was like a jungle and the greenhouse a fort. The shed

64 Osborne Rd., Farnborough, Hampshire.

had a kind of inner chamber, sealed by chicken wire and a separate door; a perfect sheriff's jail for cowboy games. As for the air raid shelter, that was pure ecstasy for our imaginations. Before long, my brother and sister had constructed a secret den down there.

George came home one day with a full size, very realistic looking rubber crocodile which he had acquired somewhere or other. This found pride of place alongside the fish pond where it alarmed several visitors.

Because he was working away so much, I did not have daily contact with my father in those days. I remember him coming home as a special event which occurred pretty regularly, but not often enough as to be routine. Sundays were fairly special because he was likely to be at home, in the day at least. This was because variety theatres were not open on Sundays, but he would still often be committed to working at a charity show, or maybe radio, T.V., or some other kind of appearance. I have clear memories of him sitting with his feet up in our dining room, watching some old film on television as he ate winkles, picking them out of their shells with a pin.

I remember him asking us, "What did the cockle say to the winkle? If I had a pin, I'd take you out!"

There was a large front room which looked onto the road. George, on a whim, decided that he wanted to have the inner wall knocked down so that it would be open plan onto the entrance hall and stairs. A modern approach back then. This was done and many late night parties took place there.

I can recall many a night as a child, laying in bed and listening to the distant sounds of late night carousing. George had recently bought an upright piano, the tinkling of which echoed into the night as he entertained his guests.

Not everyone enjoyed these parties. We had a particularly miserable neighbour, one Mrs. Freeman and her grouchy husband, who took an instant dislike to my parents and their fun loving lifestyle. Regardless of early attempts to placate her, Mrs. Freeman made it a personal crusade to complain about everything that went on in our house. Her sour face at the window and twitching curtains became a regular feature. I guess things were not helped by a musician friend of George's standing on her lawn at about three in the morning playing *Friends and Neighbours* very loudly on his trumpet.

George also decided to convert the garage into an office and was happy to leave his car on the drive. At first this office was something of a haven for him, and he would spend a great deal of time out there, tapping away on his typewriter by the light of a bright desk lamp, but eventually it got neglected and became ankle deep in discarded papers. Its place was taken by one of the spare rooms upstairs which soon went the same way.

George was in demand locally to support various functions, so it was inevitable that he would join the relevant Masonic Lodge. This meant more dinners and appearances, and the arrival of Nip Eustace, a prominent Aldershot bookmaker and entrepreneur who became a close friend. George, Nip and a select group of local high fliers transformed into a kind of Aldershot "inner sanctum", unofficial membership of which was much desired.

Another valued companion from this period was Cyril Parlane, the businessman whose friendship stretched back to the War. (He had supplied the cabs, you may recall, for George and Joan's wedding.) He and his wife, Elsie, were real party animals. Cyril would think nothing of suddenly deciding to drive to London to hit the nightclubs. This would often be following a night of heavy drinking at pubs or one another's houses. No breathalyzer in those days, of course. In fact the whole "drink/driving" scene was much more accepted back then. Not to be condoned, naturally, but that is the way it was.

George, for some reason, did not accompany Cyril on one fateful late night London visit, which was just as well, as Cyril was killed in a head on car crash on the way home. He and George had just purchased identical brand new cars, the registration plates of which differed by only one digit. This was poignant for George when he saw the picture of Cyril's wrecked car in the newspaper.

Living not far away in Fleet was another comedian who had come to prominence via The Windmill. This was Bill Maynard, known as The Sweater Boy because he also had a casual image, although he worked in a much more frantic way than George. In fact he had an odd way of moving, darting about all over the place as he told his gags. Bill's parents lived in a caravan in the area and this is what had brought him back down from Leicester. He had a nice bungalow and lived with all the trappings of his considerable television success, a career which had come to fruition when he had paired up with comic Terry Scott for the series *Great Scott, It's Maynard!* He was now working solo again and he and George socialized quite a lot when they were both in the area. By his own admission, Bill's success went to his head and he gained a reputation for being difficult to work with. Sue, Ray and I can remember going to his home where there was very little furniture. All the evidence of his celebrity status appeared to be on the surface; flash cars, etc., with little attention paid to home comforts.

"Me and your dad were considered *avant garde* comics of the day," said Bill.

Bill's career crashed to earth when he went broke in 1960. He owed a fortune in tax and found himself out of work. Going back up north, he changed direction and started finding work as a straight actor in repertory theatre. This meant he fell from earning £1,000 a week to £9 a week; quite a change in lifestyle. However, slowly but surely, he built himself up again, started getting some small film roles and eventually ended up with his own situation comedy T.V. show *Oh no, it's Selwyn Froggit!* From there he became a long running regular in the T.V. police series *Heartbeat* as the character "Greengrass".

As for George, the bookings were still coming in, although he was beginning, uncharacteristically, to look ahead. The future of variety looked grim. How much longer could it last? Most bills were now topped by pop stars or nude women. Theatres were getting tattier, audiences were diminishing...

But there was still always pantomime. In the winter of 1957 into '58 George reprised his favourite role of Buttons in *Cinderella* at the Essoldo Garrick in Southport. Iris Villiers sang like *"the happiest girl on earth"* as Cinders (according to The Stage) and the production was especially lavish with *"inspired decor and costumes"*, plus a *"first rate blend of fun... and spectacular colour"*. There was a glittering coach with miniature white ponies, a *"colour-scape of wonder in the ballroom*

George's song which was recorded by the Beverley Sisters.

scene" and a *"fantasy of butterflies and fairies, glowing in ultra violet light"*.

Of George, the reviewer said, *"George Martin's performance as Buttons shows a wealth of sincerity, and his polished combination of humour, pathos and faultless expression make him the best in the role that Southport can remember. He deserves immediate recognition for his acting ability. In addition to all this, he has written two songs which he sings with appeal, and his comedy talents are shown in a rapid kitchen scene"*.

The Ugly Sisters, Prince Charming, Dandini; all the traditional elements were present. Even the pony droppings were swept deftly off the stage by the sweetly smiling chorus girls! George's self penned songs were catchy ditties; the novelty *"I Want to be a Space Ship Pilot"* (he would make his entrance on a mini motorbike) and the charming, melodious *"Fairy Tale Coach and Pair"*.

By this time, Ray and Sue were heavily involved with their schooling so they were not able to tour around with their father as they had done in the early days. Joan was committed to her home-life as well, and George was absent for much of the time. Panto season was a bit different though, as it fell largely during the school Christmas holidays, so Joan was usually able to take the children to whatever town George was appearing in to spend a few family days together. (This proved difficult during the Folkestone panto, however, because George developed a painful touch of gout which laid him up for a while, trapping them all in the hotel.)

December 1958 saw the beginning of the run of *Goldilocks and the Three Bears* at the Winter Gardens Pavilion in Blackpool. A Howard and Wyndham production, it was written by David Croft who would eventually find fame as one of the writers (with Jimmy Perry) of situation comedies such as *Dad's Army*. The setting was Gemmell's Circus, with comedienne Betty Jumel as Meg Gemmell, and George playing another Georgie character who was employed by the circus. An actor named John Payne played a sinister rival circus owner named Heinkel. (This man was also to play a fairly significant role in *my* life eventually, and we will get to that later.) Something delayed George one day and he was late arriving for a performance. The show had already started and John Payne had been sent on as George's stand-in to cover until he arrived. George was somewhat

*Cinderella,
Southport*

put out by the fact that John Payne had already done most of George's personal act, word for word, by the time he got on stage!

George wrote a special song for this show too; *Baby Bear Lullaby*. It was used in an enchanting little scene as the baby bear is laid down to sleep, and it has always been a favourite of mine. A beautifully constructed, magical number which deserves to see the light of day again.

1959 into 60 took George to Birmingham for another lavish production of *Cinderella* at the Alexandra Theatre. With Mary Benning in the title role, George yet again played Buttons, alongside Bartlett and Ross as the Ugly Sisters. The Keepers of the Prince's Music were a close harmony quartet from Ireland; The Four Ramblers. One of them was to find fame as a major star of B.B.C. Saturday night television... Val Doonican. The stooge-like Broker's Men were portrayed by a young comedy double act who were yet to make their mark as Mike and Bernie Winters.

"It was a quiet and happy show," recalled Mike, wistfully, "no dramas or squabbles, no pregnant dancers... it was our first big show and your dad calmed our nerves and was a most kind and easy to work with performer. Later in our career, Bernie played Buttons and the experience he had gained working with George, one of the finest Buttons in the business, was a big help to him. It was a pleasure working with George, who, by the way, continually gave us funny lines to use that he had just written. Boy, we could have done with him when we got our own T.V. series!"

And still variety hung in there during the late 50s, with George sharing some traditional style bills with the likes of singers such as Edmund Hockridge and Alma Cogan. Alma was a big star with a sunny personality whose popularity was as genuinely sound with her peers as it was with her public. Ray has fond memories of sitting in her dressing room (as a child, of course!) watching her put her make-up on. Tragically, she was destined to die far too young, of cancer, whilst still only in her thirties.

I have so many memories of that period, some vivid, some vague. The smell of the greasepaint, the roar of the crowd, and all that... At the time, being so small, I guess it just kind of washed over me as being normal, but, looking back, it does take on a kind of special, magical quality and I feel privileged to have experienced it, even in such a limited way. Occasionally, we kids might be brought on stage; Ray and Sue dressed in miniature Buttons and Cinders costumes, and me as a junior stooge for the "Ahhh" factor.

"Now, we've never met before, have we?" George would ask in wide eyed innocence.

"No, dad," came my rehearsed reply, which got a big laugh.

Apparently, the first time I saw him in panto, he was getting whacked in a sketch with a big slapstick and I cried in total despair, "Don't hit my daddy!"

But my visits to the theatre, backstage or otherwise, were not that common. As I said, usually only at panto time, but the family did spend a summer with our father when he played ten weeks in a show at the Arcadia Theatre in Skegness.

We were staying in a flat on the top floor of a house near the seafront, so we kids could spend a lot of time down on the beach during the day. This was in 1958, and Ray and I (just 4 years old) acquired toy machine guns which saw a lot of action down in the sand. Sue and Ray were 8 and 7 years older than me, respectively, and we boy's activities were no doubt looked down upon by my sister who spent most of her time in the theatre. Sue had been bitten by the show-business bug very early in life. (I still have recordings of her singing *Daddy's Little Girl* and *That Certain Smile* with her dad accompanying her on piano. Also a recording of her recreating the entire kitchen scene from *Cinderella* with him.)

The Skegness show was called *Summer Serenade – the Gay Variety Revue-sical!*, advertised as "A fast moving up-to-the minute summer show; full of laughs, songs, dances and gorgeous spectacle, with an all star cast of West End artists". (So amusing now to see the innocent use of the word "gay", as was its meaning back then.) George topped the bill, but he was supported by Hill & Billie, Jean Tyler, Richman and Jackson, Jayne and Alan Howard, The Lovely Dancing Debutantes and Milton Woodward's Wonder Bar ("drinks given away free at every performance").

George always maintained that he did not enjoy long runs and said he got bored with the monotony of this particular show. It cannot all have been work and no play though. Joan remembers a lot of socializing, and a letter he wrote from the theatre in mid-season, responding to a T.V. producer's request for the orchestrations of George's song *Topical Calypso*, says, "Forgive rough typing. I was at a party last night"!

Other work from this late 50s period included a week at the Savoy Theatre Clacton-on-Sea in August 1959. The star of the show was T.V's "personality girl" Margo Henderson with support from Spanish dancers Tonia & Rafael, The Young Brothers, Duo Russmar, Reg Overbury ("The Musician with the Twinkling Feet") and Val Doonican's Four Ramblers.

George did a spot in each half of the show, firstly his normal Casual Comedian routine and then, just before Margo's entrance, as the Sergeant Major, the 2nd. spot he always used for occasions such as this. This must have been one of the last times he did it, because something happened which made him abruptly drop the routine.

The first of the famous Carry On films, *Carry On Sergeant*, had been released in 1958, and its national service army theme had proven so popular that it led to a spin-off T.V. series called *The Army Game*. This, in turn, led to another series about what happens to two of the main characters when they leave the army and take work in a hotel. This was *Bootsie and Snudge*, starring Alfie Bass and Bill Fraser, and it became a big hit. Bill Fraser's character was a bullying ex-N.C.O. and so it was no surprise that one night, during George's act, a voice from the stalls shouted, "It's *Snudge!*" Although George had been doing the character for years, he was a bit taken aback by this and decided to never play the part again.

Not that much of a blow, as it happens, because places to perform such acts were becoming fewer by the week. Variety was no longer a continuous week by week source of work. Gaps began to appear in artiste's schedules and they were all getting desperate. As traditional bills began to vanish, even the bigger names were feeling the pinch and were spreading their talents to embrace other areas.

Shows were still happening, but instead of accepted formats on the previously never ending circuit, performers could find themselves in one off productions, put on by various independent organizers. That is how George found himself appearing, in the summer of 1960, back in Clacton in such extravaganzas as *Variety*

Band Show with Ronnie Mills Orchestra and Singers. Every Friday afternoon, Ronnie Mills used to host the Junior Talent Finals, which I entered, somewhat reluctantly. I was supposed to be singing *Tom Dooley*, a popular ditty of the day, but for some reason, as I got to the microphone, I surprised the band by repeatedly singing the one line I knew of *Angela Jones*! I always was an awkward little sod!

Bill Maynard was not the only comic to find himself forced out of the business and change direction into the straight acting profession. Arthur English had been struggling for some years now, mainly because his wartime "spiv" character had quickly gone out of fashion. Another was Dave King, a smooth singer/comedian whose big time attitude had backfired on him, causing his fall from grace. He and Arthur both went on to find eventual acclaim, and new celebrity status, as actors.

The demise of the variety halls hit the spesh acts the hardest. Where could they go? Some drifted back into circus, mostly on the continent, but for many there was no choice but to leave the profession.

There was still fun to be had, however, as the dying embers sputtered to keep live entertainment in the frame. Traditionally, the entertainment profession has never gelled with family life. Always on the road, seldom at home, such was, and is, the lot of entertainers, who, naturally, have to go where the work is.

As already seen, George was very much a part of this scenario. For years now, he and Joan had been growing steadily apart as he spent more and more time away, and it is no secret that he succumbed to temptation many times whilst appearing on bills with pretty dancers and attractive female acts of every description. Comics always had a reputation as Lotharios, and seemed to be a particular target for show-bizzy females on the look-out for male company.

The comedian Bryan Burdon who, as a very young man, used to do an act with his dad, Albert, had this to say when I asked him if he had anything to tell me about *my* father...

"In those days, apart from meeting for a coffee, we went our separate ways as, unlike my dad, and your dad, I didn't drink and go to the pub after the show, but was too busy getting my leg over with the Dagenham Girl Pipers, the Luton Girls Choir, Ivy Benson's Band, the Zio Angels Troupe and, as I used to come on stage from the audience, every usherette on the Moss's and Stolls!"

Well, I think this gives some idea of what it could be like for those who had the stamina to indulge!

Early 1960s; a show with Alma Cogan, David Berglas and Ray Fell.

George no doubt had his share. One or two became quite serious affairs, apparently, as he and Joan went through the motions of keeping their relationship alive, at least to the world in general.

The winter of 1960 into 61, found the Martin family spending the Christmas period in Margate on the Kent coast during a notably freezing bout of weather. I think George was performing at the Butlin's hotel, at least for part of this time. My memory is of entering a fancy dress competition dressed as Sir Francis Drake, complete with a chin beard drawn on with my mother's eyebrow pencil. Being difficult again (but historically correct!) I objected because the real Drake had a bushy red beard, but my dad swiftly lost patience with my protests and pushed me into the line-up. I didn't win.

And another show with David Berglas, Roy Castle and Lonnie Donegan.

But it was much later that year, when George performed in the last pantomime he would ever do, that he met the woman he would spend the rest of his life with.

Chapter 11

PERFORMER TO PUBLICAN

1961 appears to have been something of a transitional year for George. Like everyone else who depended so much upon variety bookings, he was looking elsewhere.

Now free of his binding B.B.C. television contract, and no longer committed to the Grades, he had been making guest appearances on various A.T.V. shows, but a series of his own was what was really needed to re-establish himself in the public eye. There had been one off B.B.C. engagements, including a special with The Bevs (Beverley Sisters) in 1960 (fee 62 guineas), produced by his old supporter Dennis Main Wilson, and there was still plenty of radio interest. One such broadcast he did that summer was for the 21st. Anniversary of the Pioneer and Labour Corps, from an army depot in Wrexham, North Wales. He was contracted as compere for the show, as well as performing his own spot, and for this he received the grand sum of £13, 15 shillings and 0 pence, plus fares and subsistence. In May that year he also received a written offer from Producer Ned Sherrin to audition as presenter of a panel game called *Laugh Line*, but there does not seem to be a record of anything coming of that. However, Ray and I had memories of him on screen in some kind of show around that period, in which cartoon sketch boards were shown and joke captions were required to be added by a guest panel.

The chance of George's own series with independent television had come as early as March 1959, but it was an experimental format which would prove risky. Based around an American idea, the show would feature George fronting a loose variety style production where the acts would be almost secondary to the advertisement of various products. In other words, George would do a few gags, introduce a singer or some other act, and then find a link to say a few words about some new miracle detergent or health food. The manufacturers of these products would sponsor the show, of course, so, in theory, it was a win for all situation.

At the time, George saw this as a revolutionary step and everyone involved was very excited. The saviour of entertainment. Getting in at the beginning of this phenomenon had to guarantee a rosy future, surely?

The first series of *By George* ran for 6 episodes between March and June, but there was no immediate follow up. Disappointed, George went from job to job, still keeping his head above the water but wondering where his future now lay. As it happened, after a long gap, the show was brought back in April 1961 for another six episodes, which must have been an enormous relief for him. There was also a festive edition, *Christmas is Coming*, recorded in mid-December and featuring George and celebrity cook Fanny Craddock's husband, Johnny.

From there George went straight into one final pantomime booking. Back to Blackpool for a production of *Goody Two Shoes*, which was hardly one of the traditional tales. This was the only panto which none of the immediate family saw, and perhaps he had good reason to keep us at a distance.

His lady in this show was Margaret Mitchell, an ex-lead soprano from the D'Oyly Carte Opera. As a teenager she had toured the world, specializing in Gilbert and Sullivan productions and working closely with the likes of Ivor Novello. As she grew older, she developed some slight problems with her voice which took her out of the front rank of serious vocal work. Now she was appearing in panto and had re-created her image as a leggy "principal boy".

George was nearing 40 years of age and Margaret (Maggie, as she liked to be called by her friends), was a few years younger. In rehearsals they did not immediately connect with each other, but as the show progressed, they got more friendly. In fact, by the middle of the run they were intimately involved.

When the show ended in early '62, George returned immediately to planning meetings for the next series of *By George*. It seemed that the idea had really caught on. Other similar shows were popping up too, notably *Jim's Inn* starring Jimmy Hanley.

Recorded at the Associated Rediffusion Studios in Wembley, George's co-presenters were Steve Race and June Marlow, along with various other guests. Unsurprisingly, George used his influence to find jobs on the show for those who were close to him and that is why, after the first few episodes, appearances started to be made by his brother, Bill, and, of course, Maggie. Another regular was Rex Jameson, the outlandish character and notorious Guinness drinker best known in his role as "Mrs. Shufflewick". Also showing his well known face and exercising his unique vocal style was "Professor" Stanley Unwin.

George and "Mrs. Shufflewick" (Rex Jameson) at a charity event, Bagshot 1962.

These shows and related spin offs took up most of that year for George, including a 15 minute Brooke Bond Tea commercial with Desmond Morris, which was quite a milestone. The first of its kind, apparently. One perk from this venture included George bringing home a pile of rubber chimpanzee toys.

Another novelty toy which I benefited from was a mechanical alligator which was operated by a miniature air pump to make it play the drums. I remember this toothy little fellow opening one show in big close-up as the camera drew back to reveal my father operating the pump, accompanied by the jaunty theme tune.

In January, one of these spin offs was *The Furniture Show*, which speaks for itself, a show which was jointly hosted by George, a lady named Molly Love and serious social commentator Robin Day, of all people! (Seeing this in the records, I am wondering if "Day" is a typing error, as I think it more likely that it was Robin *Ray*, son of comedian Ted.)

It was all going very well. The shows were popular and it seemed like the idea of entertainment complementing advertising was spreading throughout the medium. Then, like a bombshell, it all came unexpectedly crashing to earth. A parliamentary campaign, led by one Lord Pilkington, set out on a crusade to bring such advertising magazine programmes to a halt, declaring that the format cheapened the arts. Ironic then, to see that eventually entire channels would be devoted to advertising.

Anyway, at the time, the moral high ground prevailed and an act was passed which banned all such programmes. *By George* was one of the immediate casualties and this left George drifting like a ship without a course.

He had reached the point where he thought his future really lay in the area of commercial television but it had backfired on him. The independent bosses were now hypocritically wary of him because of his involvement in something which had been outlawed, and the B.B.C. had its snooty nose out of joint. Basically, they turned their backs on George. A long period would go by before they would directly employ him again.

So, what to do? There were still live appearances, but with the demise of variety there was no longer any regularity or security in stage work. Life in general was getting complicated. There was a mortgage still to pay on a big house, and a wife and three dependant children to support, plus bills galore. George had been earning well for over ten years now and a certain standard of living had become the norm. But how could he maintain it?

In addition, his relationship with Maggie was getting more involved. She was living in a flat in Fellows Rd., London, NW3, and he was beginning to spend more and more time visiting her there. Maggie herself had actually decided to retire from show business and was managing a drinking club in the heart of the City. George was impressed by the concern she was showing for him. He felt he was getting from her the comforts he was not receiving at home in Farnborough.

Because George and Joan had been having quite a strained relationship for some time now. Since the children had reached school age, and Joan had been forced by circumstances to stay at home whilst George was on the road, she began to miss the lifestyle. She would still attend odd functions and shows, and be invited along with George to occasional events (especially if they were local) but, as a rule, their lives began to drift apart.

Inevitably, when George *was* at home, this difficult situation would often lead to arguments and accusations. Joan, understandably, was suspicious of him and he grew tired of her questions. By nature, Joan was fiery and this did not help matters when George just preferred an easy life. With the perfect excuse of being away working, he began to seek refuge at Maggie's flat on a more regular basis.

A partial solution seemed to present itself when a friend of George's put a proposition to him. Just outside of Aldershot, in the village of Ash, a pub stood on the main road to Guildford. This was the Bricklayer's Arms, run by one Pat Cuzik. Pat was a stocky little fellow and a tough businessman. He was a colourful character too, into everything, and his pub was popular with the Aldershot inner sanctum of V.I.P.s because he allowed it to be used for after time drinking sessions for those in his circle.

That circle included the likes of George, Nip Eustace and various other Masonic types, and many a happy afternoon, and late night session, took place behind the drawn curtains of "The Brickies". Amidst the laughter and cigarette smoke, and clink of glasses, many subjects were discussed, and during 1962 George's growing predicament was a major topic. Pat made it known that he would soon be vacating the pub to move to some other venture, and this sparked the germ of an idea.

George Martin could be the next the landlord.

And why not? George took to the notion pretty quickly. His parents, Bill and Lil, had been running their own pub, The Globe, in the centre of Aldershot for some years now, and his brother Bill had, not that long ago, come out of the trade. (Actually, Bill's marriage to Cynthia had ended and she had taken their son Trevor with her. Bill vacated The Angler's Rest and took a job in the entertainments department at Butlins Holiday Camps. More about that later.) Pubs were almost a family business.

In later years, George and Joan would both remember different versions of why they actually became publicans. It was a sensible move in many ways. Show-business work was rapidly drying up for George, but he was very much a social person, comfortably at home alongside a bar. As early as 1952, in an interview in Lilliput magazine, he had said, "I would like to own a pub and stand all my pals a drink. I like to have a lot of people around me." This now seemed to be a natural progression.

Joan remembers him being very keen on the idea. "The business is over," he said ruefully, "but the pub trade will thrive." He even had plans to turn the annexe next to the pub into a restaurant, where he could stage cabaret shows featuring himself and his numerous performer pals.

George would eventually say that he only took the pub for Joan's sake, because she wanted to do it, but she always denied this vehemently. It seems to me that the truth lies somewhere in-between these two viewpoints. Joan would one day become convinced that he wanted to trap her in the hectic schedule of running a pub to keep her out of the way!

George was recommended to Courage's Brewery and they were delighted at the prospect of someone with George's celebrity status taking one of their pubs. It had to be good for business. Even so, he had to attend an interview with Captain Courage himself.

As he stood in the reception area of the Captain's office, George lit a cigarette. (Bear in mind that smoking was much more socially acceptable in the early '60s.)

"Oh noooooo..." wailed the secretary, "Captain Courage does not approve of smoking!"

"Well," muttered George, defiantly, "bollocks to Captain Courage."

Despite this, George was granted the tenancy of The Bricklayer's Arms and we all moved there in January 1963, right in the middle of the worst snow in nearly 20 years.

The
BRICKLAYERS ARMS
Ash, Nr. Aldershot, Hants.

Chapter 12

CHANGING TIMES

It got off to a great start. Even in the midst of the terrible weather, opening day under the new landlord was a resounding success. Out of curiosity, to buy a drink in The Casual Comedian's new pub, punters flocked from miles around. Not only did scores of old friends and acquaintances turn out to show their support, it was a case of everyone trying to get in on the act. The car park was soon overflowing and vehicles were parked for hundreds of yards in either direction on both sides of the road.

The pub must have taken a small fortune on that first day, so it was an excellent sign of what would hopefully continue. George was in his element, holding court as he served drinks and indulging in banter with one and all. However, even then, on his first day, he was already exercising the habit of "standing his pals a drink" which was another example of his poor business acumen.

"We're supposed to be making money here," protested Joan, but George ignored her as he time and again refused to take cash from his friends.

The pub itself was an interesting building. The central part was of 17th. century origin and had been a coaching inn, apparently. Extensions had been added over the years, especially a much more modern one which made up the entire back of the structure. On one side of the recent work, at the back of the building, was a flat roof which stood over the saloon bar. The public bar stood alongside a quite spacious but dank and gloomy, bottle cellar.

Our upstairs living quarters consisted of three bedrooms and, at first, Ray and I shared one of these rooms. It was an area of low, beamed ceilings, steps and passageways, and it always gave me the creeps. With just cause, as we shall get to later.

George was like a child with a new toy. He liked playing the role of "mine host". But for how long?

Although 1960 had not been the most productive of years for George, something very significant did happen for him. Life changing, in fact, because it was the year he was initiated into the Grand Order of Water Rats, an organization which was to involve him deeply for the rest of his days.

The origin of the G.O.W.R. goes back to 1889 when a small group of successful British music hall performers owned a trotting pony called The Magpie. It was a strong little beast and began winning them lots of money in races, so the group decided to use their winnings to help fellow performers who were, perhaps, not doing so well. As time went on, they felt that their charity warranted the formation of an organization which could also be used as a social club.

One day, this jolly band were making their way home from the races, in the pouring rain, in a cart pulled by their treasured little Magpie. Familiar faces to theatre-goers, they were recognized by a passing horse-drawn cab driver.

"Ere wotcha got there?" shouted the driver, indicating their bedraggled animal.

Comedian Joe Elvin called back, "That's our trotting pony... The Magpie!"

"Magpie?" laughed the driver, "Looks more like a bleedin' water rat!"

At that moment, the group seemed to experience the same universal brain wave. They would call their organization The Water Rats, elevating a lowly creature to the highest firmament of stars. In fact "Rats" turned back to front spelled "Star". It was perfect. Why not go the whole hog and call it a "Grand Order" too?

With a motto "Philanthropy, conviviality and social intercourse", the original Rats were very few in number, but the names were impressive. Joe Elvin, Dan Leno, Wal Pink, for instance, and Harry Freeman, who was chosen to be the first King Rat, the figurehead of the Order. As the years went on, their numbers, and activities expanded. Their headquarters moved from a pub on the banks of the River Thames to, eventually, a lodge room in the auspicious surroundings of the Eccentric Club in the West End of London. Members had to be full time, well known members of the theatrical profession, male only, and the process to join was a long and complicated one. Essentially one had to be revered by one's peers within show-business.

George had long been aware of the Order. He was familiar with the small, gold Water Rat emblem which all members were required to wear in the left lapel of their jackets. It was worn with pride by a host of famous stars. Charlie Chaplin, Laurel and Hardy, Norman Wisdom, Ted Ray, Charlie Chester, Ben Warris, Fred Emney, the list went on and on. American superstar Danny Kaye was wearing his emblem during his sensational debut performance at the Palladium.

George was well established in the business by now. His social reputation was sound, he was professionally successful and highly popular, so he was certainly a candidate for membership. After a long build up, he was proposed by comedian and theatre producer Terry "Toby Jug" Cantor, the proposal being seconded by saxophonist Hal Swain. The voting procedure was successful and on Sunday June 26th. 1960, George Martin was initiated into the G.O.W.R. as Water Rat number 574.

King Rat for that year was Arthur Scott and present in the lodge room for George's ceremony were such names as his close friend Joe Church, also Arthur Haynes, Richard Afton, Barry Lupino, Clarkson Rose, Serge Ganjou, Harold Berens, George Elrick, Wilfred Pickles, "Wee" Georgie Wood and "Birdman" Percy Edwards, to mention but a few.

One of George's Brother Rats was the producer Philip Hindin, the same man who had told the Martin Brothers long ago that they would never get anywhere.

As it turned out, the pub was a short lived diversion for George's attention, which was not really a great surprise to those who knew him well. For a while he played the game, concentrating on being the genial bar host, signing autographs, overseeing the beer deliveries and doing the weekly inventory, but the lure of the boards was too deeply ingrained in his soul for him to forsake it for long.

Within a few weeks he was being tempted back to accept appearance invitations again. Old style variety bookings were more or less completely gone by now, but people were still putting on shows in theatres and halls around the country and George was still a familiar enough face to help as a draw. The club scene was beginning to take hold, especially in the North of England, and in many ways it almost replaced variety in the sense of volume of work. But it was a different kind of work. A new breed of entertainers were coming along to oust the old school. The clubs, frequented by working men and their families, were much harder places than the genteel theatres of the Moss and Stoll circuit. Performers would fight an often losing battle against noisy audiences who seemed more interested in the impending bingo games than the acts. Food was served at the tables, amidst constant P.A. announcements from club secretaries which came, usually, at inopportune moments.

Comedians, particularly, had to develop a solid style to work the clubs, and this was all about attack. The constant barracking and attitude of "Go on, entertain me!" was a hard school in which only the toughest could survive. If you didn't give as good as you got, you were dead meat.

This was not George's scene at all. He was The Casual Comedian; he needed attention, and he was not willing to adapt his laid back ways to the brashness of the clubs. Some of the old style comedians did manage to make the transition, notably Bob Monkhouse who turned into the comedy prince of clubland, but, as a rule, most of them fell by the wayside and were forced out of the business.

Material was an issue too. In variety, with so many acts on a bill, nobody was on stage for more than a few minutes. Even the top of the bill probably only did about 18 minutes, with most others being permitted about 6, tops. And theatre managers were very strict about these timings. To over run could bring severe penalties to a performer. And with so many theatres in the country, it could be a couple of years before a turn found themselves back on the same stage, so they could keep the same act going indefinitely.

Clubland was very different. Audiences were more cynical now, with a "seen it all before" attitude. Television was mainly responsible for this, and any act who was lucky enough to appear on the box was very conscious of the amount of material which was being "eaten up". And club acts could never get away with appearances of a few minutes. Comics were now expected to do an hour or more.

George observed all this ruefully and was glad that he did not have to be a part of it. He continued to perform, but with the pub behind him he felt he could be selective and stuck to those theatre bookings which still survived. Certain cabaret situations suited him too and, eventually, he would find his niche as a witty and urbane after-dinner speaker.

The face of entertainment was undergoing a radical change. Variety had shifted to television, with shows like *Sunday Night at the London Palladium* keeping the old time fans happy. Variety performers like Morecambe and Wise, Bruce Forsyth, Des O'Connor, Tommy Cooper and Mike and Bernie Winters became huge T.V. names, whilst a very few, like Terry-Thomas and Peter Sellers, became international film stars.

As pop music became the voice of the young and The Beatles took the world by storm, George began to fade from the public eye. The reason for this mystified me for many years. I could not understand why he had been riding high throughout the 1950s, having gained a first class reputation for originality, as well as his acting talent and musicianship, only to virtually vanish from the screen as soon as the '60s began.

Well, if you have read these pages up to this point, I think some of the reasons have already been outlined. The Bevs stressed in their letter that his personality was such that he would never promote himself, a trait which is not generally typical of performers, especially comedians who will usually fall over themselves to get noticed. Also, it must be acknowledged that reliability was not always his strong point and that his sense of urgency was sometimes "out of kilter". This must have irritated more than a few bookers and producers, no matter how nice a guy he was. Then, of course, there was the mistake he made by putting all his horses in the one stable of Advertising Magazine programmes, a venture which had alienated him with the B.B.C..

And so he witnessed the rise of some contemporaries who, in many cases, had for years been lower down the bill than him. But it really did not seem to bother him. He coasted on, as he had always done, taking whatever presented itself. In some cases, the jobs on offer were still lucrative and promising.

In 1962, with the ad-mag shows in full swing, he was engaged to present a short film (17 minutes) which went out on cinema release as a support to main features. It was called *Dawn in Piccadilly* and the British Film Institute synopsis describes it thus...

"Nostalgic documentary about the legendary Windmill Theatre in London's West End. Dawn Maxey, one of the Windmill girls, a dance troupe, talks about how she became one of the girls and what she enjoys about it. We see her in rehearsal and performing a fan dance. George Martin, speaking from the nearby Pop's Club, introduces the film and gives a survey of the theatre's history. We learn that great entertainers and comedians like Bruce Forsyth and the Goons started their careers at the Windmill, where the programmes were a combination of dance and comedy acts".

Having the pub probably helped him to secure a series of television commercials promoting Courage's new Keg Bitter. About 20 of these were made, with George behind a bar as a friendly pub landlord, throwing darts and pulling pints as he extolled the virtues of this beer. When told the name of the director (which I cannot locate) it had such an exotic sound that he thought, "Uhm, nice. An Italian bird!" but he was disappointed when on set he was directed by a large bloke! No matter though, because the money softened the blow. They offered him several thousand pounds upfront as a complete buy-out, or he could sign a contract which put him on repeat payments worldwide. Never having been offered such a handsome fee before, he took the buy-out, which turned out to be a big mistake because the commercials went on to be shown for years all around the globe, which would have netted him a much bigger sum.

And there was Maggie too. Leaving the pub in the hands of Joan with increasing regularity, he began spending more and more of his time at Fellows Rd.

The Bricklayer's Arms would eventually turn into a bit of a millstone around George's neck, but he actually held on to the tenancy for over four years. During that time, his fortunes were to change again as he entered the next phase of his career. Initially, by the middle of the decade, it seems the B.B.C. had decided to forgive him, because he suddenly started getting work from them again. Producer Albert Stevenson, a Brother Water Rat, gave him an attractive television job on a show called *Club Night*, which netted a fee of just under £100, and radio work took off once more. *A Look on the Lighter Side*, *Housewive's Choice*, *Start the Day Right*, *Three and Easy*, *Call My Bluff* and his very own *By George* (nothing to do with the ad-mag of the same name).

Joan could not really understand what was going on. She was busy with the pub, and regardless of her claims, my impression was that she generally enjoyed being a landlady. Hard work, yes, but it was a good social scene and she had a lot of support from the regulars. As George began to spend less and less time there, staff were employed, particularly to cover the morning and lunchtime bar sessions, although Joan would usually be there in the evenings to open up.

Even so, George did still sometimes apply himself to the pub's promotion. On one occasion a novelty football match was arranged to raise money for charity. A female team was formed which included Joan, Joyce and a group of lady customers from The Brickies, while the men's team was made up of George, Bill Maynard, Bob McGowan and various other local characters.

George wore a floral bra over his football kit for some reason, and Maynard was dressed as a Bedouin Arab. With Bob wearing a sporran and the others in various modes of outlandish dress, the match really degenerated into a kind of free for all, which I remember ending up as a big drinking session. But a lot of fun was had by all.

George with Brickies Ladies team. Joan is seated next to him and sister Joyce is standing 3rd. from right.
_(Photo by Gale & Polden, Aldershot.)

Some incidents were anything but fun, though. Not long after taking over the pub, early one evening there was a knock on the back door of our private quarters, just behind the bar area. Joan answered it, with George standing close by. Two large, brutish looking men stood in the darkness, their broad shoulders silhouetted against the garden shadows.

"You the landlord?" grunted one of them in a voice like a rasp.

George replied that he was and stepped forward, at which both the figures moved together, one of them reaching out to grab George by the shirt.

"Cuzik?" he snarled, but George swiftly realised what was happening in this case of mistaken identity, and raised his hands defensively. It took a few moments of desperate explanation before these "heavies" were convinced that they had the wrong man and that their intended target had moved on. Pat Cuzik had been involved in all sorts of things and George really did not want to know about it.

I had been forced to change schools when we moved from Farnborough to Ash, and I was now attending the local primary establishment. This was quite a wrench for me, aged 8, and well do I remember the trauma of sitting on a chair in front of a strange new classroom with all the kids sniggering at me.

Ray was attending grammar school by this time and had to make a couple of bus journeys every day to get there. Sue was not around much. There had been a few problems and she was actually living away when we moved. This was a sticky period for her and our parents, and, for various reasons, having been "Daddy's little girl" for so long, Sue actually turned against him, teenage style, for a while. It was a difficult time, but I was too young to understand the full implications until I was somewhat older.

By the mid '60s, Ray had his own crowd to hang around with, a gang who fell somewhere between being mods *and* rockers rather than throwing in their lot totally with one group or the other. They rode motorbikes and scooters, some in leathers and some in the outlandish garb of the swinging era. Ray took to wearing a scarlet guardsman's jacket, winkle picker boots, a police cape and a top hat, much to the horror of my grandmother! He and our cousin Al, with two other friends, formed a band called No Money Down which was initially a rhythm n' blues combo. They were actually rather good and began playing a string of local gigs.

We were all "Beatles" crazy at the time and I also wanted to get in on the act. I fancied myself as a singer and my father did quite a lot to encourage me. Once he put me on the phone to sing to an "agent", who I later found out was Maggie. My party piece at the time was a song which I had heard sung by Paul McCartney on the first Beatles album... not one of the band's originals but an early cover which they had taken from the film *The Music Man*; called *Till There Was You*.

Saturday night in The Brickies saloon bar was always alive with music and we had a resident trio of piano, guitar and a fellow named Nobby on banjo-ukulele. Watching through a crack in the door, and sometimes allowed to sneak into the back of the bar, I was fascinated by this little combo, especially Nobby's uke playing. George spotted my enthusiasm and bought a banjo-uke from Nobby for me to learn to play. After a few tips from Nobby, I was soon able to rattle out another party piece; *Five Foot Two, Eyes o' Blue*. I loved the uke and taught myself many more numbers, but, being the '60s, I soon progressed to guitar and had my own group by the time I was 11; The Creatures.

One Saturday night I was permitted to make my debut. Backed by Nobby's trio I belted out The Beatles' *All My Loving* to the Brickies' regulars and earned 12 shillings and sixpence in a "whip round". I was over the moon, and I think that was the moment when I became convinced that a life on stage was for me.

George had a radio series running at the time on the B.B.C. Light Programme. Called *Souvenir*, it was a wallow in nostalgia, featuring guests who George would interview in-between playing listener's requests. Maggie made an appearance, naturally, talking about D'Oyly Carte. One week, following a recording session in the bar after closing time, I made my radio debut on this show... call it nepotism! With Ray giving me guitar backing and my dad whistling the solo, I gave a spirited rendition of my *Five Foot Two*, banging away on the uke. It was broadcast on Tuesday October 18th. 1966 and I received a fee of one guinea, along with a letter from the producer apologising for the preclusion of my name from the programme!

Another notable guest on *Souvenir* was George Raft, the Hollywood actor who had become synonymous with gangster movies in the 1930s. The two Georges displayed quite a chemistry on air, even socializing in the fancy clubs of London's Mayfair. My dad wrote the material for Raft to perform during his appearance on *Sunday Night at the London Palladium*. Alas, Raft's visit to England was to end on a sour note, as he was implicated in some nefarious activities with home-grown criminals such as The Kray Twins.

The Casual Comedian's connection with The Krays was thankfully limited to one cabaret performance in their presence in a London Club. When he had finished his act, George was approached by a tough looking heavy who presented him with a bottle of champagne.

"This is from Reg n' Ron," mumbled the heavy in broad cockney, "they liked yer act."

George was appearing in shows for the Water Rats too. A terrific example of the kind of spectacle which could be produced in those days took place on Sunday February 16th. 1964 at the Grand Theatre Wolverhampton. Called *Star Celebrity Night*, to raise funds for the Order, the truly incredible bill included The Bachelors, Wilfred Brambell (of *Steptoe* fame), Ted Ray, Joe Brown and the Bruvvers, Tommy Cooper, Val Doonican, Bud Flanagan, Jewell & Warris, Beryl Reid, Frankie Vaughan, Sir Donald Wolfit and George Martin!

Chapter 13

TYPING FOR THE TAXMAN

Now that George's television appearances had receded, it seems that fellow performers began to turn to him for written material. A new comedian/impressionist called Ray Fell had his own T.V. show in 1965 and George was engaged to supply topical gags for him. Before that, he had been involved in writing Fell's spot for him to perform at The Beatles Christmas Show at the Hammersmith Odeon which ran from December 24th, '64 until January 16th, '65. (The line-up also included Freddie and the Dreamers, Elkie Brooks, the Yardbirds and Jimmy Saville.) I was thrilled because my dad obtained The Beatles autographs for me, signed "To our friend Michael" and written on the front cover of the programme. This cover was printed with a John Lennon sketch of a couple kissing under some mistletoe and I, foolish child that I was, detached the cover and pinned it to my bedroom wall.

Backstage at the concert, George and Maggie indulged in some banter with the Fab Four and George was slightly rocked by Lennon's famous sick sense of humour. Apparently, Lennon did an impression of blind singer Ray Charles which involved walking to the middle of the room, taking a bow, sitting down and extending his fingers, as if to play the piano, before leaning forward and falling flat on his face.

George also found himself writing early television spots for a brash, young new Liverpool comic named Jimmy Tarbuck. And producer John Ammonds contracted George as a writer for the whole series of *Date with Doonican*, six shows at £63 per programme. This signified the blossoming T.V. career of his old pal Val who was now on the map as a solo artiste.

With all these writing commissions coming in, along with regular radio work, George was probably not unduly worried by this turning point in his career. He would not have to be on the road so much, which suited him now that he was involved with Maggie. As for The Bricklayer's Arms, that was another matter.

George had completely lost interest in the pub by now and it was virtually being run by Joan on her own. George's dad, Bill senior, was now coming by bus every morning to open up and George himself was barely ever there. This news got back to the brewery who were understandably unhappy about it.

The large back garden had been seriously neglected and had degenerated into a wasteland. This was great for me, as a kid, because it was a playground paradise. It had a big apple tree which was great for climbing in and open ground to rampage across with my school pals. At one point we dug a huge hole, covering it over with an old garage door to make a den. We lit fires and ran amok and no one seemed to care.

I was on my own almost every night. My mother was working downstairs in the pub, Sue was away for most of the time we lived there and Ray was usually out with his teenaged friends. The living quarters were very spooky when the sun went down and I would shut myself in the front room, dreading the idea of wanting to visit the lavatory as it was at the end of a long, dark corridor. If I could wait no longer, I would run the gauntlet at full pelt, my imagination spinning into overdrive as I envisioned all sorts of horrors lurking in the shadows.

Although there was a lot of noise coming up from the bars down below, I was still often startled by various inexplicable sounds. We had a room divider in the lounge where I spent most of my time, and the ornaments on this divider mysteriously dropped to the floor on a regular basis.

My parent's room, in the oldest part of the front of the building, was usually occupied by just my mother. One night, in the small hours, she awoke from a deep sleep to see a male figure silhouetted against the light from a street lamp through the window.

Vaguely aware that she was expecting George home, she called out his name, but as her eyes focussed, she realised that she was looking at a stooped old man with a big drooping moustache. Although it was dark, she was able to make out that his face was so dirty it appeared to be covered in cobwebs.

Alarmed, she sat up in bed and switched on the light. The old man had vanished and she wondered if she had perhaps been dreaming. However, a few days later, some of the old regulars in the public bar were discussing past times in the village, recollecting how the pub's bottle cellar had, long ago, been a private cottage. For years it was occupied by an old man who was a bit of a hermit. He actually died in the cottage and nobody realised for several days.

Some of the regulars had known this man personally. Curious, and already thinking of what she had seen in her bedroom, Joan hesitantly asked what he looked like.

"Oh, he was a dirty old bugger," replied someone who knew, "kind of bent over with a big moustache. Always looked like he had cobwebs on his face."

I was not told this story until years later, but Joan soon moved out of that room and moved *me* into it! Although, thankfully, I never saw anything ghostly, I was always uncomfortable in that room and usually slept with the light on.

Sue did eventually return to live with us but she got married whilst still in her teens. This was to Billy Horton who played football professionally for Aldershot Town. I remember the headline in the local paper; "Footballer Marries Comedian's Daughter". Soon after this, Billy downgraded his sports career, moving on to play on a semi-professional basis for Trowbridge in Wiltshire. He also took a job in social services which required the newly married couple moving to Bath.

Following my Eleven-Plus exams, I left primary school and transferred with many of my school chums to the local secondary school. A lot of bullying went on there. I did not really suffer any more badly than most but there was a bit of an extra element in my situation to make me a touch more vulnerable as a target.

Because my father was not on screen very often anymore, not many of my school colleagues were familiar with his celebrity status, unless they listened to the lighter radio programmes, or read television end credits (which not many kids did). However, rumours did spread that I was the son of someone prominent in the entertainment business. When they found out what his name was, I guess it was only natural for it to be generally assumed that he was the Beatles producer, George Martin, whose name was much better known to the general public by now.

I was forever having to answer enquiries about this, feeling aggrieved when insensitive kids would then respond with rude disappointment. "My dad is *the* George Martin!" I would state, defensively, as my stock answer.

Occasionally I would get set upon by some lout who would take issue with my parentage, somehow taking it personally.

I was punched in the head once by an older boy at the swimming pool, accompanied by the words, "Just 'cause your dad's George Martin!" Whatever the hell that was supposed to mean!

As a rule though, it was not a problem. I do not remember either of my parents ever showing much interest in my schooling. Ray and Sue both had similar memories.

George could have his more enlightened moments as a father, however. In a play-about fight with Ray, one of my front teeth got snapped in two, leaving me with a gaping hole and a whistling noise when I spoke. I was devastated and really did think it was the end for me.

"I won't be able to sing anymore!" I wailed.

That night, with a dental appointment pending the next morning, I was sobbing into my pillow when my dad came into my room. He had just come home after his usual few days away and had just been told what had happened to me. Sitting on my bed, he sat me up and listened as I blurted out my sorrow. He then comforted me with some wise words, explaining how everything would be sorted out and making me laugh with some stories I had never heard before. It really was a wonderful slice of parental bonding, which has always proven to me that he could do it when he wanted to.

The annexe next to the pub, which had been originally earmarked as that potential cabaret style restaurant, never had anything done to it during our occupation. It had been used to store boxes containing heaps of George's paperwork, old scripts and piles of magazines which went back years. Over a period of months, my mates and I gradually began peeking into these boxes, getting rather excited when we discovered a horde of Playboy magazines!

On the outskirts of Aldershot, a large gasometer and other related structures needed to be demolished. This was a major project which required a specialist demolition team being brought down from London to handle the long job.

The team were like something from a film about mercenaries. They all seemed to be real characters who worked hard and played harder, establishing themselves in local digs and making The Brickies their favoured drinking haunt.

When George was around, he took to this bunch of hard men with enthusiasm. Lovable rogues, you might say, and George began to see the potential in their stories and general boisterous behaviour. This had to be the basis for a great situation comedy series for television.

Working quickly, as he always did when excited by a new idea, George typed out a synopsis for his proposed show *The Demo Boys*, writing a complete first episode along with plot lines for a further five. Using his influence and contacts, he spent quite a while promoting it but, alas, the T.V. hierarchy failed to respond positively. Even though George had based it all on real characters and situations it was rejected on the grounds of being, "Not very believable".

Fortunately, other areas had more faith in his talents and, on April 30th. 1966, he was engaged to appear at the Royal Albert Hall alongside force's sweetheart Vera Lynn, in the presence of Earl Mountbatten of Burma and war hero Viscount Slim, in aid of the 20th. Burma Reunion.

By early 1967 George was quite anxious to let the pub go, but typical of his nature, he was dragging his heels doing anything about it. Bar business was ticking over, but George's continued absence did not help. The brewery had lost patience and were putting on the pressure for the Martins to vacate.

George was getting busier and more pre-occupied with his writing commitments. He told the family that he spent most of his time living in a small room supplied by the B.B.C. at Television

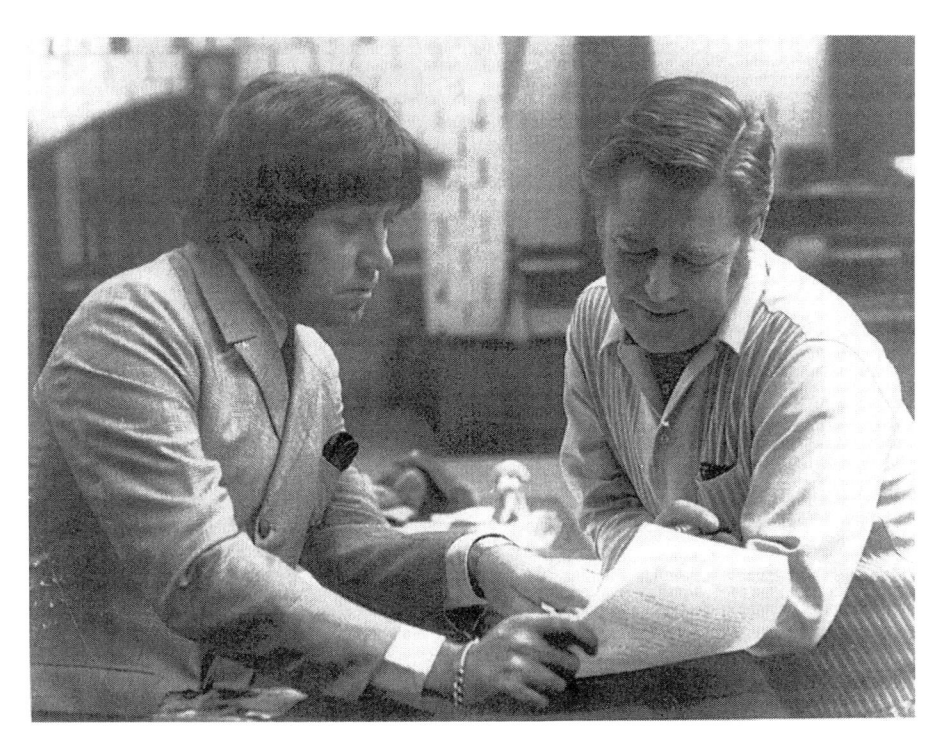

Working with "Tarby"

Centre, but in reality he was with Maggie, of course. They had moved into a bigger flat together and in April of '67 he wrote to the B.B.C. accounts department informing them that from now on all his correspondence was to be sent to 14 Leith Mansions, Grantully Rd., Maida Vale, W9, not his *old* address of Fellows Rd.! A double life indeed...

The Brickies was in need of serious attention. Damp had infested the walls, especially upstairs, and the walls were starting to crumble. The garden looked like a war zone. Potential new tenants were sent to view the premises and a deadline was set by the brewery for us to leave.

This created another dilemma as we needed somewhere else to live. George himself was comfortably ensconced in Maida Vale with Maggie, but it was not common knowledge. He was still responsible for his family, his "other life". And there were other problems too...

George had never paid due attention to his finances. Tax returns were not a priority, for instance, and although his father, Bill senior, as an ex-accountant, had battled bravely to keep his son's books in order, it was inevitable that the Inland Revenue would want their "pound of flesh".

Eventually, they placed a receiving order against him claiming £5,482 in unpaid tax.

It was an impossible sum for him to find at the time. He had never looked after his assets. Even the house he had owned in Farnborough had stood empty for about two years without any attempt being made to sell it or even let it. When it was finally sold, and the mortgage paid off, there was precious little left over.

The date for us to vacate the pub came closer and my mother, Ray and I (and the family dog; Lassie!) still did not know where we were going to live. Almost at the last moment, George's friend Nip Eustace came up with a solution. Through his contacts, and with him standing as guarantor, he found a house for us to rent. This was about a mile away from the pub, a big detached property which stood all alone like a castle at the end of a long, muddy lane, surrounded by Ash recreation ground on one side, derelict farm buildings on another, and fields on the remaining two. The address was Young's Farm.

Joan was not happy with this arrangement but the situation was so desperate she had no choice but to go along with it. We moved in, but George was not around much to help. He was busy staving off demands from the tax authorities, avoiding them as much as he could whilst still trying to work. In the end, though, it had to be faced. One of the major incidents which forced him to wake up to the reality of his predicament was when the bailiffs came to seize his car, his beloved Jaguar.

The next step, following court hearings, was bankruptcy. Naturally, the local papers made a meal of this, and it even warranted a mention in the nationals.

As for me, it did not make my school days any easier. Kids can be very cruel.

Chapter 14

BASIL TO THE RESCUE

On the same day that George wrote to the B.B.C. informing them of his change of address (April 17th. 1967), he attended a planning meeting in the office of producer Johnny Downes at Television Centre. This was to discuss the format and script of a new T.V. series for the magician David Nixon.

George and David had been good friends since working together at The Windmill and their paths had crossed a lot in the ensuing years. In more recent times, George had supplied material for him, notably during David's series *Nixon at Nine Five* in 1966. Although David Cummings was the official scriptwriter for this show, George was brought in to supply topical gags from the daily news and was initially contracted for a guaranteed three minutes of material at £50 per programme. As his involvement increased, George's fee went up accordingly and by January '67, it had doubled. (Old friends The Beverley Sisters were resident on this show too, so it was a happy gathering.)

This was the start of a very close relationship between George and David as they discovered a special working affinity. George quickly tapped into the magician's relaxed, deceptively bumbling and avuncular style, so much so that George was engaged to be the sole writer on David's next series.

Now for Nixon had a tea-time slot, aimed specifically at children, and the producer, Johnny Downes, and David himself, had something innovative in mind. They told George that they intended to introduce a novel guest to the programme who would be making a weekly appearance in a double act with David. But this was no ordinary artiste, this would be a fox puppet named Basil Brush.

George's first reaction was one of blank disbelief. "A puppet?" he responded, in bewilderment, "I don't think so..." But David and Johnny were insistent.

A few moments later they opened the door and beckoned someone in and George was instantly won over by the braying laugh which would become so famous in the years to come.

"Basil" was brought into the office on the arm of his handler Ivan Owen, who also supplied the distinctive voice, which, by his own admission was based heavily upon the comic actor Terry-Thomas. (Although, in actual fact, Ivan's genuine speaking voice was not dissimilar.) The puppet itself, with its toothy set grin and huge, wagging brush tail would obviously be an immediate hit.

This would not be Basil's T.V. debut, because he had previously appeared on other lesser known children's programmes, but this would certainly be his big break. (For the record, Ivan had also been the voice, and arm, behind another beloved puppet; the dog Fred Barker.)

The pairing of David and Basil was an immediate success and the short interlude they spent together in the new weekly show swiftly became a talking point. An unlikely chemistry but an undoubted hit. Letters started flooding in. Who was this cheeky little fox? The public wanted to see more of him. The secret seemed to be in the formula George, David and Ivan had discovered between them. Although *Now for Nixon* was essentially for children, there was something about Basil's personality, and the things he said, which appealed to all age groups.

As it happened, I made my television debut on this show. The format included a group of children who, each week, would be seen sitting behind the various guest artistes. At 13 years of age, thanks to my dad, I was one of them; for one performance only! I was quite shy about this, and being the age I was, I felt uncomfortable. It showed. Roger Whittaker (the South African whistling guitarist/singer of *Durham Town* fame) was a resident performer on the show, and he complained to my dad about my miserable expression during his spot!

Doing my best to wear a cheesy grin, I was then selected to take part in *The Train Game*. With David as the quiz master, and myself and another child competing against each other, this was a sequence involving a model train which moved up and down the track in accordance with the answering of general knowledge questions. Each contestant was represented by a miniature station and whoever succeeded in making the train reach their station first would win one guinea. (The guinea was in the form of a postal order attached to the roof of the train.)

I managed to win and caused a bit of embarrassment by reaching over to seize my prize.

"Not so hasty, Michael," smiled the ever patient David Nixon, "we won't run away with it."

I got a lot of stick at school over this!

Later that year, David was given another evening show by the B.B.C.. This was *The Nixon Line*, which ran for 26 weeks, yet again scripted by George and with a topical slot including Basil Brush once more. This series really cemented Basil's popularity with the British public and George was able to stretch his ability to find gags within the daily news as Basil could get away with murder!

The magical adviser on this series was the Irish magician Billy McComb and he, George and David made a wonderful team, devising numerous tricks and illusions, some of which involved the use of camera trickery. David would endure some criticism about this in later years, but the point is that he always made it clear when such ploys were being used. One has to remember that this was in the very early days of colour television when much experimentation was going on. David was, in fact, a fine magician and did not actually need to use technical trickery. At the time it was a gimmick.

1967. So much going on for George; personal problems battling alongside a major shift in his career. Moving from the pub, bankruptcy, the balancing act of living a double life between Joan and Maggie... and with so much to involve him professionally too.

David Nixon and Basil Brush – George became their right arm.

His commitments with David Nixon were enormously time consuming as the shows were much more than straightforward variety productions. But George enjoyed his work and was always happy when able to seek refuge in planning meetings and the endless socializing which accompanied such a life.

One such highlight occurred when David and George were invited to perform for the Queen and the Duke of Edinburgh when they held a 25th. coronation anniversary celebration at Luton Hoo House. Aided by George's topical gags, David did a routine talking to himself on a giant screen in which he produced a convincing replica of the monarch's crown of state. As a Royal memento of thanks for attending, George and David were each presented with a pair of classy cufflinks and a brace of pheasants.

Right in the middle of this hectic schedule George somehow found time to get away from it all. On August 10th. he left for a three week tour of South Africa, performing in a show with Hollywood star Cyd Charisse (who was said to have the "longest legs in the business") and her husband Tony Martin (no relation). They worked theatres in Cape Town, Johannesburg, Durban and venues all over the province, but George had mixed feelings about the place.

Many aspects he found fantastic. The culture, climate, spectacle and attitude impressed him, but this was at the height of the apartheid system and George was shocked by much of what he experienced. He found it hard to accept the humility and cowed behaviour of the black servants in the hotels and always made a point of being pleasant to them. One evening he engaged a young black singer in friendly conversation, but later on he received a visit in his room from a pair of official looking white men who introduced themselves as representatives of some government department.

"Mr. Martin," they said, icily polite but meaningful, "welcome to South Africa, but, please, may we ask you to respect our policies?"

Confused, George enquired what they meant by this, at which he was told, in no uncertain terms, "Don't consort with the *kaffirs*!"

This was quite a lesson and it disturbed him. At the time, however, when in South Africa, as a visitor you had to tow the line.

For all its luxury and easy going life style for the white population, there were many underlying layers of violence. George had the feeling that the country was like a powder keg waiting to explode.

One night, he got talking to a couple in a bar. They got on well and he ended up going back to their apartment for a night cap. After a while, the couple got drunk and started arguing. When it all got too heated, George made his excuses and left only to hear, the following day, that shortly after his departure the wife had shot her husband!

George had another new experience during this tour too. Socializing with the show's musicians one night, he became aware that they were all high on marijuana.

"Give it a try, George," said one of them, offering his spliff.

George shook his head. "Not for me, mate. I'd sooner stick to my Bells whisky."

"Go on... " urged the musician as others egged him on, "You should try everything once."

George resisted for quite a while, but in the end they wore him down and he took the spliff with a shrug.

Taking a puff, he looked at them all blankly.

"What now?" he asked of their expectant faces.

"Take another drag... a deep one. This is good stuff."

Doing as he was told, George sat for a moment waiting for something to happen. Handing back the spliff he shook his head and shrugged again.

"Well, I guess its not for me. I can't feel a thing."

Everyone laughed and the moment passed, but George finished his drink and decided to go to bed. Closing the door of his hotel room he was suddenly overcome by a strange, weightless feeling. Rocking on his heels, the room started to slowly spin and the walls began to close in on him. He knew Bells whisky would not affect him like this!

Falling back onto the bed he found himself staring at the wardrobe, along with an overwhelming feeling that it was the most beautiful thing he had ever seen.

In the future he would say, "My one and only experience with drugs? It made me fall in love with the wardrobe!"

Chapter 15

DAVID AND BASIL

Returning from South Africa, George plunged straight into work on the new David Nixon series. But there was other work on offer as well. It is interesting to note that a radio show called *Follow the Stars* booked George and Bob Monkhouse together on the same fee of 14 pounds 8 shillings and 9 pence each, whilst Rolf Harris, in the same show, received only 6 pounds 11 shillings and three pence! There was also a show called *The Entertainers* which used George on a fee of 52 pounds and 10 shillings to cover "script, research, record selection and programme presentation".

George had also been heavily involved in fund raising events for the Water Rats, so much so that in November, at their Annual Ball, he was rewarded with the Rat of the Year cup. Attending many functions, George was now openly taking Maggie with him. It was generally assumed, within show business circles, that they were an item. Busy with the pub, Joan had not been seen for years but George was playing a dangerous game.

To quote Dec Cluskey of The Bachelors; "I knew that Maggie and George were not married... that was the norm with all that gang. It was quite common for artists in those days to have two separate families. We never seemed to meet George's family..."

It did not seem to bother George. Looking back, it does appear odd that he thought he could just carry on getting away with this dual existence. It was as if he felt that his family in Ash would never find out about his activities on the entertainment social scene.

Inevitably, things would change, but he was happy to coast with the situation while he could.

However, it was not a secret to everyone in the Aldershot area. From early on in his relationship with Maggie, George's close relatives knew what was going on. It must have been difficult for them, at first, because they had all known Joan from the early days, even though by the '60s their paths did not cross much any more. Bob and Joyce, Bill, even George's parents were aware of Maggie, and eventually became very friendly with her as she was the one who now attended family parties with the Martin brood.

As George juggled with this complicated state of affairs, Christmas became an awkward period. He had not worked in panto for several years, so, technically, he should have been free to spend time with his *bonafide* wife and children, but there always seemed to be some excuse to cover his absence. My memory of the festive holidays of the mid to late 60s is of my father making fleeting appearances at home, always in a rush to get off somewhere else. The reality, of course, was that he was anxious to attend the more attractive surroundings which involved Maggie. Often, I found out later, this was closer to home than my mother and I imagined... just up the road in fact, at boozy parties in Aldershot, usually at Bob and Joyce's flat where they lived above their dry cleaning business. I am not sure quite how it happened, but one Christmas my dad took me to this flat where a packed, jolly party was in full swing. It was only a brief visit, but he introduced me to a very well spoken, larger than life, show-bizzy lady who beamed at me and made quite a fuss. I did not know it at the time, but this was my introduction to Maggie. All I remember is that I was taken home to my mother while my father, no doubt, returned to the party.

Joan had her suspicions but was not in a position to do much about it at the time. One night, while my mother was busy serving in the bar of The Brickies, Maggie phoned her. She had obviously had a few drinks and was engaged in an enormous row with George, presumably about confessing all to his wife. None of it made sense, and Maggie was rather incoherent. George, who it seems was with her, refused to come to the phone, so Joan told her to get lost. (Or words to that effect!) George denied everything, of course.

George's brother Bill had come through a domestic crisis of his own. Splitting up with his wife Cynthia, he had left his own pub, and made the heart rending decision to let his son Trevor go off with his mother. Cynthia had begun a relationship with the family doctor, whom she married, and went to the far-east, with young Trevor, to begin a new life. Much to everyone's surprise, Bill and the doctor's ex-wife, Sybil, began seeing one another and they got married too.

Very concerned for Bill's welfare, the family generally thought this direct swap of partners to be a big mistake but, happily, it turned out well. Bill and Sybil had a long and contented life together, producing three daughters, Laura, Andrea and Freya.

Straight from the pub, in the late 1950s, Bill took a job in entertainment's management at Butlins Holiday Camps. With his track record of performing experience, and being much more business minded than his elder brother, Bill soon climbed the ladder of promotion and became a leading light of the company. Eventually he became Butlins top booking manager. As well as being a boss, Bill still loved to be on stage and he trod the boards at the camps as often as he could. (His portrayal of the drunken chairman in Old Time Music Hall shows was legendary.) At one point he formed a double act with an Irish Redcoat named Dave O'Mahoney. Dave went to Australia and made his name on T.V. there before returning to England to become famous as the raconteur Dave Allen. In April 1966, George wrote the pilot for Dave's first British television show.

Bill would often book his brother to make star guest appearances at the camp's theatres. By this time, Butlins was one of the only places that still booked shows which resembled the old variety format. One of the entertainment's managers was a colourful character named Rocky Mason, an ex-boxer. Rocky had this to say...

"Your dad and Maggie Mitchell came to do a show in the Queen's Theatre, Butlins Margate. A five act bill. Maggie was down to follow Rex Roper (a cowboy style lasso performer) and go on just before George, who was topping the bill. Impressionist/comedian Victor Seaforth was on stage doing his act when Maggie decided to relax her throat. It was very quiet. (As it always was when Victor was on!) Victor was almost on the tag line

of his Toulouse Lautrec impression when Maggie's voice, doing the scales, rang out through the theatre! To say Victor was livid would be an understatement! He brushed angrily past me as I went on to introduce Rex, giving Rex the quickest intro of his life as I heard loud voices raised. I quickly dashed behind the proscenium arch to pull Victor off Maggie! Suddenly, George appeared, and it was all I could do to prevent him from having Victor for dinner! I got Maggie to the safety of her dressing room before introducing George, and then spent the break between shows trying to pacify everyone. I thought I had achieved this until the second house when Victor went on to do his big spot, the Quasimodo routine. I was standing in the wings, holding the chimes and padded stick to play the Notre Dame bells when your smiling father appeared, with a teaspoon. As Victor uttered the words "Its the bells that have made me deaf"! your dad reached past me and played a perfect rendering of Three Blind Mice! I had to get a stage hand to go out and take your dad off and close the show."

Basil Brush had become such a phenomenon it was only a matter of time before he got his own T.V. series and this happened in mid 1968 when Johnny Downes engaged George to write the scripts for the B.B.C.'s *Basil Brush Show*; 12 thirty minute programmes.

Siblings... George, Joyce and Bill at a Rat's "do".

Transmitted in an early evening Saturday slot, it was much more than a children's production. In fact, Basil became something of a cult and Basil fan clubs were formed by units of the British Army and ships of the Royal Navy. He was also adopted by several squadrons of the R.A.F. and an appreciation society was inaugurated in the Scilly Isles. Before long, no lesser body than the Admiralty had invited the furry puppet to attend the commissioning of the ship H.M.S. Fox as official mascot!

It was the beginning of a long, successful career for the foxy little fellow. Over many series, the format of the show remained the same; Basil indulging in cheeky back chat with his human side-kick before introducing guest acts (which included top pop groups of the day promoting their latest single), sketches (which often had lavish historical settings) and the weekly instalment of an adventure story. These stories (which George created) would be read by the side-kick to Basil, who would make regular interruptions as he commented on the progress of the plot.

The first was *The Saga of Des P. Rado*, a kind of Indiana Jones figure who would get into all kinds of hair-raising scrapes. Stories that followed in subsequent series included *Basil de Farmer*, *Basil the Buccaneer* and *Bulldog Basil*. Each character had his own song (all written by George) with a rousing chorus. The medieval knight's ditty went thus…

"Basil de Farmer, the knight in shining armour,
Fought against injustice with his sword held high.
And all his enemies, used to tremble at the knees
And everywhere they went they heard his battle cry…
Have at ye varlets… hooray!"

And all the kids in the studio audience would join in heartily.

Basil's side-kick in the first series was the actor Rodney Bewes (who played Bob in situation comedy hit *The Likely Lads*). Mr. Rodney, as Basil would address him, apparently had a rather large ego and was prone to name drop. According to George, he even wanted the next series re-named *Rodney and Basil*! As it happened Mr. Rodney did not make it to the next series and his place was taken by Derek Fowlds. Derek was much more suited to the role and his amiable, but much put upon, Mr. Derek became a popular fixture for the next few series.

Many years later, at a Water Rat's Ball, Derek was to tell me, "Your dad taught me how to drink!"

Every year there was a new Basil Brush television series and George's involvement as sole writer lasted for well over a decade. He and Ivan became close friends and George and Maggie spent a lot of time at Ivan's beautiful country home at Send near Guildford. Because, of course, Ivan became a rich man thanks to Basil's success; not only from the T.V. shows, but also from numerous theatre appearances, all of which were also scripted by George.

Ivan and Peter Firmin (who actually made the puppet) saw, very early on, the potential of merchandizing products around the name of their character. Toys, pillow cases, tooth brushes, games, mugs, etc.. Generously, they offered George the chance to join them in partnership but, inexplicably, he declined. A classic example of his lack of vision when it came to business. He simply could not be bothered. A shame, because Basil Brush merchandise was certainly a major factor in making Ivan his first million.

The 10 years between 1968 to 1978 were to be particularly lucrative for George, mainly thanks to his ongoing partnership with David Nixon and Basil Brush. Whatever either of them did, on stage or screen, George would be there to supply the words and songs for them.

David switched from the B.B.C. to making shows for the independent television companies, but Basil remained loyal to the "Beeb" and turned out his annual series like clockwork. David would still regularly guest on B.B.C. light entertainment shows, however, such as those fronted by Rolf Harris and Moira Anderson, and George still supplied David's material. (During this time, George also wrote regularly for Rolf himself, as well as Harry Worth and numerous other artistes who would come to him for topical stuff.)

Tonight with David Nixon went into production in January 1969.

This was an A.T.V. show, recorded out in the provinces of Borehamwood Studios in Hertfordshire. There were 16 shows, with George as script writer and John Wade as the magical adviser, involving guest stars such as Norman Wisdom in various illusions. By the autumn of the same year, the show had been commissioned for a further 16 week series.

Also from A.T.V., from the same studio, came *Tonight with Dave Allen*, which went out late on a Sunday evening. Producer Colin Clews and Dave himself had come to George with a request for weekly "special comedy material". Dave and George went back a long way, ever since the Irish comic had worked in that double act with Bill at Butlins, but Dave had progressed a lot since then. This new show was a lot of fun to work on. Dave was a progressive, anarchic funny man who was not frightened to take risks; a ground breaking approach at the time. He loved to push boundaries, but was never offensive. The show was adult in tone and included guests in an interview format, usually "edgy" celebrities like actor John Cassavetes or James Caan who had recently made his film debut in the John Wayne western *El Dorado*. Caan was actually quite an accomplished knife thrower and Dave Allen bravely stood against a board while Caan threw knives into the surrounding wood. At the last moment, Dave stepped aside and the actor plunged his final knife right into the spot where Dave's chest had been seconds before!

The show was renowned for its outrageous stunts and oddball guests. Dave would always try to take part in the stunts and on one occasion escaped from a car submerged in a gigantic water tank. Another time he attempted to emulate a man who could swallow a dozen raw eggs in a couple of gulps, likewise an eater of light bulbs! Apart from star names, he would also interview characters such as the President of the Flat Earth Society, a lady who specialized in past life regression and a man whose enormous snake escaped into the studio. The show also saw the British T.V. debut of Tiny Tim. With his long, flowing hair and assertions to the "purity of a good life", Tiny Tim made quite an impact with his falsetto renditions of old favourites like *Tiptoe through the Tulips* accompanied on his ukulele.

George always felt that his contribution to this show was not like working at all. He and Dave would meet for lunch at the L'Epee Dor restaurant in the Cumberland Hotel at Marble Arch, where they would laugh their way through the afternoon, maybe settling on an idea or two for that week's show. Earlier in the week there would have been a planning meeting in the producer's office where they would sift through the many proposed ideas which were sent in by the sack load. As they talked and formulated some kind of script, George would produce a whisky flask from his briefcase, adding a generous tot to their plastic beakers of tepid coffee; "Just to warm it up a bit"!

One week, live on air, Dave suddenly lunged out of camera shot, dragging George into vision. Taken completely unawares, George had a clipboard under his arm as Dave held him in a headlock, ruffling his hair as he dragged him around the set shouting, "George Martin, ladies and gentlemen!"

Tonight with Dave Allen – promotional stunt. *(Photo by Colin Jones)*

Many side lines came from the shows George was involved in. One, in 1969, was the offer of a daily story to be printed in The Daily Sketch featuring Basil Brush. George took this on but found that his other commitments made it difficult for him to honour the deadlines. He turned to my brother Ray, who had writing ambitions, and was by this time working in an office job in the City. To ease the pressure, George asked Ray if he would like to write the stories. Glad of the opportunity, Ray did so and they went into the paper with the dual credits of father and son. Plot lines reflected Ray's interest in history, and Basil found himself in the age of the Vikings!

Many of the sketches in the Basil T.V. show were historically based too, as George wracked his brain to find new situations for the character to exploit. One week Basil was with the 7th. Cavalry fighting Sioux Indians at the Battle of the Little Big Horn and Ray came up with a classic line to tag it. As Mr. Derek, in the role of General Custer, staggered into shot crying out that he had been scalped, Basil took one look at the single lock of blonde hair hanging from his bald head and quipped, "Ah ha, Custer's Last *Strand*! Boom! Boom!"

This was typical Basil humour which only he could get away with. There were always plays on words, such as when Mr. Derek started talking about the breeding of birds and Basil asked him, "Bred any good rooks lately? Haaa!, Haaa!"

By 1970 the little fox had released his first record album for E.M.I., an L.P.called, simply, *Basil Brush*. George was heard on this album as Basil's sidekick, "Mr. George", of course. He also wrote most of the songs, such as *Basil the Bard*, *Basil's Bicycle Song* and *Whenever the Circus Comes to Town*, along with revivals of his *Basil de Farmer* and a new airing of his old panto favourite *Baby Bear Lullaby*. There were parodies too, with George's new lyrics to classics such as *Froggie Went a Courting* and *How Ya Gonna Keep 'em Down on the Farm?*

George was adept at writing parodies and he regularly used this technique when scripting shows, especially for Basil. Probably owing to Maggie's influence, he was fond of using Gilbert and Sullivan tunes and would cleverly score whole routines around pastiches of such operas as *The Mikado* or *Pirates of Penzance*.

He was a fine song writer with a creative ability to compose catchy, emotive melodies and nice lyrics. As well as *The Small Shepherd Boy*, which The Beverley Sisters had recorded, he also penned beautiful ballads such as *Comes Autumn, Tears of an Angel* and rousing chorus songs like *Those Good Old Days of Music Hall*. Singer Pat Stark was fond of a song he wrote for her called *Raggedy*

Barrel Organ to sing in a Basil Brush costermonger sketch. I liked an early effort of his, a bizarre novelty number called *Tears in my Ears* which went like this…

> "Every night, I get tears in my ears from lying on my back and crying over you.
> Don't seem right, that a bod on his tod
> Should have to go through all the heartaches like what I've been going through.
> I hear that ever constant drip like water down a plug 'ole,
> Its very hard to get to kip with water in your lug 'ole.
> Every night, I get tears in my ears from lying on my back and crying over you!"

But there was one song writing assignment which he was never very proud of. In fact, he just took the money and declined to have his name included in the credits. This was for a collection of bawdy ditties he supplied for the book *More Rugby Songs*!

Chapter 16

A DOUBLE LIFE

All this work must have helped enormously, coming at just the right time to help him through the period of his bankruptcy, although, presumably, he must have been having to pay the Inland Revenue substantial sums to clear his debt.

The writing had certainly become his main source of income, but he still appeared on stage when the opportunity arose. Sunday variety shows at Butlins' theatres were still coming in, as well as the occasional special. The London Borough of Hackney engaged him, for instance, to appear for one night at the Assembly Hall Stoke Newington on Saturday November 1st. 1969 in *The George Martin Show*, with full supporting bill.

And there were more radio shows... *Now and Then*, *Be My Guest*, *Sounds Familiar*, *Listen at Lunchtime* and *Listen at Teatime* too!

As the years went on, George found a couple of particular niches which suited his performing style. One had arisen just by chance when he had become more heavily involved in television production. He found himself acting as the "warm up" man for studio audiences at the various shows he had written. George's laid back persona and calm way of talking to a crowd were just what was needed to relax the public who were, probably, in a television studio for the first time. Using gentle humour and a "matey" style, George would explain exactly what was happening, filling in the recording breaks and introducing the stars of the show.

Because he was so good at this role, other producers began asking

George if he would do the "warm ups" on their shows and he soon found that this had become another handy string to his bow. I remember him taking me along to one in the early days and it was quite an education for me. It was *The John Davidson Show* at Elstree. John Davidson was a smooth American singer who had been given his own British T.V. series, although his fame did not really take off in the U.K.. I recall his guests were the American impressionist Rich Little and French singer Mireille Mathieu. Homespun talent was supplied by the "lovely Aimi MacDonald" who was very popular that year. (1969.)

In the artiste's hospitality room, I was impressed by the glitzy atmosphere. Television people were, and are, very much a rule unto themselves. My father introduced me to Paul Anka (the writer of *My Way*) but I was more excited by the fact that I recognized him from the role he had played in the war film *The Longest Day*. What sticks in my mind though is the fact that he was eating a greasy chicken leg as he shook hands with me, covering my fingers in gunge. He did apologize, however.

George also became much in demand as an after dinner speaker. This was another area of performance which suited his style perfectly. Having honed his speeches to a fine art for the many events he had spoken at over the years, George could now adapt his words and mannerisms to suit any occasion. Complete strangers at company dinners could be taken in completely by his urbane persona as he convinced them, over the cigars and brandy, that he had known them for years. The secret was in doing one's homework upon arriving early at the event. Ask a few questions about various characters known to the assembled guests, discover their traits, strengths and weaknesses and re-structure the basis of one's speech by personalizing it. By blending this with his rock solid reputation for finding humour in the day's news and he was onto a winner every time.

This was a period when he began making an effort to keep in regular touch with his official family. By that, I mean me, mainly, because I was the minor member. Perhaps he was feeling a bit guilty.

He was still away most of the time, but he started to invite me, quite often, to various things he was involved in. Consequently, I travelled with him to some shows, such as a theatre appearance he made at Butlins Clacton, where Bill was entertainment's manager. We stayed overnight, but my main memory was of watching him, Bill and the camp compere, Terry Dale, having fun over endless rounds of drinks. That was alright though, because I was well used to such a scenario and actually enjoyed being an observer. (Not that I understood *everything* they talked about!) I also went with him to a charity Boxing Gala in aid of the Water Rats, somewhere in the Midlands.

There was also a long period when he would arrive at Young's Farm on a Saturday night to take me and my mother out to dinner. This actually became a ritual which I really looked forward to and on the odd occasion when he was unable to make it, I was bitterly disappointed. We would sometimes go to a Chinese restaurant in Windsor. Chinese food was still quite a novelty in those days, so it was rather exciting, especially as George knew the management and they would always make a fuss of us. One night he surprised us all by asking my mother to dance and they ended up with a big circle of punters around them, clapping along as they danced a very energetic Charleston! I never realised he could move so fast! This was rare however, because he would seldom be seen on a dance floor.

Another place we frequented was the Silver Park Club in the Fleet area. This was a private member's establishment, lavish and upmarket, but the owners were old friends of my parents, so, once again, we were made very welcome. After a long, drawn out meal, there would always be an after time session which would stretch way into the small hours. I vividly remember how I would get so tired waiting for these nights to end I would actually feel physically sick, my eyes burning from the ever present cigarette smoke. Every now and then, my dad would lean over to me and ask if I was alright, offer me a drink and tell me we were about to leave. No one seemed to be unduly worried, and I just accepted it. I did not feel hard done by. It was just the way it was.

When we finally got home, it would be about 3a.m., and then another ritual would begin. George seldom ate much at these meals, maybe some spare ribs or a plate of oysters, and this was probably because he had eaten with Maggie before picking us up. However, back at Young's Farm, he would usually have a cheese sandwich and a glass of milk, then I would go to bed and lie there listening to the inevitable raised voices which would emanate from him and my mother. Joan had more or less worked out his situation by now, and so the late night accusations would begin. He still dug his heels in though, and stubbornly denied everything in his calm, infuriating way.

Finally, the time came when it seems he felt he must come clean. I had my own theory about what had happened between my parents, but still being only 15 years old, I suppose I was undergoing a form of denial and tried not to think about it too much.

A kind of "showdown" was arranged, although I was not told what to expect. My mother, in her terse way, merely announced that she and I were going to London to "face your father with a few truths". Somewhat bewildered, I went with her on the train to Waterloo and we made our way to the West End where Dad met us at the L'Epee Dor, the restaurant where he had those planning meetings with Dave Allen. Ray had been summoned too, and we all had a luxurious, but rather tense, lunch.

George was obviously uncomfortable during this meal, because he knew what was coming. It was still a mystery to me at the time, however, but I was soon to be enlightened. The conversation, so far, had been rather strained, but we all climbed into George's car and he drove us along the Edgware Road to Maida Vale, then we climbed three flights of stairs to the flat he shared with Maggie.

To her credit, Maggie tried hard to be charming. She greeted us all with a big smile, ushering us through to their tastefully furnished lounge, but my mother was having none of it. She was hostile from the word go. Her face set hard in anger, she began snapping out insults from the moment she crossed the threshold.

Maggie owned a miniature white poodle (Mitzi) which was totally unused to such confrontational scenes. Yapping and running around my mother's heels, it did not help the situation at all. As Joan sat down, Mitzi tried to jump on her lap but was met with a sweeping arm and a cry of "Piss off!" which flung the little dog half way across the room.

Now the gloves were off.

"Come on, Joan, there's no need for that," said George.

Maggie's Achilles' heel had been struck. "Don't you dare hurt my dog!" she railed, in her upper crust voice, "I will put up with a lot from you, Joan, but *not* that!"

Oh dear, it was all downhill from there. Ray and I sat in chairs on opposite sides of the room, raising our eyebrows helplessly as our parents battled it out, with Maggie caught in the middle.

The accusations flew thick and fast, but George delivered his point of view without raising his voice, unlike Joan whose justified outrage was spat out with considerable venom. Nothing could really be denied anymore, although George did his best to offer some kind of defence. Accused of lying by both the women in his life (or those who were *present* anyway!) he merely said, "Well, I will stretch the truth if I feel it will help a situation..."

That was pretty feeble and Maggie responded with her own observation, "Stretch the truth? George, the lies fall off you like from the back of a lorry!"

At one point, Joan made a remark about Maggie's superior airs and graces.

"I'll have you know," sniffed Maggie, indignantly, "that my father was a coal merchant."

"Oh?" Joan flew back, quick as a flash, "So that explains why you're a slag!"

Unnecessary, perhaps, but admittedly quite witty!

And so it went on. The outcome did not really seem to solve anything, save for the fact that the whole situation was now out in the open. George dropped us back at the station and my mother made me promise that I would never visit that flat or see "that woman" ever again.

For a while, I honoured the promise to my mother, but it was an impractical vow. George would still come down to take us out most Saturdays, and he and Joan maintained an uneasy truce, presumably for my sake, but as I got older I started travelling by train to London on my own. I would visit my father at the various studios where he

For Thames T.V.; the production team of David Nixon's show. Ali Bongo (Magical Associate, seated), Bobby Chapman (Production Asst.), Royston Mayoh (Producer/Director), Barbara Dudley-Evans (trainee P.A.), David and George.

was working; the B.B.C. Television Theatre at Shepherd's Bush for the *Basil Brush Show* or Thames Television Studios at Teddington, Middlesex, where production began in 1970 on *David Nixon's Magic Box*. At first just seeing him at the studios was fine. We would take breaks in the pub and have lunch, and dad would introduce me to all the celebrities, who were generally very pleasant to me, but I quickly began to feel that it would be nice to also see him in more informal surroundings. George sensed this and eventually suggested that I go to the flat with him.

I felt like a bit of a fraud doing this, but I did succumb and my visits to the flat for cosy dinners with my dad and Maggie became quite frequent. It was a long time before my mother found out.

I grew quite fond of Maggie although she never really lost her patronising attitude towards me. Accompanying them to a Water Rat's event at the Dorchester Hotel (the first black tie dinner I ever attended), she even suggested that I call her "Mother" for the evening, to "save confusing people" she said, but I refused to comply with that one.

George's involvement with The Water Rats had been growing deeper and in 1970 he held the office of Prince Rat, just one step below the top position in the Order. There was only one place for him to go from there.

And yet, it was still a side of his life which he liked to keep apart from us in Young's Farm. Although he was seeing us on that regular weekly basis, plus the fact that my visits to London were growing more frequent, we had no idea that he was in line for such an honour.

In late November 1970, the day after the annual Water Rat's Ball at Grosvenor House in Park Lane, I saw a headline in the newspaper; *Comedian George is made King Rat*.

It was the first I, Ray or my mother knew of it.

Genuinely proud of him, I got on the telephone to offer my congratulations.

His reply was quite frosty. "How did you know about that?"

It was as if I had touched a nerve. A part of his life which was separate to the relationship he had with me, his youngest son.

Everything was fine after that, and he warmed to my questions, but I would never forget his initial response to my "well wishing".

It was quite a lesson.

Dear Friends,

I am delighted to welcome you this evening to the first Rats' Revel to be held in Bedford.

The motto of The Grand Order Of Water Rats is "Philanthropy, Conviviality and Social Intercourse", and on an occasion such as this, we Rats enjoy conforming to the second and third maxims, because you can't beat a reunion with old mates and meeting new friends, can you?

Since its inception in 1889, The Order has faithfully pursued the first of its declared objects, Philanthropy, and on behalf of the G.O.W.R. I offer you all our grateful thanks for your support.

As one illustrious Elder of our Order, the late FRED RUSSELL said, "It would ill become us to boast of the good we try to do for others; it suffices if it is registered in the hearts of those it has been our privilege to befriend."

I wonder if the Father and Founder of our Order, JOE ELVIN, had any idea when he suggested forming "The Pals Of The Water Rat" at the Magpie Hotel, Sunbury-on-Thames in 1889, how much pleasure and pride he had bequeathed to certain pro's during the following years. It's difficult to describe the feeling I had when that treasured, little golden emblem was pinned to my lapel at my Initiation. I wear it everywhere I go, both onstage and off. Mind you, it's going to be a bit dodgy if I ever get a job in "Oh! Calcutta!", but I believe there are a few good tattooists still operating.

I extend our gratitude to Water Rat CHARLES LANE and THE BEDFORD ROUND TABLE for organising this evening's fun, and to the Artistes appearing (both Rat and non-Rat), the Theatre Management and Staff, and everyone who has contributed to make this an evening to remember.

Enjoy yourselves, good friends . . . that's what we're here for!

GEORGE MARTIN,
KING RAT, 1971.

One of many events hosted by George during his year as King Rat.

With HRH Prince Philip the Duke of Edinburgh, who was made a Companion Water Rat.

The cover of the Annual Ball brochure, at the end of George's year in the chair.

Chapter 17

FAMILY JUGGLING

During the early 1970s, George followed fashionable trends and changed his image. As he passed his 50th. birthday, like so many other middle aged show-biz types at the time (especially if they worked regularly in television) he began to adopt a particular look. He let his sideburns reach the bottoms of his ears and grew his hair a bit longer. Light coloured safari jackets were all the rage, as were flared trousers, although George's clothes of this style always maintained a crisp, well pressed appearance. Sometimes he would wear a neatly ironed kerchief around his neck, but he never neglected to display his gold Water Rat's emblem which he wore proudly, pinned to his lapel. If he was not wearing a jacket, he had another emblem which he would wear on a chain. (There is a rule in the G.O.W.R. which states if a Water Rat meets a Brother member not wearing his emblem, he is obliged to fine him.)

He now always smoked his Player's cigarettes in a holder and well do I remember the way he would sit at a bar, nonchalantly holding it between his fingertips as the smoke curled in lazy patterns around his head. It all added to his general aura of casual sophistication, an image which he seemed to carry very easily. Men warmed to him as an instant friend, women were charmed by him. When in a restaurant he possessed this intangible ability to take control without being overbearing. It came so naturally to him.

And yet, although he was at his best in social situations, if anything ever riled him, he could show a very different side to his nature. More of this later.

1971; George's year in the chair as King Rat was a very eventful one. The King Rat, as figurehead of the Order, is expected to support the Rats in everything they do, not least of all to oversee the lodge meetings as well as to be out and about promoting their aims. George took the position very seriously and made a huge effort to make himself available, even though he was so busy with his work commitments. He arranged numerous fund raising events and shows, travelling all over the country. There were midnight matinee

A typical show-biz gathering. Left to right; Paul Raymond, Frankie Howerd, George, Bill, Billy McComb, Tommy Cooper and Bob Andrews in the front. (Is that the ghost of Dan Leno looking over George's shoulder?!!)

performances and stunts such as when the Rats took over the Guinness Brewery for the day. A particularly satisfying moment must have been when he was able to personally present HRH Prince Philip, the Duke of Edinburgh (a Companion Rat) with a cheque for £10,000 for his Award Scheme.

The highlight of his reign as King Rat was the Annual Ball in November, as described in the opening pages of this book. Although Sue attended the event, it was never on the cards for Ray and I to be there.

Brother Bill, who had become a Water Rat in 1967, decided to end his association with Butlins in George's year as King Rat. Bill was in a senior management position by this time, but had become somewhat disillusioned with the way the company appeared to be heading. Before he left he arranged a job for Ray as a Redcoat at the Barry Island camp. (Although Ray was married by now, he was feeling unfulfilled by his London office job and wanted to take steps into a career in entertainment.)

Bill planned his move from Butlins carefully. He bought a greengrocery business in Aldershot, presumably as a back-up to support his continuing career in show-business, but shortly after taking this commitment he was offered a full time position as the administrator of the G.O.W.R.. This meant travelling to London every day to run the Water Rat's office. He was also managing his own entertainment agency, Fay Promotions, as well as leading a trio on Fridays and Saturdays at the Hawley Hotel in Surrey. A busy man indeed. (On top of all this, he and Bob had opened a club in Aldershot called The Ritz; something else George was offered a stake in, only to decline it.)

Productive times for the Martin Brothers, but tragedy came in 1972 when their parents both died within a few weeks of one another. Bill senior suffered a stroke and failed to regain consciousness, and Lil succumbed to cancer.

They were buried in the same plot as their daughter Rita.

George said, with much poignancy, that he was actually pleased that his dad had not come around from the stroke.

"If he had survived and been left paralyzed, I don't think I could have stood it."

In view of what would one day happen to him, these words were laced with awful irony.

Regardless of the family meeting in Maida Vale which was intended to clear the air, the situation did not really change.

George and Joan remained married although there was no longer any secret about his life with Maggie. How could there be? George carried on taking us out for regular meals, although the gaps between his visits steadily grew wider. I left school in 1971 and began a 3 year course in film and television production at an art college in Guildford. There were problems again with our home at Young's Farm and, once more, my mother and I (and the dog!) were facing eviction.

This was partly due, I believe, to a change of landlord who had plans for the property, plus issues of unpaid rent. Of course, George was supposed to be paying this. I am unsure of the circumstances, but it seems that this led to a falling out between him and his old friend, Nip Eustace, who was the guarantor.

We were rescued, at the last hour again, when a big, rambling town house was found for us in the centre of Aldershot. A ramshackle, creepy place; but at least we had plenty of room. My bedroom was at the very top of this four storey building and I was often kept awake at night by the sound of pigeons trapped in the walls and mice scurrying around the floor. Indeed, my childhood was filled with unique home environments!

Ray had enjoyed his season at Butlins and came back with so many tales of fun that I decided to join him the following summer ('72) back at Barry Island. I was able to do this in the long break at the end of my first college year, although Ray had been promoted to assistant entertainment's manager and I was a basic general duty Redcoat.

It was a great baptism of fire into the world of entertainment and I was able to appear regularly in shows for the first time. Up to this moment, I was absolutely convinced that I wanted to be a film director, but following this season, I felt a "hankering for the boards" again. I loved it so much that I went back the following year.

A lot of the older management people knew George and Bill. Also many of the visiting cabaret and theatre artistes, so Ray and I would often find ourselves discussing our dad with the likes of Tommy Trinder and Bob Monkhouse.

One of the dancers in the resident revue company was the daughter of the comedian/actor Dave King. King was obsessed with the Wild West, to the extent that he had named his children after Red Indian tribes; therefore the one at Barry Island was Cheyenne, her sister being Kiowa.

The Butlin publicity machine decided that it might be a good idea to present a feature about variety comic's kids following in their footsteps. They suggested that Cheyenne, Ray and I could pose for a cosy picture together for a potential newspaper item, but the delightful dancing diva sniffily refused to have anything to do with it. She was brought to earth shortly after this, however, when dancing the Apache in the Pig and Whistle Show-bar. Thrown across the floor during this vigorous routine, she broke her knee and was carried from the stage wailing in agony. I am not proud of the fact that I had a chuckle about that.

In the meantime, George was busily working. It had now reached the stage where his commitments to Basil Brush and David Nixon almost filled up his entire year, with regular series being re-commissioned. And there were lots of other offers to stop the few gaps in his diary. He would often be asked to structure one off productions, such as the *T.V. Times Awards Show* as well as a "six minute per show" contract for *The Black and White Minstrel* series, which was hugely popular at the time.

In late 1973, Derek Fowlds moved on from Basil Brush and the new sidekick became a young actor named Roy North. George's fee rose considerably to accommodate this change and he was now guaranteed £250 per show. The David Nixon shows had a format which consisted of regular guest magic acts, plus resident performers such as singer Anita Harris and comedian Freddie "Parrot Face" Davies.

July saw George engaged to appear on the television panel show

Looks Familiar, a nostalgic quiz in which veteran performers were grilled by presenter Denis Norden for their memories about variety and old films. Sharing the sofa with Roy Hudd, Ted Ray, Joe Loss, Renee Houston and Joan Turner, George found several excuses to mention the G.O.W.R. and actually got gently chastised on screen by Norden for his constant "plugs for the Water Rats"!

In November, George was heavily involved in the planning for David Nixon to be the subject of a *This is your Life* programme. Along with Ali Bongo, David's new magical adviser, he coerced with presenter Eamonn Andrews production team to devise a situation which would entrap the unsuspecting David with a total surprise. This took the form of a filmed insert which, ostensibly, was intended for the Nixon Christmas Special. Luring David to the headquarters of the Magic Circle where the sequence was to be filmed in the Club Room, the set up was to involve Ali Bongo appearing as Santa Claus from a sack. The pay off was David's complete shock as he was faced by Eamonn as Santa, instead of Ali.

This is your Life, *David Nixon.*

Whisked off to Thames Studios for the recording of the actual T.I.Y.L. show, David's guests included Basil Brush and several members of the G.O.W.R., including Tommy Cooper. David had been initiated as a Water Rat in 1970, with George as his proposer. When brought forward by Eamonn to speak about his friend, George praised the magician for his professionalism and charitable nature, describing him as a "gentleman and a gentle *man*".

Early in 1973, well into the second year of my course, I had to produce and direct a television programme. For my subject matter, I chose to make a documentary about my Uncle Bill.

Bill was very accommodating about this, and patient too as it involved disrupting his busy schedule. I took a crew of fellow students up to the Water Rat's H.Q. at the Eccentric Club in London's high brow St. James' district to film him at work in the office. George was there too for a few sequences. I also took a lot of photographs of Bill doing his stuff in his grocer's shop and at the Ritz Club, as well as at the piano with his trio at the Hawley Hotel.

This all culminated in a day at the college's T.V. studio when an interview was recorded between Bill and George. They were really on form and I was so proud of them. It was just an ad-lib session as they spoke about Bill's interesting life and show-business in general but it created a great spark. Bill had even brought in some items from the Rat's museum... Stan Laurel's dress suit, Little Tich's boots, the dummy from the vent act Coram & Jerry, etc.. The two brothers were in their element and chatted for about thirty highly entertaining minutes, true pros that they were.

One of the things which really impressed me was the way they won over my colleagues, some of whom were typical left wing, cynical students. By the end of the day, everybody seemed to be full of praise and respect for the Martin brothers.

It was satisfying to know that I had managed to capture some magic moments on video tape, so imagine my horror when, a few weeks later, one of the college lecturers came to me and sheepishly confessed that he had somehow accidentally wiped half of the interview!

Friday March 2nd. 1973; the recording of Profile; Bill Martin. Doing their impromptu vent act, Bill manipulates the head of Jerry, as George operates "Coster Joe", the dummy once owned by Fred Russell, renowned as the "father of ventriloquism".

When George and Bill got together the result was always something a bit special. If Bob was around to complete the trio then it was *really* something. This would often happen during the regular gatherings at the Ritz club, or parties at Joyce and Bob's flat (or maybe Bill's house or George and Maggie's place). These were times when, after a few drinks, they would be persuaded (it never took *much* persuasion) to go through the paces of the old Martin Brother's act. The harmonies were still tight and it was great to see. The three of them were so close.

Although only a small place, the Ritz Club played host to some terrific events. George brought David Nixon to the opening night

Bill, George and Bob, reviving The Martin Brothers at the Ritz Club, Aldershot.

and there were often Water Rat's fund raising occasions fronted by George and Bill. It became quite a magnet for celebrities who were in the area, especially if they were resident in a show at the local Princes Hall. Eventually, Bob, Joyce and Bill found it necessary to transfer to bigger premises, around the corner to the considerably more spacious Owls Club. This was the point when the venture changed from being just a social exercise to a proper business move.

Now that I was older, I would sometimes be involved in these social shindigs. Ray got a job as an entertainments officer with P. & O. Cruises and went to sea, but while still at college, I would often catch the train to London to meet my father. As previously stated, this would usually be at one of the studios where I would spend a lot of time sitting on the sidelines watching him at work.

Ivan, the voice and arm behind Basil Brush, was fiercely protective of his identity. For years he was a secret and would never be photographed with the puppet. In fact, he was so into the character that even when they were doing basic read-throughs, he insisted on having Basil on his arm so that he could get the right "feel" for his performance. After a while, the Basil puppet started to get a bit tatty and threadbare and Ivan had another identical one made, but it never felt the same to him and he neglected using it. I recall how odd it was being in Ivan's dressing room and seeing Basil lying "lifeless" upon a chair.

Watching the production of the show was an interesting experience. George would do the warm-up in the evening to the studio audience which, in Basil's case, was mostly made up of children. He would speak to them in his familiar, chummy way, adapting his style to suit the younger crowd. During the recording breaks, when the next scene was being set, George would try to involve the guest artistes in some banter with the kids. More often than not, the stars were receptive to this, with one notable exception. I remember how unapproachable and difficult the singer Gilbert O'Sullivan was when George tried to get him to join in.

"Its been a hard day, hasn't it, Mr. Gilbert?" asked George in a friendly fashion, his "umpteenth" attempt to break the ice.

Sour faced on his piano stool the singer snarled back, "I think it's much harder for them sitting out there."

There were a lot of parties at George and Maggie's flat too, and I would sometimes be there. They really knew how to throw a party and always did it in style. Many nights I would catch the last train home to Aldershot, groggy on my feet and full of red wine.

I completed my course in mid-summer 1974 and Bill found a seasonal job for me as a Bluecoat in the entertainment's department of a small holiday centre he was involved in, down at Westward Ho! on the north coast of Devon. Bill was not actually working there; he just had connections. The entertainments manager was Terry Dale, the Butlins compere I had met during that trip to Clacton.

On one memorable occasion mid-season, George and Bill turned up with Ray. Ray had been home for a short leave from P. & O. and was about to join another ship at Southampton. For some reason, it transpired that the Martin brothers were able to give him a lift to the docks and they had all decided that it would be a wheeze to take a huge detour and drop into Westward Ho! on the way.

It was quite a night! Apparently they had stopped at just about every pub en-route. When they finally arrived at the camp in the late afternoon, they were in high spirits, to say the least. George was driving his huge green Pontiac convertible with the hood down. He was wearing a cowboy hat and the three of them made quite an entrance.

Terry Dale was overjoyed to see them, as was the general manager of the site, "Red" Killand, another old friend from the Butlin days.

George with Lord Delfont and Her Majesty the Queen Elizabeth at a Royal Variety Performance.

That night in the show-bar, Bill got on the keyboards and George did his act, sort of. It was very informal and they were all showing the effects of a full day's drinking, but it was still great fun. At some point, George tried to drive his car on the beach and, when the bar closed, we all ended up being chauffer-ed around the countryside to various other places to continue the partying. I don't recall much detail, but I do remember that we all sobered up quite quickly at one point when whoever was driving us around the dark country lanes sped straight across a blind traffic junction!

When they left the following day, amidst much bonhomie, they apparently visited more pubs all the way to Southampton. The rest of the season was quite an anti-climax after that!

And so the '70s progressed, with George Martin as one of the leading British television scriptwriters of the decade. He also became Preceptor of the G.O.W.R., a position which in many ways is regarded as even more prestigious than King Rat, because it is recognized as being "Father of the Order". For his ongoing devotion, his Brother Rats also awarded him the Badge of Merit.

George brought several high profile names into the Order. David Nixon, of course, who became King Rat for two consecutive years (1976/77), and he also proposed boxing champion Henry Cooper. David proposed the singer Matt Monro, with George as Matt's seconder. Other successful initiates of George's were dancer Lionel Blair and ventriloquist Keith Harris, but he was upset when his attempt to get Brother-in-Law Bob into the Order failed.

George, as Preceptor, had to carry out the solemn welcoming speech during the initiation of Peter Sellers. Although Water Rat's lodge meetings are all about fun, they never-the-less take their rituals seriously, so it did not go down too well when Sellers began larking around during the ceremony. George battled vainly to keep it all dead straight, but it was very difficult when up against the star's infamous "mickey-taking" and myriad voices; Pakistani, Bluebottle and Fred Kite! Sellers was notorious for being unable to take *anything* seriously and before long he petulantly resigned from the Order over a trifling matter.

Many Water Rats had stories and warm recollections of George Martin. Property businessman Tom Anderson, a Companion Rat, first met him in the 1950s through Terry Cantor.

"I have many happy memories of your gifted dad..." he said, speaking of one such time when the Rats did their shows at the La Reserve nightclub in Sutton Coldfield. A coach had been booked to take the Rats, in evening dress, to the venue and, "... at once your dad was the life of the party, saying *"This is the poshest pub darts outing I've ever been on"*. He never stopped on the journey... what a start to the evening."

When they got to the club, Tom said he had to go to the Gent's just to have a rest from laughing. "Your dad and brother Bill sang their version of *It Happened in Monterey* as *It Happened to Monty Ray*... it was a night I would never forget."

Helped onto the coach at the end of the evening, George's head was slumped on his chest, "More than a little *Brahms*," said Tom. Michael Robbins (Arthur from *On the Buses*) shouted out "George Martin is a poof!" to which George managed to briefly raise his head and respond, "Oh no, I'm bisexual. I like soldiers just as much as I like sailors!"

"He was an amazing man." carried on Tom, "One night at a Lady Ratling's Party at the Cafe Royal, George was led onto the stage (completely impromptu), given that evening's newspaper and dared to do his act without any preparation. He did about 20 minutes without pausing, with a newspaper he had never seen before. His contemporaries all stood and gave him a great ovation. His wit in lodge was unequalled."

Comedian and producer Kenny Cantor (son of Terry) said, "George was probably the most under-rated comedian of his time, mainly because he was so nice a guy without any undue forcefulness. He went on his way and was extremely successful without having to jump up and down to be seen."

"Without doubt the finest topical comedian of his day. He was always a kind and caring man," said singer Clive Stock, "one of the most loved performers in the profession. His friends and fellow artistes held him in high esteem... George was the host of a broadcast Gwen and I did from Birmingham and when we had finished our spot, he said to the audience; *"Did you notice they had an unusual gimmick for singers these days? Voices!"*... a first class wordsmith, we will never see his like again."

Another singer, Mike Redway, spoke of having worked with George on *Worker's Playtime*, amazed by the fact that he was just sitting with a newspaper, at a typewriter, minutes before the show would be broadcast live. "How stressful, or laid back, was that? There we were, having rehearsed our songs for the show a hundred times or more, and there was this guy casually picking bits out of the paper, which I soon found out he could turn into very amusing stories for the audience. Just being around people like him was an education in professionalism."

Bryn Williams, one of the U.K.'s top toastmasters, called George "one of the loveliest blokes that anyone could meet" and told of a Royal event at the Lakeside Country Club in Frimley Green, Surrey, where George set up a humorous stunt. David Nixon and George were in the line-up of various celebrities waiting to be introduced to Princess Anne and her then husband, Captain Mark Phillips. As the Princess exchanged small talk with George, she was about to move down the line when Basil Brush popped up from behind his shoulder.

"Hello, your Royal Highness!" piped up Basil, "Fallen off any good horses lately? Boom, boom!"

With the Royal demeanour only slightly shaken, the Princess shot back, "You don't fall off *good* ones."

Dec Cluskey of The Bachelors said, "My new born baby daughter, Victoria, spent her first night out of hospital in George and Maggie's flat; in the bottom drawer of their chest of drawers! We stayed with them quite a lot... our kids adored them."

George and Maggie would also occasionally travel down to Dec's beautiful country home, The Old Bakehouse in Horam, Sussex, to stay there and baby-sit the children when Dec was away with his wife, Sandy.

"I can still see George, floral shirt over his trousers, with the flagon bottle of red wine gently warming at the back of the gas fire in the lounge. To this day I like my red wine slightly warm. Certain folk in life just seem to still be around. George and Maggie were such a part of our family that I have no sense of them not being with us."

Bert *"Play in a Day"* Weedon recalled, "He was a very dear friend. One of the nicest men in show-business, and certainly one of the funniest."

Actor and legendary straight man Nicholas Parsons said, "I followed your father into the Windmill. He had a wonderful, laid back style; one of the very first to work like that. He was always totally charming."

And David Nixon's widow Vivienne had fond memories of the many social times she spent in George and Maggie's company.

"George, Maggie and Mitzi (the poodle) came to Innisfree (David's home in Chipstead, Surrey) socially loads of times," she said, "when we would all sing along to Gilbert and Sullivan. George always called David 'Dave'; the only person to do so as 'Dave' simply didn't suit David. To us, as a family, your papa was just

The Bachelors (John Stokes, Con and Dec Cluskey) with George and magician David Berglas. Bob McGowan is looking over David's right shoulder.

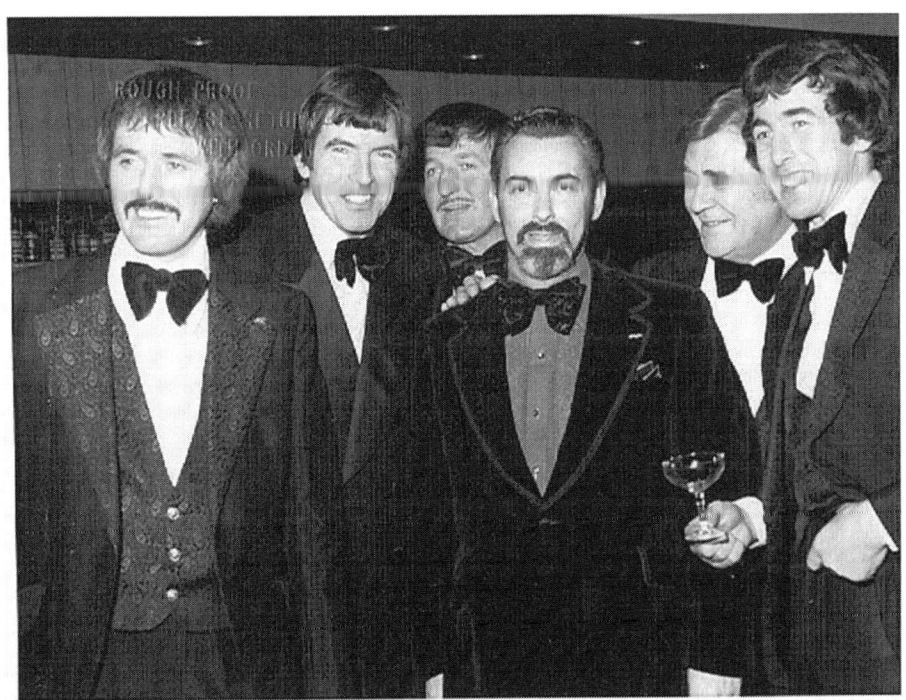

lovely George – we all adored him – he was easy going, funny and always welcome."

It is nice to hear this kind of thing, of course, but my mother had very different feelings about him, which is, perhaps, understandable. For a long time I found it hard to accept the situation of my parents breaking up, but, when I look back on it now, I realise that they had already been leading separate lives for many years. Difficult now to ever visualize them as a happy couple, because they were poles apart. What happened to the laughing teenagers who danced together to the *Chestnut Tree* song way back before the war? I mentioned this to my father once, stressing that they must have had an affinity once, and he sighed, ruefully, "Well, we were just kids..."

Sad, but so often true in life.

By the time my mother and I moved into the Aldershot town house, George's ritual visits to take us out dried up altogether. This was not a conscious decision. It just seemed that weeks passed, then months, before we accepted that this phase of our lives had moved on.

I was still seeing him, but only if I made the effort to travel to London. That said, he continued to appear in Aldershot but only to visit the club owned by his siblings. More often than not, I would not even know he was there and would find out by chance by seeing his car parked outside Bob and Joyce's flat.

On one such day, early in 1976, having spotted the evidence, I went to the club hoping to see him there. In actual fact, he was absent, but I was reliably informed that he was in town. Phoning Bob's place, George came on the line.

"Hello dad. I'm at the club. I was hoping to see you."

"Not tonight, son. I'm relaxing. Maybe next time, eh?"

I was incensed. At the time, this seemed like the last straw. I had not seen him for weeks and his blasé attitude with me, I felt, was taking the Casual Comedian act just a step too far.

The following morning I wrote him a letter in which I poured out the depth of my feelings and disappointment. It was strong stuff and, on reflection, I went too far, but I was upset and still pretty young. Accusing him of not caring, and throwing words like "audacity" at him, I even went so far as to venture that he probably spent more on Mitzi's collars than he spent on me! Ray was back from sea by now, and he advised me not to send it, but I felt very strongly that it was time our father was enlightened a little.

Much to my surprise, he replied almost immediately; a long letter in which he eloquently put across his point of view. He began by stating how pleased he was to see that I could put my feelings so strongly in writing, adding "... it seems you said everything but Happy New Year". Defending every point I had raised, his letter was cleverly non-commital with all the elements of the charm he was so famous for. The only part of my letter which seemed to raise his hackles slightly was my use of the word "audacity"... "Wrong choice when addressing me", he wrote, plus he claimed to be mystified by my, admittedly, rather stupid accusation about Mitzi's collars.

He concluded with affection, but leaving me with the impression that nothing would change. "Don't reply to this letter, son. Let's just see each other whenever we can..."

It was quite a turning point for me and I decided that I was not going to contact him for the foreseeable future.

As it happened, I was to leave home shortly after this. I had already spent several seasonal periods away working at holiday camps and had graduated from college with my diploma in Television and Film Production. Unable to secure employment in T.V. or film work, I managed to get a job working in the advertisement department of The Stage newspaper and I moved to London to share a flat with my wife to be, Val, whom I had met when we were both Redcoats.

I had no contact with my father for about six months, although I was more or less aware of his movements. What really hurt me, deep down, was the fact that he made no effort to contact me. To this day I wonder if we would ever have spoken again had I not relented, one evening, long after I had moved to London.

I phoned him and he seemed pleased to hear from me, in his easy going way. He was surprised to be told about my situation, my job and my location, but he acted as if there had never been any kind of rift between us. It was as if I had been with him only the day before.

It was then that I was overwhelmed with a huge feeling of understanding, as if everything suddenly slotted into place. The charm of George Martin was a very hard thing to by-pass, and did I really want to? He was his own man. Maybe not the most perfect of fathers, but a special bloke, to be sure. Perhaps it would always be "out of sight, out of mind", living for the moment and taking life as it came. I was proud of him and I loved him to bits, and I am sure he cared, in his own "casual" way...

By George, it would have to do!

Chapter 18

ALL CHANGE

On February 25th. 1974, the day before his 52nd. birthday, George embarked on a three week tour of the Far East with David Nixon and Ali Bongo. The trip was sponsored by the airline BOAC, which had recently changed its name to British Airways. Part of the deal involved the trio agreeing to present promotional appearances and prominently display BA shoulder bags wherever they went. In return they received first class flights and accommodation.

Beginning in Hong Kong, they performed at various venues, including the Lee Theatre (which was televised) and the Magic Studio in Kowloon. An ex-Windmill girl named Pat Raphael owned the "Bottoms Up" Club in the city. George and David had both worked with her and were warmly welcomed at the club. Beautiful Chinese girls clad only in tiny G strings sat in the middle of the club's circular tables, acting as hostesses. When David did some card tricks for the clientele, he handed a card to one of these girls and she concealed it inside her G string.

"Now shuffle it," said George.

The club later featured in the James Bond film, *The Man with the Golden Gun*.

They also went to Singapore, via Bangkok, appearing at the Victoria Theatre and the Hilton Hotel along with the full military band of the Gordon Highlanders. In Kuala Lumpur they did a show at the University and, upon returning to Singapore, they entertained troops at the Nee Soon camp.

George, David and Ali were impressed by the good manners of oriental audiences, but amused when a local orchestra had problems with their Western band parts. These particular musicians knew only one familiar tune and so one show was accompanied by endless renditions of *When the Saints go Marching In*! At another performance, the audience were so courteous that they seemed uncertain when to actually applaud. They only did so when a Thai gentleman in authority loudly ordered them to *"Crap"*!

Whose Baby? was another Thames T.V. vehicle hosted by David Nixon, with George on board as his writer. (The format of this show involved a panel who had to guess the identity of featured children's celebrity parents.) George's input on anything which David did resulted in various stages of upgrading his status. From supplying "special material" he progressed to scriptwriter, then Script Associate, then also Production Associate. This last title had been suggested by the most regular producer/director of the shows, Royston Mayoh, who thought it would be a good idea for George to be officially permitted to have a voice on the studio floor during rehearsals.

David was most appreciative of George's efforts, recognizing that his old friend from the Windmill, "knows me very well". On one occasion, David showed his appreciation by sending George a gift of three crates of fine Burgundy wine.

In the summer of '76, Val and I had problems with our flat in Clapham, but George found a place for us which was located just around the corner from his local pub, The Heroes of Alma in St. John's Wood. This meant a new phase in my relationship with my father because I was now in a position to see him regularly. I was still working, 9 to 5, at The Stage newspaper, but most evenings I would find him in the bar of The Alma. Abbey Road Studios (the one favoured by The Beatles and numerous other big names) stood just a block away, so the Alma was a popular haunt for musicians and famous faces.

This was a happy period and I really enjoyed being able to nurture a proper relationship with my father, at last. He and Maggie grew very fond of Val and we would often go to their flat for dinner, or to the parties they hosted. (Sometimes these parties would have a theme, such as the one they would throw on Burns Night when they would have haggises sent down by train from Scotland. George would then "pipe" the haggis into the room with his accordion and we would consume it with "neeps n'tatties"!) Their poodle, Mitzi, was very spoiled and could not be left alone, so we would also be engaged to "dog sit" when they went out, but we didn't mind at all because they always left us wonderful food and drink and we could relax in luxurious surroundings watching their colour television. (A novelty back then.)

The pub scene was fascinating because it was tucked away in an attractive little mews, frequented only by "those in the know". Consequently, celebrities were happy to use it. It was not unusual to be sharing the bar with personalities such as Hank Marvin, Dame Anna Neagle or members of bands like Wings. George seemed to know everyone.

On the corner, opposite the pub, stood a big house where certain members of the young acting fraternity lived. This crowd included such faces of the day as Robin Askwith (from the "bum bearing" *Confessions* films) and sexy actress Linda Hayden, who had made a name for herself as a naughty schoolgirl in the film *Baby Love*. Dennis Waterman was a regular visitor too. There were some wild times in that house.

The pub's local customers all seemed to be interesting. Choreographers, actors, newspaper editors, racing drivers, private detectives, theatrical agents... We had some good sessions in there, with George playing his accordion and other musicians, like trombonist "Laddie" Busby, joining in.

And throughout all this, George remained 100% loyal to his two main sources of income, David and Basil. Any other work offered always had to fit around his commitments to them. As a rule, this tended to work out fine but there was at least one occasion when a conflict of interests arose.

George's role as a performer had long ago taken second place to his role as a writer. He even gave a newspaper interview once in which he said he was "getting too fat to be seen". There were still occasional requests for him to appear in shows as The Casual Comedian, but apart from charity appearances for the G.O.W.R., warm up spots for the T.V. shows he was involved in, or high profile after dinner speeches, he had more or less accepted his new position "behind the scenes".

However, he had agreed, at my suggestion, to take a page in The Stage's annual publication *Showcall*. This was an entertainment industry directory of artistes, agents and suppliers, and it appeared to act as a reminder to many in the business that George Martin was still in the frame "to be seen". A few engagements came in from it, with one offer being particularly significant.

A T.V. drama producer, who remembered George's earlier career, was making a serious play with an action/thriller theme. He thought that George would be perfect for a major part playing a crime boss! Well, this would have been a real departure from George's normal role in show-business and the offer came as quite a shock to him. He seemed reluctant to pursue it, but deep down I am sure there was an actor desperate to come out. After all, Arthur English, Dave King and Bill Maynard had all managed to succeed, and he was potentially as dramatically good, if not better, than any of them.

His audition was successful and he was formally offered the part. When he first told me, I was delighted, loving the idea that this could open up a whole new career for him, but he was not so sure. The filming dates clashed with the next series of David Nixon.

As it happened, David and Royston Mayoh were really pleased for him, both insisting that it would not be a problem. They were sure that it could be arranged for George to work around the dates and were more than happy to accommodate any thespian ambitions he might harbour. "Go and do it," they urged.

But after a few days, George decided to turn the part down, insisting that he wanted to put all of his energy into David's show.

"It would have been too distracting," he explained, "and not fair to David."

So that was it. We never got to see George Martin the "Crime Boss" and it was the last chance he ever got to stretch his dramatic muscles on screen.

However, he was still able to stretch them in real life.

Showcall *entry... reproduced by kind permission of* The Stage *newspaper*

By 1977, George was getting a fee of £500 per programme for the *Basil Brush Show*, and this was to be his peak. The format was rock solid and as familiar to the British viewing public as fish and chips. Basil, as a character, was riding on the crest of a wave and it seemed as if this success and contentment would last forever.

Alas, all things must change, but no one predicted the unfortunate path fate would tread.

Basil's stage appearances were as popular as his T.V. shows and George had always supplied the material. There were pantos, tours and guest invites of every description. George was even commissioned to compose a string of verses for a block of Basil Brush birthday greeting cards for Royles.

Mr. Roy moved on to try and further his acting career, and things were never quite the same after his departure. A young actor named Elliott Cooper took Roy's place for one of the theatre tours, but for some reason he did not make the transition to the next T.V. series and Ivan Owen chose a Mr. Howard and, eventually, a Mr. Billy.

For quite a while now there had been signs of instability in the success story of Basil Brush. Ivan was an extremely nice man; gentlemanly and courteous, humble too. He had, from the very beginning, always made it a priority to keep himself well out of the public eye. Although he possessed a great sense of humour and could be excellent company, he was also a Christian Scientist with strong principles.

When Ivan developed cataracts on his eyes, he faced the dilemma of facing an operation or going blind. Apparently his faith prohibited him from undergoing such surgery, but rather than lose his sight, he went ahead with it and George always maintained that this was when everything changed.

Having had a close working and personal relationship with Ivan for years, George quickly began to notice some radical changes in his friend's character. It seemed to George that Ivan had "lost his faith", the result being that he had emerged from his surgery with a harder edge.

Of course, through Basil, Ivan was one of the leading lights of the B.B.C.'s programming; an important part of their Saturday evening scheduling, along with *The Generation Game, Morecambe & Wise* and *Match of the Day*. Ivan knew he held some power when negotiating his contracts, but his demands gradually became increasingly unreasonable. For quite some time, the independent T.V. companies had been trying to poach Basil, and Ivan tried to use this as leverage to get his own way. Because of the appeal Basil had achieved with an adult audience, alongside children, he felt the time had come for his show to rise a notch in status. He no longer wanted the show to be transmitted in the traditional "tea-time" slot; he wanted 8pm., the prime position for family viewing, the coveted slot inhabited by the likes of showbiz Royalty such as Eric and Ern.

The B.B.C.'s Programme Controller, Bill Cotton Jr., was having none of it, but Ivan dug in his heels and started acting like a prima donna. He did not like it at all when George failed to support his demands. George knew a good formula when he saw one and felt certain that Basil should remain just where he was.

Apparently, Ivan took this rather personally. The first cracks in the writer/star relationship started to show when Ivan began allowing Basil to voice "ad-libs" during the shows, some of which were a touch unsavoury. For instance, in one sketch, Basil made a derogatory remark about Americans, the sort of thing which George would never have put in the script. George was then upset by some American friends of his asking if this was how he really felt about them.

George addressed this problem with Ivan but he failed to take it on board, so George pressed the point home more strongly, stressing that he was uncomfortable having his name credited for some of the things Basil was now saying. Still Ivan took the attitude that he was the star and he could say what he liked.

This began to cause quite an atmosphere between them, especially when Ivan started to question more and more aspects of George's writing, something he had seldom done before. He had always trusted George's judgement, but now George felt he was "nit-picking" for the sake of it. Ivan was now regularly demanding change and a fresh approach whilst George argued "why fix something if it ain't broke?"

Matters came to a head during a social gathering after one of the shows when Ivan became quite obstreperous with George during an argument about Basil's future. Frustrated, Ivan lost his temper and blurted out, "You've been living off my back for years"!

George could scarcely believe his ears, especially as this wounding remark had been made in front of others. Taking Ivan to one side, George gave him a sound dressing down, demanding to know how Ivan could dare speak to him like that, and requesting an immediate apology. By all accounts, Ivan seemed to regret his words and he did apologize, but it was now obvious that the relationship between the two of them had changed forever.

Things reached the point where George actually requested that his name be taken off the credits, and by the 1978 series, Ivan had brought in other writers and George's contribution had been reduced to just 5 minutes per show.

The atmosphere between the old friends had become exceedingly frosty which made working conditions increasingly difficult. It was all very sad and George felt let down and hurt. He and Ivan began threatening one another and by 1979, Ivan was telling the B.B.C. bosses that he no longer wished George Martin to be associated with the *Basil Brush Show*. According to the records, the B.B.C., acknowledging the fact of how much George had contributed to the show in the past, were also worried about possible legal problems. Regardless of Ivan's wishes, to avoid the potential of George slapping injunctions on Ivan, it was felt that George should be used in "some capacity or other". That is how, for his final series with Basil, George ended up suffering the indignity of being contracted for just 2 to 3 minutes per show.

With another series looming, George was summoned to the office of the Head of Light Entertainment where he was plied with champagne and told, with all the pleasantries which could be summoned under the circumstances, that his services would no longer be required by Basil Brush.

It was a most tragic and ignominious ending to a long and auspicious partnership and I do not think George ever really got over it. Saddened and understandably bitter, he moved on, but the loss of Basil was a huge blow to him. All he could do was take comfort in witnessing how the show declined rapidly without him in a leading role. A top T.V. critic of the day summed it all up with this scathing piece in a national newspaper...

Headlined *"POOR OLD BASIL IS MERELY A PUPPET"* it read; *"No more George? From its inception years ago, The Basil Brush Show was written by comedian George Martin who brought it from obscurity to national fame. But for the new series, which started on Saturday on BBC 1, George has got the elbow and has been replaced by 4 script writers and a script editor. This is a perfect example of that T.V. sickness, over-manning. Why have 1 man if 5 can do? No wonder the BBC is going broke. A chat with the tea lady would have produced better results than this trivia. I asked George why he had been sacked. He said the BBC wanted a new look for the show. Maybe they don't want Basil Brush to be typecast... the show has lost it's intimate individuality, and is now a disjointed, nondescript variety show. Basil has ceased to be a personality in his own right and is now merely a puppet"*.

Ivan's demands grew more vocal and he was soon telling the press that he was leaving the B.B.C. for Thames T.V. who were going to give him the later spot he desired. Thames T.V. then denied any such offer, which embarrassed everyone concerned, prompting the B.B.C. to make the decision to end their association with Basil Brush.

Before long, Basil/Ivan were struggling to secure any kind of television engagement and they ended up re-appearing in the type of kiddie's schedules where they had begun so many years before.

For George it brought a form of rueful satisfaction, but it was still, ultimately, very sad.

Losing the Basil Brush connection proved to be a double blow for George because just a few months before he had also lost his other major employer, David Nixon.

David had been suffering from ill health for quite some time, but his work load was as heavy as ever. Although very ill, he had still managed to attend the Water Rat's Ball on November 26th. 1978 and the next day he had honoured a commitment to record his contribution to *Basil Brush's Magical Christmas*. (This was to be

David's last television appearance. Ironic and synchronistic considering the close connection between him, Basil and George.) That same week, on Friday December 1st., David died at home.

Working at The Stage newspaper, the trade journal of show-business, I heard the news quickly via our Editor. Knowing what a blow this would be to my father, I immediately telephoned him, but he had already received the news.

I think it was about the only time in my life when I heard him really lost for words. He was completely devastated, his voice choked. It was then that it truly came home to me just how close a relationship he and David had enjoyed.

Fresh from this personal tragedy, George went into the New Year to face increasing confrontations with Ivan, so he also had to accept the fact that his earning potential may suffer too.

There was still other work, of course, but could it ever replace the recent decade or more when he had been earning regular big money from two major T.V. shows? (He was employed in '78 as a writer on Tommy Cooper's new T.V. show; *Cooper, Just Like That!* but it was only for the run of the series.)

In February '79, he made another appearance on Denis Norden's *Looks Familiar*, this time on the nostalgia sofa with old variety pals Michael Bentine and Chic Murray. He also occasionally broadcast in his familiar role as a topical comedian on Richard Baker's *Start the Week* radio show (a nice opportunity to get back to his roots).

In addition, his numerous connections started to bring him more regular bookings as a "warm-up" man on a variety of T.V. shows, but what he really needed was another long running production.

Just as the final nail was hammered on the lid of his Basil Brush career, another opportunity arose which, at first, looked like a life-line for George. Now that David Nixon had passed on, his crown as the King of British television magic was to be taken by a character whose style was very different.

Paul Daniels, being a generation younger, had emerged from the world of club entertainment rather than variety. Having honed his talents in this harder environment, his way of working was more about "attack", rather than David's gentle, relaxed persona. But Paul was skilled in all aspects of magic and illusion, along with a rapid, no nonsense style of comedy patter. Sharp and interesting, he was David's obvious successor.

Having worked at Granada T.V., Paul was now ready to take on his first B.B.C. series. The producer was an ex-Basil Brush man, so it was an obvious move for him to ask George, along with Ali Bongo, to join the team. After all, if anyone knew about magic shows, it had to be David Nixon's old crew, surely?

I remember this period and I do recall my dad, in the bar of The Alma speaking, with some discomfort, about his role on the show. Paul was difficult and hard to work with, he said. I certainly know that George did not seem too unhappy when the series ended.

But this is where it all gets strange and complicated, because Paul remembers it like this...

"My memory of your dad is of a man who used to pop up on our T.V. screen quite frequently, dressed casually, opening a newspaper and entertaining us with gags all about what was in the paper that week. Very funny guy... I left Granada T.V. to join the B.B.C. and John Fisher, the producer and a keen amateur magician, needed an ideas team. He thought it would be a good idea to bring in the David Nixon team of Ali and your dad. Ali for the magic and your dad as scriptwriter. On paper, not a bad idea because David had been so popular.

"I sat quietly (I know... not like me at all) for quite a while as they plotted and planned and then I had to stop the meeting, as all I was listening to was 'David would do this, David would do that...' I pointed out that it was a bad idea to remake the David Nixon Show because I wasn't David Nixon, I was me. What I wanted was the Paul Daniels Show, done in my style.

"Ali stayed, your dad chose to leave."

I thought this odd because the B.B.C. archives state that George was contracted for the whole 6 part series on a fee of £400 per show. Also, John Fisher himself remembers it differently. He told me, very clearly, that he was not the original producer but had been brought in, by the B.B.C.'s top brass, after a couple of shows were "in the can" to see if he could improve things. The first producer, Brian Penders, had been the man who employed George and Ali.

Straight from producing *Parkinson*, John was asked to watch the recorded material which the powers that be were not happy with. John thought them to be the "worst shows he'd ever seen", as Paul was not being used to best effect. It was all wrong and John felt he could do better. In this way he (in his own words) "inherited George Martin" who was already under contract.

John "turned the whole thing on its head" and explained that the problem appeared to be a clash of styles. Paul did not really need a writer as such, so George was more or less redundant. "Basically, he had nothing to do," recalled John, "and he would turn up at the studio without any real role."

Of course, this was not George's fault and John confirmed this strongly. "Don't get me wrong," he stressed, "I had great respect for your father, but by the end of the series there was no place for him".

John then wrote to me, saying, *"The thing to emphasise is that George ceased to work on the Paul Daniels Show, but he was never replaced by another comedy writer"*.

And so, another door closed.

Chapter 19

DECLINE

As the 1980s dawned, George's future did not look too bright.

It was the beginning of the sweeping changes which were about to affect the British entertainment profession as "alternative comedy" took hold. On reflection, in much the same way as a new breed of comedians came crashing through the scene at the end of World War 2, now another batch of brash upstarts were emerging from universities and all walks of life to rattle the traditional principles of show-business.

Comedy Clubs were all the rage now. Performing "stand-up", as "comicking" was now dubbed, became highly popular. It was important for the new funny men and women to reject all the old standards. Dress code took a nose dive as it became an unwritten rule for performers to shamble on stage in "scruff order". Tee shirt and jeans, so that they could be perceived as "real". Gags, as such, were not told anymore. Now it was all about observational humour. And foul language. Suddenly, every stage act seemed to find it necessary to punctuate every sentence with a string of four letter words. No reason for this, as far as I could see. The shock element soon receded and I, for one, just found it rather tiresome. But, to be cool and fashionable you had to say "fuck" regularly. Ho, hum.

The female comics mainly seemed to concentrate on gynaecological material for their routines, which resulted in many audience members feeling uncomfortable, although few dared to admit it for fear of ridicule. Lots of political satire too, especially as the Thatcher administration of the time made such a good target.

Channel 4, in particular, seemed to spearhead the rapid advance of the new comedy generation, although old Auntie Beeb quickly caught on to the idea that she had better tag along. New shows were commissioned and new T.V. stars born over night. Most of them seemed to shout a lot and be aggressive. Although much of what they did was clever and original, the over-riding tone of it all was of anger and cruelty. Performers did not seem to want to be "likeable" anymore; just "smart-arse" and shocking. And politically correct, of course.

This resulted in a rapid and almost total rejection of the "old school". Within a few short years, television no longer seemed to be run by veterans who knew the entertainment business. Suddenly accountants and university graduates with their own political agendas ruled the roost.

Gradually, the stars of yester-year began to vanish from the public eye. Quite a few of them had died by now (Tommy Cooper, for instance, whilst doing his act during a live T.V. transmission!) but the old timers who survived on the box mainly only did so by relegating their variety talents to fronting game shows.

Therefore, the outlets for George's services were diminishing. He did secure a job with Southern Television as writer for a new series starring ventriloquist Roger de Courcey and Nookie Bear, but Roger was not happy with the way the company appeared to be trying to turn him into a children's entertainer, so the association was short lived.

George also wrote for the comedy duo The Krankies, particularly when they made appearances on *Crackerjack*, but it was all pretty hit and miss. For the first time in his long career, George actually began to struggle to find work.

And he was saddened by the way show-business was going, missing the standards and the warmth he had always known. Even some of the old hands had decided "if you can't beat 'em, join 'em", sometimes unnecessarily, as was the case with Dave Allen. Allen had always been a clever "edgy" comedian, but did he really need to start soiling his act with colourful expletives? Most people thought not. He remained popular but disappointed many.

And then there was Jim Davidson who became a big star during this period. Although young, he was regarded as "old school" by the alternative fraternity. They hated him and the feeling was mutual. His material was abrasive in a different way, but it was probably his youth and swift success which made him so disrespectful.

George was appalled by some of his behaviour. Employed to warm-up Davidson's T.V. show, George shook his head in disbelief as the young comic moved through the studio audience, shaking hands with them and smirking at some old woman, "Sorry if its wet, love, I've just had a piss!"

Val and I got married in 1978 and we bought our own place in East London, but we were still seeing my dad and Maggie on a regular basis. My mother had not had any personal contact with him for several years. She was bitter and made it clear that she would not

With Nookie Bear and Roger de Courcey.

welcome him at the wedding. Not wishing to create any kind of potential scene, he and Maggie were present on the day but they stood at the back of the church during the ceremony and then hovered furtively amongst the tombstones in the churchyard with my mother's scathing eye trying to seek them out! Needless to say, they did not attend the reception.

Around this period there had been an embarrassing incident involving the national press. The Stage had printed a report on a charity gala which included a picture of Arthur English and his young fiancé standing in a cosy group with George and his "wife", Margaret Mitchell. Within a day or two, the Features Editor, Sydney Vauncez, came to me with a letter in his hand asking, "Can you confirm for me, is this your mother?"

Indeed, the letter was from Joan. She was incensed that the paper had printed false information and was demanding a retraction in the next issue. This was duly done, much to the annoyance of my father, but what could he expect? Why they were still married was a great mystery to everyone who knew the truth. And that was just about *everyone* by now.

But that was not the end of it. Always desperate for a sordid little story, one of the Sunday papers got hold of it and sent one of their reporters down to Aldershot to hound my mother. She slammed the door in his face, but he hung around the area for a couple of days, sitting outside Joan's home and trying to get into Joyce and Bob's club. No one would co-operate with him so it must have been a frustrating time for the sad sod.

That weekend, the Sunday People had to make do with a pathetic piece of copy headlined *"Ouch! It Wasn't the Comic's Wife!"*, illustrated by a picture of George which was well over 20 years old.

I left The Stage and turned professional in the entertainment profession in May '79, feeling that I could now support myself with the gigs I was doing in a duo, supplemented by work as a background artist/extra or Walk On in the film and television business. It was a lively scene in those days, protected by union membership, so I kept busy.

George actually got me a couple of jobs, firstly as a costermonger in a cockney musical sketch during his final days on the *Basil Brush*

Show, and then a significant role in a new show for A.T.V.. It was actually a pair of shows called *Arrivals* 1 and 2. George had been engaged by producer/director Royston Mayoh as one of the writers. The format centred around an imaginary airport departure lounge and sketches involving various characters punctuated by spots by artistes new to television.

Working under my Equity name of Mike Vinden, I was part of the company performing the sketches, most of whom were hardened pros such as Hope and Keen, Ronnie Dukes and Carole Lee Scott. As I had got the part through pure nepotism, my father was not keen that it should be general knowledge that I was his son, so he instructed me to call him George during the run. Even so, most of the cast and crew gradually picked up on the truth, but it was not an issue.

This was a big break for me, but, to be honest, the shows did not really work. They were disjointed and the sketches were not that funny. I hated the thought, but it seemed that George Martin was losing his touch. To rub salt in the wound, he was also acting as warm-up man for the studio audience and, to my dismay, he seemed to struggle with it and did not really connect.

I could not understand the reason for this. For years I had watched him perform and he always did well, but something had happened. His magic spark, his natural audience charm, the talent which had come so easily to him was missing. Perhaps it was something to do with the blows he had suffered in recent times with the loss of David and Basil. Whatever, I found it hard to watch and it made me very sad, especially when I heard comments being made by one or two members of the cast who were still unaware of my relationship with him.

"This guy just isn't funny," muttered one.

It hurt me deeply.

Chapter 20

SALAD DAYS OVER

George's world had changed.

The show-business he had known and loved was evaporating all around him. His old friends were dying, retiring or losing their influence as the new generation took over. Of course, he still had the Water Rats as a refuge and was as involved as ever, the one place where pros could still gather and indulge in an atmosphere of how it used to be.

He was nearly 60 years old and confused by modern tastes. His laid back nature made it more difficult for him than some contemporaries who had actually moved with the times. Bob Monkhouse was a classic example; he always stayed at the top of his game by adapting to trends. Frankie Howerd was rediscovered by university audiences and enjoyed a huge comeback at the end of his life.

But for George, it was all too much. Some would call it laziness, but he simply did not want to change. In many ways he was out of touch and seemed beyond caring.

That said, he by no means became a dejected character. He enjoyed life, loved a drink and would often still be on form, but his day to day existence began to take on a routine it had never had before.

If he was not working on something (and that was becoming the norm), he would probably sleep in late and then drive the short distance to the Alma for a midday drink. There he would chat to the locals, maybe bump into an old friend who was working around the corner at Abbey Road, and make his way home, but he was always back in the pub again by evening opening time. It was a regular sight to see him sitting in the corner of the bar, clutching his cigarette holder and doing the crossword in the evening paper. Any thoughts he had which he wished to remember he would jot down in a kind of shorthand, using a black felt pen on the white surface of his Players cigarette packet.

There were a series of setbacks too. A pantomime he scripted for Harry Worth got into financial trouble and George ended up not getting paid. (Harry got *his* money, however.) George also found himself booked by an agent he did not previously know to tour The George Martin Show around the West Country. This offer had come out of the blue and was very welcome, and so he and Maggie, and their budgie Mickey (which had taken the place of the deceased Mitzi) took off for a series of shows in a variety of venues. Although he was glad to get back to performing, George was somewhat put out by the quality of some of the places he had to work. Clubs, halls, community centres; it was not what he was used to at all, but, apparently it all went rather well. That is until the agent disappeared and George failed to receive a penny.

Understandably, this rocked his confidence somewhat and did not help with his growing feeling of disillusionment.

Money was getting tight. He was back in trouble with the Inland Revenue and was being chased for unpaid taxes from the years when he had been thriving. When we went to the flat for dinner these days, we noticed that the quality wine which had always been a nightly fixture had been replaced by cheap lager. And the arguments between George and Maggie were getting more frequent.

While still working at The Stage, a couple of significant incidents had occurred. I dealt with the advertisements and there was a directory of artistes which took the form of small pictured boxes which ran over a double page. One of them featured a comic named Jan Harding, a brother Water Rat and good friend of my father's and my Uncle Bill, who actually part owned a villa in Spain with him. Suddenly, Jan changed the copy on his weekly directory advertisement and started calling himself The Casual Comedian!

Unbelievable that he would steal somebody's billing. Bewildering too. Why? I immediately told my father, and he was stunned, but I don't think he ever challenged Jan about it.

On another occasion, a big Royal event took place at the Lakeside Country Club and the Water Rats were heavily involved. The entire back page of The Stage was taken to promote the event, along with a huge list of thanks for all those who had worked on the project. George's name was prominent on that list, but just before it went to press, the advertisement manager told me that he had received a call from Andrew Neatrour, a high profile Companion Water Rat with close Royal connections, with an instruction to take George's name off the list.

Once again, a blow to George. He was under the impression that Neatrour was his friend. Ah, so fickle, the world of show-business!

(Actually, it is just worth saying that the advertisement manager I mentioned was an ex-actor named John Payne; the very same man who had stood in for George in the Blackpool panto years before, when he had performed George's act!)

A few T.V. warm-ups were still coming in, but I got the impression that George was starting to get an unwelcome reputation. Doing extra work, I sometimes found myself there when he was working on another production and I would meet him in the bar. He seemed to be slightly tipsy, something I had never witnessed before when he was in a working situation. Professionalism had always been his first consideration. I was shocked when the producer actually had to come and usher him out of the bar to go to work.

Popping into the studio to watch him perform, it was a surprise to see him leaning on the microphone stand, not exactly drunk, but showing the effects. He got way with it but things like this were obviously being noticed. He began to wonder why people were often asking him if he was "Ok now".

Ironically, Bill had become the "King of the Warm-Up Men" and was widely acknowledged as the top man in the game. This was odd because George had introduced him to the scene. Initially reluctant, Bill had taken to it with gusto and was now in demand for all the top shows. It had become his main source of living, and a lucrative one too. He was also doing some writing for shows and taking the occasional part in situation comedies.

This meant that I regularly saw Bill at the studios as he was usually doing the warm-up for lots of the things I was working on. He told me that he was getting worried about his brother and that word was going around the business that George had developed a drink problem.

Well, he had certainly always enjoyed a drink but it had never been considered a problem before.

Perhaps realising what was happening, George decided to go on a bit of a health kick. He bought an exercise wheel, which involved a kind of prone, push up routine, but this proved too much effort so he bought himself a bicycle. The idea was to ride to the pub twice a day instead of taking the car, and he did make the effort. Somehow though, the image of him on a bike was not an easy one to swallow. It did not seem right; bicycle clips and wobbling around whilst wearing a Russian style fur hat was just not him and he chastised me once for "taking the piss"! Unsurprisingly, the bike phase passed quite quickly.

He also grew a beard which did not suit him at all. It was grizzled and multi-coloured and made him look like Gabby Hayes. Bill asked me, "What's the beard all about? Is he trying to get parts?" Fortunately, the beard phase did not last long either.

I can see him now, sitting at the dining table, relaxed and idly watching the television with Mickey the Budgie on his finger, as if he did not have a care in the world. He loved the comfort of his own home and he slowly became more and more reluctant to venture out, especially in the evenings. Whenever the phone rang, after dark, he would always say to Maggie, as she answered it, "I'm not in!" When I appeared in pantomime just across the river in Battersea, my first professional show, it was a major operation to talk him into making the effort to come and see it, even though it was obviously important to me to get his opinion. I got him there in the end.

As things got tighter and he saw me (and Ray) doing lots of little T.V. and film bits (which were sometimes well paid), George announced that he thought that he might sign up with a couple of the agencies we were with. I immediately did not like the thought of that and Maggie commented, "Has it come to this?"

She was right to be concerned. For someone in George's position in the business to be seen doing background work would be the "kiss of death". No matter how desperate he felt things were, if word got around that he was now "in the crowd", that would definitely make his status take an irretrievable nose dive.

Even so, he approached some agents, just two as far as I can remember, both of whom knew him by reputation. One was even a local at the Alma. I think they both felt uncomfortable taking him on and neither had the nerve to actually offer him any actual "extra" work, thank God. One of them even said to me, "I'm saving your father for anything special that comes along". Unfortunately, nothing did.

I was so worried about him. It seemed dreadfully unjust, after a lifetime in the business, having seen so much success, to witness my father struggling in the latter part of his life.

It put an enormous strain on his relationship with Maggie too. George and Joan had finally got divorced and he and Maggie got married in a fairly low key ceremony at Marylebone registry office. It was a good excuse for a party and we all had a fun filled time back at the Alma with loads of booze, food and music. George got on the accordion, of course, and had the pub in the palm of his hand, just like in the old days.

But the rows between him and Maggie got worse by the day and often turned nasty. Val and I began to dread going to visit them because the evenings inevitably seemed to follow a pattern these days. It would all begin pleasantly enough, just as it had always done, with nice food and chit chat. George might have been out in the day, working somewhere with a bit of luck, and was now in his quiet, relaxed mode. Then Maggie would make a comment which would cause him to bite. Sometimes it was vice versa, but I usually saw it as Maggie because he would prefer to sit in silence. This is often what irritated her.

His argument would be that he had been talking all day, in planning meetings or something, but she would say she had been alone and needed someone to talk to. He started to get a bee in his bonnet about "making conversation", and having no patience with "small talk" which frustrated Maggie even more. She would then get drunk and start getting very vocal and dramatic saying things like she had given up her career for him, and what had it got her? He would reply, in his calm but forceful way that the "salad days are over" and that she was finished in the business long before he met her.

Sometimes he would look at me and say, infuriatingly for Maggie, "Sorry son, its all started a bit earlier than usual tonight."

Oh dear, hurtful stuff, and it was most uncomfortable to witness. Maggie would usually end up in tears and Val and I would exchange helpless glances before making our excuses to leave. If we stayed the night we soon got used to the way they were with each other the next morning. By then they were full of the joys of spring again as if it had all been a bad dream. It was hard to fathom how they could still be together after some of the things which were said in their vitriolic arguments.

All of this was a huge worry for family and friends and everybody did what they could to offer support. Maggie made the point that no matter how hard things got, it would always be important to give the impression that everything was just fine. This she managed to do, up to a point, and the pair of them continued to keep up appearances when they attended the various events and functions they were invited to.

Fortunately, although he sometimes mentioned his "worries", George was able to detach himself. He maintained his dignity and kept his cool. Once in the pub, when I was expressing concern for him, he said, "The way I look at it is this... money problems, whatever, I've still got my friends. When I'm having a good time with them, nothing else seems to matter."

A strange philosophy perhaps, but one which seemed to work for him. His laid back persona had always been one of his main strengths in the popularity stakes.

But he was certainly no pushover, and for all his charm, he was capable of lashing out when the need arose.

Bill used to tell a story about when they were in a restaurant together and an American at the next table started loudly insulting

On their wedding day, George and Maggie with Sue, Mike and Ray (products of George's first marriage). Photo by Gary Horton.

Great Britain and the British. George reached the point where he had heard enough and he challenged the man, suggesting that if he didn't like the country, why didn't he go home to the States? The argument raged on until the American demanded that they go outside to settle their differences. George agreed and they went downstairs to the exit. Opening the glass door to let his antagonist out, George took one look at the pouring rain, slammed the door and locked it! "Sod that, I'm not going out in that weather!" he said, walking back upstairs and leaving the drenched American hammering on the door!

One evening, George and Maggie were relaxing in their flat watching television when they heard a commotion on the landing. Although he was in his dressing gown, George ventured out to see what was happening and was confronted by a scene on the floor below. There was a man in a violent argument in the hallway with a female neighbour. He was getting quite rough with the woman and she was upset, so George called out to the man to ease up. When the man responded with abuse, apparently George launched his entire 14 stone down the stairs onto the man, knocking him down. He then sat astride him, holding him helpless until he promised to behave.

George could certainly move quickly when he wanted to, although on the face of it, such behaviour would seem to go completely against his nature. It must have been reserves of energy and confrontation which were still hanging on from his sporty youth!

Another example of this came one lunchtime at the Alma when George was drinking quietly with Brendan, the pub landlord. There were not many customers in, but a rowdy group of young men were becoming "out of order" as they sat at the outside forecourt tables. These were not kids but well spoken "yuppie" types who were rather drunk and spoiling for trouble. They were not familiar faces and Brendan went out to ask them to calm down. They reacted nastily, swearing and voicing threats. When Brendan told them they had better leave, they stood up and a couple of them went to the boots of their cars and took out weapons, pick-axe handles and the like.

It was a hairy moment, but George and a couple of the other regulars stood alongside Brendan to support him.

"Ridiculous really," mused George later, "we were a bunch of fat old men up against this bunch of hoodlums."

A lot of shouting ensued and one of the yobs picked up a bar stool which he waved threateningly. Finally, he flung it with all his might at the glass partition alongside the bar, but George, moving with the unexpected grace of a young gazelle, somehow managed to reach up and grab it in mid air. It bruised his arms rather badly but the yobs immediately turned tail and sped off in their cars, leaving George being hailed as the hero of the moment.

An even more dramatic confrontation took place in Shepherds Bush market one afternoon, when George and Maggie were strolling through the crowds between the stalls. Maggie was wearing a valuable pendant on a chain around her neck, when suddenly an athletic looking black youth grabbed it and tore it away from her. The wrenching motion nearly pulled her over and drew blood on her neck, but the youth was away into the crowd like lightning.

Once again, George found inner strength and took off after the thief like Daley Thompson! It was probably the first time he had run anywhere since that charity football match for the Brickies back in the early '60s, but he was determined to not let this guy get away with it. Overweight but pounding away, George called out to the stall holders for help and one obliged by pushing the spurs of his barrow into the thief's path. It worked because the youth hit it at speed and went sprawling to the ground. A second later, George was on top of him, twisting his arm up behind his back and forcing his face into the ground.

Unfortunately, the thief must have passed the pendant on to an accomplice as he ran because he did not have it with him He struggled and swore, demanding to be released, but George was not going to let him go. Somebody went to call the police but the atmosphere soon became threatening as a crowd of black people gathered around.

"Let him go, man!" they were snarling and, "Is he hurting you, brother?"

"Bloody right I'm hurting him!" growled George, "And I'll break the bastard's arm if I have to!"

Support for George came from several of the stall holders and other passers-by who began giving abuse back to the thief's contingent. It seemed like ages before the police arrived, with George holding his wriggling captive and doing his best to avoid a race riot. As soon as they took charge of the youth, one of the policemen nodded his head and said, "Oh yes, we know him. One of the Balham Boys. They come up here every week for the mugging."

Ah, yes, Dad, what a character you were. I remember it all so well. Your blissful expression as you sat at the piano, entering some kind of Nirvana as you found the right chord; your sense of humour and intellect which made comedian "Wee" Georgie Wood describe you as "that master of James Thurber humour" in his Stage column. Informed and thoughtful, yet not one to read great literature, George Martin *did* like to stretch his mind.

And yet he could still make a statement like "What is the point of philosophy? With a degree in philosophy, all you can then do is teach other people philosophy!"

I used to argue with him about that one, but the fact is, he was actually a rather accomplished philosopher himself. Self taught!

Chapter 21

SWANSONG

In the early 1980s, there were still a few young performers in the public eye whose style resembled their variety forebears. One rare example was Keith Harris.

Keith had learned his trade in the world of Northern clubs but had been noticed by T.V. producer Peter Dulay. Dulay, an advocate of the old school, who had managed to retain some influence, was impressed by this pleasant young ventriloquist's charm, probably seeing it as an antidote to the hard edge of modern comedy. One of the very few traditional shows which was still managing to hang on in the T.V. schedules was *The Black and White Minstrel Show*, a production soon to be consigned to the depths of oblivion for its "political incorrectness". In actual fact, it was an innocent slice of hokum, intended only as fluffy, mindless entertainment, but, unfortunately, the concept of "black faced" white chorus singers crooning minstrel ditties to pretty girls was rapidly becoming unacceptable.

As producer of the show, Dulay had been looking for a new act for the Christmas edition and Keith seemed to fit the bill. He worked mainly with two "dummies", a green duck which wore a nappy, and a manic monkey, and they were named Orville and Cuddles respectively. Knowing that George Martin (who had written for the Minstrel Show in the past and had also worked on Dulay's *Cooper, Just Like That!* show) was now available, Dulay took him to see Keith working in cabaret at the Savoy Hotel in London.

George instantly took to Keith and the feeling was mutual. *"We bonded well and he came up with some good ideas,"* said Keith, *"he really understood me."*

Pleased with his television debut, the B.B.C. gave Keith his first series and George was engaged as the writer. Things were looking up.

"I also used your dad for any other T.V. stuff which came in for me, like when I played the ringmaster for Billy Smart's Circus. He wrote lots of little magic things for Orville and Cuddles. And he liked a few 'bevvies', eh? Happy memories... it was always good. I remember once when he was with me for my panto in Windsor. We were walking down the street late one night, on our way to get a meal, and there were two fellers rolling in the street fighting. As we passed, your dad said with a chuckle, 'No dancing, please!' I never found anybody as good again and I'm still using a couple of his lines."

Keith was present when George proposed to Maggie. It was in Scarborough when they were staying with Keith. *"He got down on one knee, the whole bit, and then did this gag thing about not being able to get up again!"*

Keith Harris was prominent in British light entertainment for quite some time, but the routines he did with the baby voiced Orville started to grate on some people. In the cynical '80s, his popularity started to recede and, like so many others, his T.V. appearances began to dry up. Twenty five years later he was still making a living but had to adapt. This included the necessity of touring Orville in an adult show which he called *Duck Off*.

"Your dad would turn in his grave," mused Keith.

George had never really made "keeping fit" a priority. He enjoyed life but had not indulged in sport or serious health regimes since leaving the R.A.F.. Being a keen sportsman in his youth, plus a laid back attitude to his problems, probably kept him on his feet in later years.

There had been a few illnesses, but nothing of a serious nature. In the mid 1960s he had been hospitalized with appendicitis and he told me on the phone once, "Your mother is giving me an ulcer!", but apart from that he seemed to keep reasonably fit. That is for someone who smoked and drank as much he did.

He felt he was as fit as he needed to be. Apart from those occasional bursts of energy when he chased a mugger or something, there was not much call for him to exert himself. As a rule, walking to the bar seemed to be his main source of exercise. He went in David Nixon's swimming pool once, attempted to swim a length and felt he was having a heart attack! With that in mind, he actively pursued a policy of taking it easy.

Consequently, on reaching middle age, he began to pile on weight. Never grossly so, but he certainly expanded somewhat and would occasionally go on a bit of a diet. He enjoyed his Players cigarettes too much to cut down on them, likewise his Bells whisky.

However, the older he got, he began to feel the effects of a lifetime's neglect. Short of breath and feeling tired, he had a medical check-up and was diagnosed with high blood pressure. This was considered such a concern that his doctor put him on the drug Warfarin, plus he was ordered to wear tight stockings to help with his circulation. This did not make him lose his sense of humour and he would joke about being in an accident and what people might think when they found him wearing stockings under his trousers!

The Keith Harris Show had brought him back into the arena somewhat, but he was nowhere near as busy as he would have liked to be. In between Keith's requirements, and other occasional engagements, he had long gaps of inactivity. A by now rare appearance in cabaret at a Royal Navy mess also had an effect on his confidence. It was a rowdy affair, apparently, and just a few minutes into his act he began to suffer a heavy nose bleed which forced him to leave the stage. The officer in charge of the booking was unsympathetic and started talking about "breech of contract"!

"I have to face it, son," he said to me one day in the pub, during a rare moment of despondency, "my career is winding down. The ideas don't come to me like they used to..."

I did not want to hear this, but no matter how much I tried to encourage him, I knew, deep down, that he was right. The salad days *were* over. Where could he go from here?

But there was to be a Swansong.

Completely out of the blue, he was contacted by The Beverley Sisters. The Bevs had retired quite some time ago, but their daughters (Joy's Vicki and Babette, and Teddy's Sasha) had formed their own trio and were having some success as The Foxes. Just by chance, during a Foxes appearance at Peter Stringfellow's club, The Bevs had been persuaded to go on stage and revive their act and it had been a huge success, especially with the gay fraternity. Encouraged, the Bevs dusted off their old routines and decided to make a comeback.

George had always stayed in touch with them, even though he might not see them very often anymore, but they had a special show coming up at the Queen's Theatre in Hornchurch Essex and they wanted him to appear in it. Not having actually performed his act for some months, he was understandably a bit dubious about taking this on, but the girls were special old friends and he must have felt flattered to be asked.

Once committed to the date, George gave it his full attention and worked with the Bevs to ensure that he got it right. This included buying himself a full football strip and boots to bring back a routine he had done with them on television some 30 years ago. Joy had been famously married to the England football star Billy Wright, so the skit involved heavy reference to this, with George making an entrance as Billy.

As the date drew closer, George began to get nervous, something I had never seen before.

"I hope I can remember the act," he muttered. He seemed unwell and I was very worried about him.

On the day of the show, September 15th. 1985, I travelled over to the theatre, determined to lend my support. My nephew, Gary Horton, was there too. He was my sister Sue's eldest son, and this would be the first time he was to see his grandfather perform his proper act.

In his dressing room, George still seemed apprehensive and concerned about being up to the job. Gary and I wished him luck but, quite honestly, I was feeling nervous myself, especially when I saw him take a swig of whisky from a flask he had tucked away in his briefcase. "Just to loosen me up," he grinned, unconvincingly.

We took our seats in the auditorium and were encouraged to see a nice full house. They were George's kind of crowd too. Sixty some-things and Bev's fans who would remember him from his variety days. I crossed my fingers and uttered a little prayer...

We need not have worried. The Bevs were on top form, working the crowd as if they were still teenagers. George came alive on stage and interacted with them perfectly. The years seemed to fall off him and he was really in his element. The Billy Wright routine, the accordion, the parodies, the pipe and newspaper along with up to date topical gags. It was 1956 all over again, and as the audience cheered, clapped and laughed themselves hoarse, I felt a lump forming in my throat.

So The Casual Comedian could still cut the mustard after all.

What a tonic for everybody, not least of all George himself who was justifiably proud of having given such a good performance.

I was so happy that it had turned out well. Hopefully, this might prove to be a turning point and another boost to his flagging career. Anyone made aware of what he had achieved in Hornchurch that night would have to acknowledge that George Martin was not a spent force.

As Christmas approached, George seemed to find a new lease of life, but as 1986 dawned, he started to look unwell again. A new Keith Harris series was pending, so at least work was coming in. That said, George's finances were in a mess once more with lots of debt, not least of all to his old sparring partner, the Inland Revenue.

In January, I had a problem in my house with some wiring and he offered to come over and take a look at it for me. He had been an electrician by trade, remember, and knew what he was doing. I had quite a shock when I saw him. His complexion was positively grey and he looked weary. When standing on a chair to fix my wiring, he began to gasp for breath and I told him he must get down. He laughed it off and insisted on finishing the job before suggesting we go to the pub for a well earned drink.

Unusually, he was willing to walk, saying, uncharacteristically, that the fresh air would do him good. However, on the way around there, just a ten minute stroll, he appeared to get a bit distressed and had to stop and sit on a wall for a moment to recover.

Although we got to the pub eventually and relaxed over that drink, I was feeling really anxious. He tried to make light of it, but I could tell he was not himself. Money worries seemed to concern him more than anything, and he sighed, "I really don't know what's going to happen, son..."

On a positive note, he was happy about the Hornchurch show with The Bevs.

"Yes, just like it used to be," he smiled wistfully, "my kind of people. You know, if it's the last show I ever do, I can't complain..."

"Don't be silly, dad," I began to protest, but he was already asking what I was drinking.

He drove away from my house in the late afternoon, hoping to miss the traffic, because it was quite a journey right across town from East to West.

On Saturday February 8th. I received a telephone call at about 8am.. It was Maggie, and I could tell immediately from her voice that something was wrong.

"Michael," she said, struggling to control herself, "your father has had a stroke."

Chapter 22

THE FINAL CURTAIN

I guess it was inevitable. My worst fear...

He was taken to St. Mary's Hospital in Paddington where he lay in bed, semi-conscious, as the family rallied around. Bill, Joyce, Bob, Sue, Ray, me...

Maggie was tearful but composed as she told us what had happened.

The new Keith Harris show had just gone into production and George had commenced work on it. He had been in his office at the flat "beavering" away on the first script all day. Maggie said he was totally pre-occupied, as he always was when working, but she was concerned that he did not seem well. She had left him alone to get on with it, looking in on him occasionally.

That evening, they settled down for dinner, placing a table in front of the television set as they usually did when on their own. With the meal set out in front of them, they ate quietly, but Maggie noticed that he was paying a lot of attention to his right arm, looking at it with a puzzled expression. He began to massage it, squeezing his fingers and trying to manipulate them.

She asked him what was wrong and he made light of it, unwilling to talk. As the evening wore on, Maggie noticed that the few words he was uttering had begun to sound slightly slurred. She felt a cold shudder, fearing what was happening, and she told him so. He agreed to her phoning the doctor, but the doctor did not seem overly concerned and said to just keep an eye on him.

Whether or not acting on his symptoms earlier would have made a difference, I guess we shall never know, but, as it was, he collapsed alongside the toilet in the early hours of the morning. Maggie immediately called an ambulance and he was rushed away.

Indeed, he had suffered a massive stroke which had paralyzed his right side and robbed him of his speech. Over the first few days, as he was monitored in his hospital bed, we all hoped that he might improve. We were told that stroke symptoms are sometimes temporary. Instead of the embolism destroying brain cells, victims can be lucky and the cells are just bruised, enabling total or partial recovery of faculties.

However, as time went by, it became horribly obvious that this was not to be the case with George.

Initially he was dazed, totally bewildered by what was happening to him. He got angry and frustrated and acted out of character as he struggled with the terrible dilemma of not being able to express himself. As I wrote at the time, "For a man whose whole world revolved around words and socializing, it was a cruel blow".

It was awful to see him like that. There was a great sadness in his eyes as he looked around helplessly, totally dependant upon others. Not him at all. I could not avoid continually thinking of what he had said when his own father had suffered a stroke.

Of course, he received plenty of well wishing visitors; at least in the early days, but he was not capable of responding well and would just sit looking at them blankly. One of the earliest visitors was Benny Hill. He and George went right back to their earliest variety appearances together, and I was touched that Benny should take the trouble to make the trip. Benny was rich and famous but was now a sad man himself, unable to understand why he had become a victim of the "alternative cull" of old favourites.

Naturally, George's Brother Water Rats turned out in droves to try and cheer him up and lend support, but it was not easy. Keith Harris had been left in a difficult position, having lost his writer at the start of his new series. On the face of it, it may have seemed callous, but Keith had to find someone else quickly. However, Maggie said she was deeply upset when Keith apparently brought this someone in to the hospital when he visited George, and introduced the man as his replacement. When they left, George had tears in his eyes.

As the weeks drew on, the time came when the authorities needed to make a decision about what to do with George. By now his predicament was obvious. He was paralyzed and unable to speak; an invalid, and as recovery did not seem to be an option, a place would need to be found for him to reside.

Living at the flat with Maggie would be an impossibility. He would need specialist care and, in any case, the flat was on the third floor with no lift. The first thought was that a place could be found for him at Brinsworth House, the marvellous care home for retired performers in Twickenham. George being involved with the Entertainment Artistes Benevolent Fund, as well as being an active charity campaigner and trustee for the G.O.W.R., Brinsworth would be happy to welcome him, but the problem was a practical one. The home simply did not have the facilities to support someone with George's disabilities. So, as a temporary measure, he was moved to another hospital in Ladbroke Grove.

After a few more weeks, an ideal place was finally found. As an ex-service man, George would be eligible for a place at the Royal Star and Garter Home on Richmond Hill in Surrey. With a magnificent setting looking down on to the River Thames, the Star and Garter was a perfect solution for a terrible situation. The building itself was grand and imposing, but with a feeling of warm hearted care. I immediately got the vibe that if one had to be in a home, one could not really do much better than this.

George got his own cosy room which had a wonderful view across the landscape. By now he seemed to have more or less accepted his situation and had started to regain some of his old charm. Although he could not speak, he had learned to be more expressive with his face, and with the use of his one good arm, he was able to gesticulate to good effect. He was also able to vocalize with emotive "ooh" and "aah" sounds, the result of which was often quite comical. He certainly did not lose his sense of humour, nor his taste for Bell's whisky which he was able to sample in the home's own bar. It was gratifying to be able to see him still enjoying himself in such an environment.

It was a surprise to witness him seemingly content to give up cigarettes, something I thought I would never see, but he never touched one again after the stroke. I remember a visit when the current King Rat Alan "Fluff" Freeman was present and he wickedly pulled out a packet of fags, running the sticks through his fingers and pushing them into his mouth whilst crowing, "Mmmm, bet you'd love one of these, eh, George?"

But George just responded with his benign smile and a shake of the head.

He became a very popular resident at the home. The staff all seemed to take to him and he made friends with several of the residents who, naturally, were all suffering from different forms of disability. Lots of age groups were present, some of whose problems dated back to World War 2, but there were others too like a young soldier who had been shot in the head in Northern Ireland, and an ex-S.A.S. man who, after surviving God knows what dangers on active service, had ended up breaking his spine when he fell from a window he was cleaning!

George's visitors gradually diminished as time went by, but this has to be understandable. It was difficult to see him if on one's own as, obviously, the conversation was all one sided. Sometimes I could see that he was getting uncomfortable about this, as although he had always been a good listener, he did not like to be talked *at*. Some of these people said that they found it hard to see George incapacitated and felt they could not handle it. Others admitted that they would not be able to visit him at all because they wanted to remember him as he was. A selfish viewpoint, but valid.

But there were others, apart from immediate family, who continued to visit him regularly for the rest of his life. Certain Water Rats were familiar faces in that bar and in his room and a special thank you comes from my heart to The Bevs who seemed to be there like clockwork every week, bless 'em.

The months turned into years and the only comfort which could be salvaged from George's predicament was that he did adapt and appeared to find a quality of life. I would take him into the garden

The Bevs; faithful friends to the end.

in his wheelchair on fine days and sit with him. It was a calm and reflective time and I would tell him what I had been up to, but I always instinctively sensed when he had heard enough. Once or twice I took my two boys, who were very young at the time, to visit their grand-dad, but that did not really work. It is a huge shame that they never knew him when he was in his prime.

Sometimes he would be taken away from the home for various reasons, to let him experience a change of environment, but I am not sure he always enjoyed this. The Bev's daughters, who were fond of him, arranged to have him brought to a show they were doing supporting '60's stars Gerry and the Pacemakers at Wimbledon Theatre. I went along too, and I remember his pained expression as he sat at the back of the stalls, his face creased in tolerant agony at the volume. It must have been purgatory for him!

In 1989, a huge effort was made so that he could attend the wedding of Bill's eldest daughter, Laura. This was a lavish affair because Bill really pushed the boat out to give her a magnificent, traditional wedding with all the trappings. George did seem to get pleasure from this and wore a contented, happy expression all day, especially when he was reunited with his and Bill's old chum Dave Allen, who was a guest.

Dave Allen, Bill, George, Laura and her husband Greg.

At Christmas time, George would be taken to Bill and Sybil's house for the festivities. This would turn into a happy and highly emotional family gathering. Everyone made a huge fuss of George and he seemed to enjoy it a lot, especially when Bill and Bob sat on either side of him to revive The Martin Brothers again. Although unable to form words, he hummed the harmonies perfectly!

But one of the most significant excursions came when it was arranged for him to be taken to a Water Rat's lodge meeting, the first one he had been able to attend in over two years. Although it was difficult to get him up the stairs into the room, once there the evening was a success for all involved. With King Rat Bernard Bresslaw presiding, it was reported in the G.O.W.R.'s newsletter thus, *"The entire lodge immediately erupted in a great emotional wave of genuine affection, warmth and brotherly love, rarely, if ever, seen before. A standing ovation and deafening applause which echoed around the room... and there in our midst, was Past King Rat, Badge of Merit, George Martin, sitting in his special chair at the end of King Rat's table. PKR George, although unable to reply vocally, sat there wreathed in smiles, with tears of joy trickling down his crumpled face and acknowledging the plaudits by giving us the 'thumbs up' sign."*

He lived for five more years, the vast majority of it being in the confines of the Royal Star and Garter Home. The G.O.W.R. gave Maggie plenty of support and his true friends continued to visit him. Every now and then a face would turn up from his distant past, just to say hello. They usually only made it the once. By the end, he was truly institutionalized, and I used to wonder what thoughts were still going around in his mind. As I have already stated, he appeared content, happy even. Perhaps he saw his predicament as a great Heaven sent release from the troubles which were weighing up against him. Sometimes he seemed to be elsewhere, in fact a lot of the time, in the depths of his mind, he probably was, still living the active life of The Casual Comedian. One thing was for sure, he could certainly look back on some enjoyable memories...

Late in 1991, we were told that he had cancer. From then on, the visits to see him had an extra poignancy about them, but outwardly

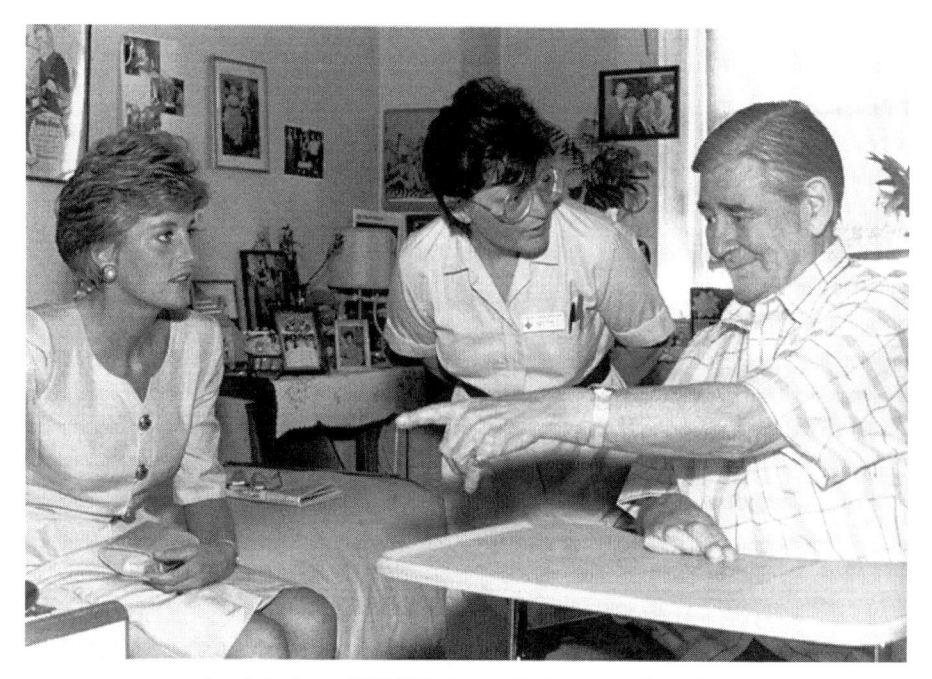

A visit from HRH Diana, Princess of Wales.

he seemed the same. Eventually he was on a lot of medication and the last time I saw him he was in bed giggling like a schoolboy.

With a broad smile he squeezed my wrist and was in a really good mood, largely "away with the fairies" because of the drugs, but still aware of what was going on. When I left him, it was with a feeling of finality.

The next day, November 4th, as I rehearsed with my duo partner, I got a phone call from Ray's wife who had just heard that my father had died.

Chapter 23

REFLECTIONS

George Martin was 69 years old when he passed on. Not a huge age, especially as he had spent five of those years trapped in a damaged body, but it had been a full life.

As the heyday of his fame was long gone, no mention of his death reached the national press, but the entertainment trade journals thought it significant. He also made the Aldershot News, complete with a picture, but I think it was only because of the tribute Arthur English paid to him.

The day after George died, a much more important death (for the general public) took place when the tycoon Robert Maxwell fell overboard from his yacht in the Mediterranean. (Strangely enough, Maxwell had a strong family connection because Bill's second daughter, Andrea, had worked as his personal assistant for years.)

George's funeral took place on Thursday 14th. November at Streatham Park Crematorium. The G.O.W.R. had taken over the arrangements and it was a true show-business affair attended by many Water Rats, Lady Ratlings, numerous friends from all walks of life and a gaggle of mysterious faces, several of them female. So much of his life had been a mystery to us...

The chapel was packed, standing room only, and with so many well known personalities, it resembled a checklist of the entertainment profession. The Welsh comedian King Rat Wyn Calvin spoke solemnly about the loss of a much loved Brother and the magician David Berglas, as Preceptor of the Order, gave a moving valediction. Vocalists Robert Earl and Bruce Trent sang beautifully. Then George's close pal, the one who was often thought in variety to be his "blood" brother, Joe Church, stepped forward to speak. It was a heartfelt speech, full of just the right blend of humour and pathos, and at the end of it, Joe, always a "softie", broke down and wept. It was too much for Sue and I and we put our arms around each other and joined him. I saw tears in Ray's eyes too.

On the back of the Order of Service programme, the Poet Laureate of the Rats, PKR Charlie Chester, had written...

To the Memory of Past King Rat
GEORGE MARTIN, B.M., Past Preceptor

The Empty Chair in Lodge now stands,
And we, with heavy hearts
Give silent salutation as a Brother now departs.
George Martin,
The Casual Comedian leaves the stage,
And only those who knew and loved him well, can gauge
The loss that we now share.
And we remember all too well
The cross he had to bear.
Actor, writer, musician, wit
These attributes were only part of it...
And though he took them all within his stride
He reached the prime of life and was denied.
For then he had a different world to face
The time when his great courage took first place.
And yet, let those with memories not despair
For there is much to share...
We know he made his name for all of that,
And then the crowning claim... to be King Rat.
He leaves us now and prayers go to the Lord
That in the life beyond
His limbs and voice will be restored...
And George, as you now sleep,

Your family and Brother Rats your memory will keep;
And though there will be weeping for a while,
The legacy you leave will be a smile...
To Maggie and to Brother Bill and all those you held dear,
We tender them a comfort, with a love that is sincere.
So travel on dear George, to where all earthly troubles cease,
We ask the Lord, in one accord...
To rest your soul in peace.

I guess its the same feeling for most people when they lose a parent, but, to me, the world seemed an odd, empty place without him.

Ray collected his ashes from the undertaker and we discussed what should be done with them.

On a cold, misty December morning Ray and I made our way to Aldershot cemetery. We were the only ones there, I think, and the atmosphere was bleak. Trudging through the headstones, we found the Martin family plot and stood silently reading the inscriptions for Bill, Lil and Rita.

We wanted it to be a tender moment; a final tribute to our dad as we scattered his ashes onto the grave of his dad, mum and sister, but it did not go smoothly. For a start, I was surprised by just how much volume of ash there actually was. As we attempted to make a team effort to upend the urn and pour our dad's remains evenly across the plot, a breeze blew them around in a haphazard cloud. The distribution of the ashes seemed to go on forever and by the time we had emptied the urn, a white, powdery mess was all over the place.

It formed a thick crust over the surface of the grave site and looked awful. We had to leave it though, and a short while later, Bob told us that on his next visit to the plot he found that the ashes had frozen into a coagulated lump which stood out like a jagged coal heap. Fortunately, he took some soil from the surrounding area and was able to disguise our handiwork.

At first, I felt bad about this, and somewhat stupid, but, on reflection, I think it was The Casual Comedian having his last laugh.

On Sunday May 3rd. 1992, the G.O.W.R. staged a tribute show for George at the Churchill Theatre Bromley.

Maggie was allotted a dozen tickets for the family but because a rift had grown between her and us (George's children), she gave them away to friends. Bill, however, arranged for some extra tickets for us, although Sue was unable to attend. Bill could not go either, because he was abroad.

Ray and I turned up on the night with our cousin Al, (Bob and Joyce's son) only to be told that our tickets had been re-allocated to someone else's demands. We were speechless. The show was a total sell-out and there we were, in the theatre foyer, with herds of punters flooding past us to take their seats.

"Who are you anyway?" asked the indignant box office attendant.

I turned around and pointed to the huge picture of my dad which was displayed prominently above the entrance to the stalls. Underneath it was a notice which stated that the whole night was dedicated to his memory.

"We are *his* sons and nephew," I said, but it cut no ice at all..

Eventually we managed to track down the G.O.W.R.'s administrator who I had spoken to that very week to arrange the tickets. He was embarrassed but unable to offer an explanation as to what had gone wrong. In the confusion, he disappeared, leaving us completely flummoxed. To this day it has never been explained to me what happened.

With Don Shearman's Orchestra already playing the overture, we had begun to resign ourselves to the unbelievable notion that we were going to be denied entry to our father's tribute show, when somebody came to the rescue. A young man in a bow tie approached us and said, "I believe you are George Martin's sons?"

Confirming this, we were pleased to hear that this man was the Front of House Manager and was the son of Buddy Logan who George had worked that double act with in Canada during the war.

"My father was always so full of praise for your dad," he grinned and I replied that the feeling was mutual. When we told him about our problem, Mr. Logan Junior was very concerned and promised to do all he could to get us in to the show, but with the opening act about to come on stage, this was a tall order.

"Follow me," he said, and he led us to the lighting box where he ushered us in to find a position looking over the shoulder of the engineer through his viewing panel. Apologising that it was the best he could do, Logan Junior left us to it. He *had* done his best, but it was far from satisfactory. Ray and I looked at each other in despair, and not a little anger.

From what we could see, on either side of the engineer's head, the show got off to a great start with a jolly group of Water Rats taking the stage for the opening. Then came The Bevs, on form, as usual, followed by an introductory bit of patter from Roy Hudd...

It was going to be quite a show, but from our position we felt like outsiders, as if we had sneaked in via the fire exit. Ray was particularly incensed and muttering, "I can't stand this," he walked out.

Al and I stayed put for the remainder of the first half, watching spots from trumpeter Joan Hinde, Davy Kaye, Henry Cooper, Bernard Bresslaw and the current King Rat Bert Weedon, then we made our way to the bar where we found Ray, seething.

It had been quite an insult to us, but at least the show was successful. Although we never went back in for the second half, apparently it maintained the standard and there was terrific response to Len Lowe and David Lodge (who made much of the raffle), singer Lyn Paul, comic Charlie Smithers and the top of the bill, Frankie Vaughan.

Afterwards, we hung around for a while for the drinks reception and told those who would listen of our grievance, but although we received much sympathy, the moment was gone. Maggie was swanning around like the star of the show with Henry Cooper on one arm and Danny La Rue on the other. Always in her element in such a situation, her reaction to us was cool, to say the least. When I mentioned dad's funeral she icily snapped, "Oh, were you there?"

Afterwards, I said to Ray, "Do you think we should try to get into the Rats?"

Without hesitation he replied, "I think our time has passed."

The main plus side of the evening was that the show raised over £8,000 for charity.

For a while I had to endure various colleagues in the business saying things like, "So now you've inherited the Martin fortune". They meant it good naturedly, but many believed it. How wrong they were. A lot of money had passed through George's hands for sure, but by the end there was nothing left but debt.

Ray cleared out the office in the flat, so all we inherited really were boxes of old scripts, and his accordion which needed repairing before it could be playable again. (This proved to be financially unviable.) Bill, Bob and Joyce cleared a lot of outstanding debt for Maggie, plus the G.O.W.R. continued to look after her in her new role as a PKR's widow, but she still harboured a grudge against we Martin offspring.

After a while, I decided that this was ridiculous and I made the effort to go and see her to "bury the hatchet". She received me warmly this time, and appeared pleased that I was offering to clear the air. However, she remained convinced that we had somehow "wronged" her and had been a "disappointment". I honestly do not know how she arrived at this conclusion but I am glad that she was able to end her days knowing that at least a little oil had been poured upon the troubled waters.

It was sad because she became a quite a lonely figure, still suffering with money problems, a far cry from the days when she and George had been riding high in show-business circles. Of course, real friends still helped her but it could never be the same and, for somebody like Maggie, it was extremely hard. Although a long term tenant, the flat's landlord was determined to get her out and was being rather heartless about her predicament. When the dining room ceiling collapsed and she ended up virtually living in the kitchen, it was the final straw.

As I sat with her over coffee in that kitchen, she put on a brave face, but I felt I could hear the distant ghosts of all those happier times which had once resounded within those walls.

On January 9th. 1994 I was initiated into the G.O.W.R., an immensely proud moment for me as I really did feel an ethereal empathy with my dad as I stood in that lodge room for the first time. (My proposer was Bill and my seconder Joe Church.) That night I was told that Maggie was in hospital in intensive care with liver failure, and that I had best go to see her immediately.

I went the next day and was shocked to see a yellow, skeletal figure, fed by drips and gasping for air. She was heavily sedated but I think she knew me as I showed her the Rat's emblem in my lapel.

Within three days she died.

So, on a physical level, few mementoes remained behind of George Martin.

Not even a headstone to mark his final resting place.

There are some audio recordings of a few of his radio broadcasts but no filmed record of his act. It seems that virtually none of his television appearances were archived, although I was told that one of his "Ad-Mag" programmes was preserved; not that I have been able to locate it. The *Looks Familiar* shows he appeared in still exist, for anyone who is willing to pay a rather steep fee for a copy, also his appearance in that B.B.C. sketch with Terry-Thomas from the 1956 show *We Are Your Servants*. In the early '80s, a T.V. documentary about the Water Rats was made and he is seen talking, briefly, on that. Some silent black and white film footage too, of the Water Rats in attendance at Arthur Haynes' funeral in 1966, and, if you look quickly, George can be spotted walking out of the church with Jimmy Tarbuck.

Not much to show for a long, distinguished career as a performer. Of course, his real legacy remains in the credits as a writer for so many high profile light entertainment shows.

And then there is that elusive short cinema film about the Windmill, *Dawn in Piccadilly*, which I finally managed to track down. The British Film Institute has a copy but informed me that it has been assigned what they call "Master Status" and, for preservation reasons, is therefore unavailable for viewing. Well, I am all for preservation, but what is the point of preserving something if no one is allowed to see it?

So it would seem that the magic of George's casual variety act must remain in the memories of the few people still alive, at the time of writing, who actually saw him perform. Their words are all we are left with as evidence that he was rather special.

The last time I spoke to Bob Monkhouse; I was engaged as what is known as a "dummy contestant" on his game show *Family Fortunes*. Bob was a genuinely nice man with an encyclopaedic knowledge of the entertainment world. "George was a big influence on me in my early days. Always very generous with a gag," he said, "I could never understand why he didn't become a much bigger name than he was."

Says Ed "Stewpot" Stewart, "I liked George's line 'Radio is the mother of television, and they're still looking for the father!' I use it to this day!"

And when I met up with comedian/actor Joe Baker in Hollywood he said, with a twinkle in his eye, "Me and your dad had a lot of fun in the old days. I could tell you a few things, but it wouldn't be right"! This meeting took place at the Magic Castle theatre club, a magnificent venue which was being managed by another old chum of George's, Billy McComb.

"Ahhh, me n' your pop," drawled Billy wistfully, in his lilting Irish brogue.

We still occasionally receive residual payments for repeats, extracts and DVD sales of some of his old shows, and up until a few years ago money would come in from his PRS song-writing royalties, but it is getting less and less. What really frustrates me is when his name comes up and most people still confuse him with the Beatles' George Martin.

I know his heyday was a long time ago but it is important for me to preserve his memory. Regardless of my proud relationship with him, I think he deserves his place in show-biz history. He earned it.

Perhaps the last tribute should come from Royston Mayoh whose words seem to sum it all up;

"George was a superb human being, apart from being a very important writer in T.V.. His work was so good that the performers who benefited from it always looked as if they were ad-libbing. That was just one of his many talents."

In the late 1950s, Royston was a T.V. cameraman at the ABC Studios in Didsbury and, as a hobby, he and his writing partner, David Lamb, would submit material for all kinds of T.V. and radio shows of the day.

Royston continues, *"The Ponderosa was a late night cabaret club in*

Chorlton, a suburb of Manchester. George Martin was advertised as **top of the bill** *there and as George was a regular on 'Workers Playtime', I couldn't wait to see this popular 'family' radio performer work live, and was especially intrigued to see how his very individual 'material' would go down with a northern late night (and largely drunk) audience. I was convinced that in order to survive he would have to include some raunchy gags and perform very differently to his more ordered and casual theatre and radio style.*

How wrong was I?

George was nationally famous for his incredibly laid back and casual style so he did what he did best. Instead of faking large amounts of false energy and trying to shout over the audience, 'George Martin' was 'George Martin' right from his introduction, which incidentally was made by the resident Ponderosa compere Ray Cameron who, sadly, is no longer with us but lives on through his son Michael MacIntyre.

After Ray's announcement, George strolled onto the stage taking forever to get to the mic stand, and instead of the audience shouting predictable abuse like 'Get on with it', the applause grew louder and louder and suddenly it was apparent that here was a performer who owned the stage and who was actually able to manipulate and win over an audience just by sheer charm and authority.

George stood there with his pipe and just talked. The audience were captivated and all too soon his act was over and he strolled off, just as slowly, to rapturous applause.

I went backstage to meet this remarkable comedian, and discovered that off stage he was a quiet, humble and kind gentleman with a presence and charisma not normally found in Manchester Club Land.

It was a good few years before I was promoted to Trainee T.V. Director from my previous job as a T.V. cameraman with a hobby. Suddenly that 'hobby' had become my job! What bliss. Within months of my apprenticeship, I was asked to sit in on the studio element of 'Candid Camera' hosted by the star of BBC's 'What's my Line' panel show, David Nixon. It is impossible for me to fully describe the extraordinary impact on my senses during these 'heady' days as each day was even more full of new discoveries and new people than the last; so to see a familiar face, albeit in an unfamiliar setting, was a joy to behold.

It was, of course, GEORGE MARTIN, the very George Martin that I had seen and met in the Ponderosa Club. After re-introducing myself (and to my utter amazement he actually remembered that first meeting) I discovered that he was not there as a performer but rather as a writer and collaborative adviser to David Nixon.

Before a programme actually started rehearsing in the studio there was always an 'office' meeting where scripts and running orders were, privately, discussed and finalised. These meetings were only attended by the Producer, the Director, the Star and the Writer. The crew were not invited, and, because, up until this time I had been very much crew, all this was new and mysterious.

I soon learnt that this 'writer' George Martin, was an expert at discussing and 'reading' other peoples styles and characteristics and one of the finest diplomats I had ever witnessed.. '… I think he may react better if we re-wrote the question….'…. 'Perhaps we could tighten this link up without losing any of its meaning….', '….I may well be wrong, but would these two items in the running order have more value if we transposed them..?' These are examples of the typical George Martin style of contribution to a production meeting. Anyone else, less diplomatic, or wet around the ears, like me, would have simply charged in and said '….We need to change the question…', '…This waffle needs a major cut…' '… These two items are, blatantly, in the wrong place…' which, while to the point, stood a very good chance of creating a negative atmosphere and thus reducing the creative value of the meeting.

Yes indeed, George Martin had a lot to teach, and it was my good fortune to find that I was allocated onto programmes where George was Associate Producer and/or Writer. The bonus was that if George was involved in the creative production team he was also co-opted as the person to get the live studio audience in the right 'mind-set' for the show, This used to be called 'A Welcome' but later became known as 'A Warm-Up'.

It was years later when I became Producer/Director of the 'The David Nixon Magic Show' that I discovered a rare talent of George Martin which stunned me on a regular weekly basis. On each episode of this show, David Nixon had many guests, and they were not just conjurers and illusionists, but unpredictable and unlikely guests who would be a big surprise for the audience both in the studio and at home. They would be interviewed by David and either wittingly, or unwittingly, become a part of a David Nixon magic trick performed in David's' own individualistic style.

Of course I knew that most of David's 'jokes' and 'one-liners' had been created by George, but what I didn't know was that George had also provided the guests with their own 'one-liners' and 'jokes'. This may sound obvious and easy, until you realise that each and every personality has an individual style of presentation, speech, timing and emphasis. What will work for one personality will not for another. George was the first writer that I had ever met who had the knowledge, talent and wisdom to be able to write 'bespoke' material for each and every individual personality that ever appeared on David's show.

Later George did the same on the 'Basil Brush Show' with Basil's guests. What many people might not know is that Basil Brush would never have been an item were it not for George.

My last recollection of George was visiting him, after his stroke, in Richmond. Many old pros would sit and regale joke after joke for George, in the full knowledge that although the stroke had, cruelly, taken away his beautiful voice, he was very much still with us. He sat without making a sound, but his eyes told us all what he was thinking and that he was still enjoying meeting his friends.

In this day of the fast turnover celebrity culture, it is wonderful to look back at those who had a lasting and influential talent. It is true to say that the whole world of entertainment would have been a more lack-lustre industry without their inspiration.

GEORGE MARTIN is, and will always be, at the very top of my personal list of influential comedy writers, performers and, above all else as a friend."

All things must pass, times move on and tastes change. And yet, paradoxically, things often have a habit of coming full circle.

Although George struggled with many aspects of modern show-business, he probably would have been gratified to witness what eventually happened. That is to say the line between 'mainstream' and 'alternative' gradually grew more and more indistinct until it merged into one. The difference disappeared. Following the revolution, when all the old standards were rejected and cool young 'stand-ups' would never consider "selling out" by appearing on the Royal Variety Show, there came a time when it all became acceptable again. An honour, in fact. At last, it seemed, a simple basic fact was recognized; something is either funny or its not.

Some of the most reactionary and outrageous performers began to make appearances for Royalty, as well as on 'family friendly' T.V. shows. And old gags make return visits constantly, albeit that they might be given a more 'up to date' slant. Of course, so much has an "edge" to it now. People are harder to please as we live in a culture of "seen it all before". But humans are still humans and, essentially, they want to be entertained.

Bob and Bill had both gone by 2006. The Martin Brothers were no more. It was the end of an era.

And as for George Martin; ultimately, with echoes of his signature tune, he certainly did a whole lot more than spread just a *little* happiness...

GEORGE MARTIN
"The Casual Comedian"
February 26th 1922 – November 4th 1991

Index of Names

Abicair, Shirley 74, 76
Afton, Richard 54, 117
Allen, Dave 141, 145, 146, 152, 190, 214
Allen, "Pop" 49
Ammonds, Jon 126
Anderson, Moira 144
Anderson, Tom 170, 171
Andrews, Bob 160
Andrews, Eamonn 164, 165
Andrews, Julie 64
Angers, Avril 89
Anka, Paul 150
Askey, Arthur 8, 64
Askwith, Robin 179
Attwell, Winifred 57, 91
Ayres, Emily 6, 9, 15

Bader, Douglas 30
Bachelors, The 125, 172, 173
Baker, Joe 224
Baker, Kenny 72
Baker, Richard 186
Bandy, Kenneth 47
Barker, Fred 134
Barnett, Lady Isobel 83
Bartlett & Ross 103
Bass, Alfie 105
Bassey, Shirley 86
Bear, Nookie 190, 191
Beatles, The 119, 123, 124, 126, 129, 178

Benning, Mary 103
Benson, Ivy 107
Bentine, Michael 65, 67, 186
Berens, Harold 117
Berglas, David 107, 173, 217
Beverley Sisters, The 82, 83, 94, 100, 108, 119, 133, 147, 206-208, 212, 213, 221
Bewes, Rodney 143
Bey, Ali 63
Billy, Mr. 182
Blair, Joyce 43
Blair, Lionel 43, 170
Bogino Troupe, The 57
Bongo, Ali 154, 164, 177, 178, 187
Boyer & Ravel 63
Brambell, William 125
Breeze, Alan 56
Bresslaw, Bernard 215, 221
Brightmore, Alwyn 19
Brooks, Elkie 126
Brough, Peter 64
Brown, Burton 88
Brown, Joe 125
Brush, Basil 134-136, 142-144, 146-148, 163, 164, 168, 172, 179, 182-186, 192, 193, 227
Burdon, Albert 106
Burdon, Bryan 106, 107
Busby, Laddie 179
Bygraves, Max 35, 64, 74

Caan, James 145
Calvert, Penny 49
Calvin, Wyn 217
Cameron, Ray 225
Cantor, Kenny 171
Cantor, Terry 117, 171
Cassavetes, John 145
Chamberlain, Neville 16
Chaplin, Charlie 117
Chapman, Bobby 154
Charisse, Cyd 137
Charles, Ray 126
Charlesworth, Alice 5
Chester, Charlie 57, 117, 218
Chic & Mandi 43
Church, Joe 78, 117, 218, 222
Church/Stark, Pat 147
Clark, Petula 89
Clews, Colin 145
Cluskey, Con 139, 173
Cluskey, Dec 139, 172, 173
Cluskey, Sandy 172
Cluskey, Victoria 172
Cogan, Alma 103, 107
Colehan, Barney 86
Cooper, Elliot 182
Cooper, Henry 2, 170, 221
Cooper, Tommy 40, 70, 71, 119, 125, 160, 164, 186, 190
Cooper/Law, Margaret 50
Coram & Jerry 165
Cotton, Billy 56
Cotton, Bill 183
Courage, Captain 114
Courtenidge, Cicely 78
Craddock, Fanny 109
Craddock, Johnny 109
Crazy Gang, The 67
Creatures, The 124
Crier, Gordon 54
Croft, David 101

Cummings, David 133
Custer, General 147
Cuzik, Pat 112, 113, 122

Dale, Terry 151, 168, 169
Daniels, Paul 186-188
Daniels Trio, Joe 76
Dare Devil Peggy 8
Dagenham Girl Pipers, The 107
Davidson, Jim 191
Davidson, John 150
Davies, Freddie 163
Dawson, Les 2
Day, Robin 111
De Courcey, Roger 190, 191
Delfont, Bernard 51, 67, 70, 169
Desmonde, Jerry 45
Deveen & his New York Blondes 60
Dixey, Phyllis 59
Donegan, Lonnie 90
Doonican, Val 103, 105, 125, 126
Dowler, Cyril 57
Downes, Johnny 133, 134, 142
Driver, Betty 70, 72
Dulay, Peter 203, 204
Duo Russmar 105
Dudley-Evans, Barbara 154
Dukes, Ronnie 193

Earl Mountbatten of Burma 130
Earl, Robert 218
Ebonaires, The 57
Edwards, Jimmy 40, 61, 62, 86
Edwards, Percy 117
Egan, Bill 11, 15, 17, 79
Elliott, Patricia 76
Ellis, Vivian 74
Elrick, George 57, 117
Elvin, Joe 116, 117
Emery, Dick 40
Emney, Fred 117

English, Arthur 41, 42, 48, 94, 106, 180, 192, 216
Eustace, Nip 98, 112, 132, 162
Eva & Nick 56
Evans, Joan 15
Evans, Wilbur 57

Fairbanks, Douglas 8
Fell, Ray 107, 126
Ferrari, Frederick 57
Fields, Gracie 67, 91
Firmin, Peter 144
Fisher, John 187, 188
Flanagan, Bud 1, 125
Fletcher, Cyril 78
Formby, George 67
Forsyth, Bruce 40, 49, 86, 119, 120
Four Ramblers, The 103, 105
Fowlds, Derek 144, 147, 163
Foxes, The (Vicki, Babette & Sasha) 206
Fraser, Bill 57, 105
Freddie & the Dreamers 126
Freeman, Alan 212
Freeman, Harry 117
Freeman, Mrs. 97

Ganjou, Serge 117
Garland, Judy 67
Gay & Barry 60
Gerry & the Pacemakers 214
Gilbert & Sullivan 147, 173
Goons, The 65, 120
Grade, Leslie 51, 67
Grade, Lew 51, 64, 67, 89
Grant, Pauline 56
Green, Hughie 2

Haley, Bill 90
Hancock, Tony 63, 64
Hanley, Jimmy 110

Harding, Gilbert 83
Harding, Jan 195
Harris, Anita 163
Harris, Keith 170, 203-205, 207, 209, 210
Harris, Rolf 2, 139, 144
Hay, Will 1, 67
Hayden, Lynda 179
Hayes, Gabby 197
Haynes, Arthur 1, 81, 117, 223
Hearne, Richard ("Mr. Pastry") 62
Henderson, Dickie 2
Henderson, Margo 105
Hewitt, Doug 14, 15, 24
Hewitt, Florrie 15, 23
Hewitt, Jack 17, 23
Hill, Benny 41, 87, 210
Hill & Billie 104
Hinde, Joan 221
Hindin, Philip 38, 117
Hitler, Adolf 16
Hobbs, Betty 63
Hockridge, Edmund 103
Holliday, Michael 84
Hooper, Frank 39
Hope, Bob 67
Hope & Keen 193
Horne, Kenneth 83-85
Horton, Billy 128
Horton, Gary 206
Houston, Renee 163
Howard, Jayne & Alan 104
Howard, Mr. 182
Howe, Len & Audrey 91
Howerd, Frankie 160, 194
HM The Queen Elizabeth the 2nd. 136, 169
HRH Diana the Princess of Wales 216
HRH The Duke of Edinburgh 136, 157, 161

HRH Princess Anne 172
Hudd, Roy 163, 221
Hughes, David 57

Jackley, Nat 91
Jacques, Hattie 64
Jameson, Rex ("Mrs. Shufflewick") 110
Jewell & Warris 57, 125
Jumel, Betty 101

Kardoma 67
Kaye, Danny 67, 117
Kaye, Davy 221
Kelly, Barbara 83
Kester, Max 39
Killand, Red 169
Kimber, Bobbie 72
King, Cheyenne 163
King, Dave 106, 163, 180
King, Kiowa 163
King, Hetty 57
Krankies, The 190
Kray, Reg 124
Kray, Ron 124

Lamb, Dave 224
La Rue, Danny 221
Laurel & Hardy 8, 70, 117
Law, John 50
Law/Cooper, Margaret 50
Lee Scott, Carol 193
Lennon, John 126
Leno, Dan 1, 117, 160
Lester, Harry 57
Levis, Carrol 35
Lewis, Jerry 67
Little, Rich 150
Little Tich 165
Littler, Emile 87
Lloyd, Reg 44

Lodge, David 221
Logan, Buddy 31, 32, 220
Logan, Jimmy 32
Lord Pilkington 111
Loss, Joe 163
Lovely Dancing Debutantes, The 104
Lowe, Len 221
Lupino, Barry 117
Luton Girls Choir, The 107
Lymon, Frankie 90
Lynn, Vera 2, 89, 130
Lynne, Gillian 56

MacDonald, Aimi 150
MacIntyre, Michael 225
Madden, Cecil 87
Main-Wilson, Dennis 39, 51, 54, 108
Mann, Joan 81
Mantovani 2
Marks, Herbie 57
Marlow, June 110
Marshall, Jack 13, 15, 22
Martin, Andrea 141, 217
Martin, Benjamin 4
Martin, Bill 2, 7, 9, 23, 32, 37, 38, 44, 76, 87, 110, 113, 140-142, 151, 160, 161, 163, 165-169, 171, 195-197, 199, 214, 215, 217, 219, 220, 222, 228
Martin, Dean 67
Martin, Eliza 4
Martin, Fred 4, 5
Martin, Freya 141
Martin, George 1-228
Martin, George (Producer) 129, 224
Martin, Kate 5
Martin, Laura 141, 214
Martin, Mike 1-228

Martin, Ray 34, 44, 50, 57, 67, 70, 81, 99, 101, 103, 104, 123, 127-129, 132, 161, 200, 206, 209, 218, 220
Martin, Rita 8, 9, 23, 32, 33, 161, 219
Martin, Sue 3, 34, 44, 50, 57, 67, 70, 81, 99, 101, 103, 104, 123, 127-129, 132, 161, 200, 206, 209, 218, 220
Martin, Sybil 141, 215
Martin, Val 175, 178, 191, 198, 199
Martin, Tony 137
Martin, William (Bill) Sr. 6, 7, 16, 33, 37, 38, 113, 127, 131, 132, 161, 219
Martin, William (1800s) 4
Martin Brothers, The 38, 39, 40-44, 46, 117, 166, 167, 215
Martin/Hewitt, Joan 14-18, 22, 23, 28, 30-34, 37, 44, 46, 50, 52, 53, 57, 67, 70, 77, 82, 85, 86, 88, 101, 104, 106, 107, 112, 113, 115, 121, 122, 127, 128, 132, 135, 139, 140, 151-155, 162, 174, 191, 192, 198
Martin/Seymour-Jones, Trevor 113, 141
Martin/Vinden, Lil 6, 7, 23, 37, 52, 113, 161, 219
Martin & McGowan 25, 33, 34
Martino, Al 78
Marvin, Hank 179
Mason, Rocky 141, 142
Mathieu, Mireille 150
Matthews, Jessie 47
Maxey, Dawn 120
Maxwell, Charles 39
Maxwell, Robert 216
Maynard, Bill 80, 98, 99, 106, 121, 180
Mayoh, Royston 154, 178, 180, 193, 224
McCartney, Paul 123
McComb, Annie 3
McComb, Billy 3, 135, 160, 224

McDevitt, Chas 90, 91
McGivern, Cecil 55
McGowan, Alan 2, 43, 123, 220, 221
McGowan, Bob 2, 25, 26, 28, 31, 32, 37, 38, 42, 43, 44, 76, 121, 140, 161, 166, 167, 170, 173, 174, 192, 209, 215, 219, 222, 228
McGowan/Martin, Joyce 2, 7-9, 16, 23, 32, 43, 76, 121, 122, 140, 142, 166, 167, 174, 192, 209, 222
Medlock & Marlowe 56, 57
Middleton, Cynthia 76, 113, 141
Miller, Max 35, 64
Milligan, Spike 65, 67
Mills, Nat (& Bobbie) 57
Mills, Ronnie 106
Mitchell, Guy 56, 57, 67, 78
Mitchell, Warren 62
Mitchell/Martin, Margaret (Maggie) 2, 109, 110, 112, 121, 124, 126, 127, 131, 135, 139, 140-142, 144, 152-154, 162, 166, 168, 172, 173, 178, 191, 192, 195, 197-201, 204, 208-211, 215, 219, 220-222
Mitchell Singers, George 56
Monkhouse, Bob 57, 87, 118, 139, 163, 194, 223, 224
Monro, Matt 170
Moore, Roger 2
More, Kenneth 40, 86, 87
Morecambe, Eric 3, 55, 119, 183
Morris, Desmond 111
Murdoch, Richard 87
Murray, Chic 43, 186
Murray, Rob 57

Neagle, Dame Anna 179
Neatrour, Andrew 196
Nelson, Bob 60

Nixon, David 83, 133-136, 139, 144, 145, 154, 163, 164, 166, 170, 172, 173, 177-180, 185-187, 193, 205, 225-227
Nixon, Vivienne 173
No Money Down 123
Norden, Dennis 163, 186
North, Roy 163, 182
Novello, Ivor 109

O'Connor, Des 61, 119
O'Sullivan, Gilbert 168
Osborne, Leonard 35
Overbury, Reg 105
Owen, Ivan 134, 144, 168, 182-185

Parlane, Cyril 22, 98
Parlane, Elsie 98
Parsons, Nicholas 173
Paul, Lyn 221
Payne, John 101, 103, 196
Peggy & Bobby 44
Penders, Brian 187
Perry, Jimmy 101
Pertwee, Jon 57
Phillips, Captain Mark 172
Phillips, Woolf 57
Pickles, Wilfred 117
Pink, Wal 117
Pinky & Perky 86
Powell, Sandy 64
Presley, Elvis 91

Race, Steve 110
Raft, George 124
Raphael, Pat 177
Ray, Johnny 89
Ray, Robin 111
Ray, Ted 111, 117, 125, 163
Raymond, Paul 160
Redcliffe, Reggie 60

Redway, Mike 172
Reece, Brian 86
Reid, Beryl 125
Richard, Cliff 91
Richman & Jackson 104
Ritter, Tex 57
Roberts, Ken 44
Robbins, Archie 56
Robbins, Michael 171
Rooney, Mickey 67
Roper, Rex 141, 142
Ros, Edmundo 2
Rose, Clarkson 57, 117
Ross, Chic & Candy 91
Rothwell, Talbot 54
Russell, Fred 57, 166

Savage, Edna 89
Saville, Jimmy 126
Scott, Arthur 117
Scott, Terry 99
Seaforth, Victor 141, 142
Secombe, Harry 40, 65, 67, 87
Sellers, Peter 40, 65, 87, 119, 170
Shadows, The 91
Shaw, Sandie 2
Shearman, Don 220
Shek Ben Ali 60, 91
Sherrin, Ned 108
Sinatra, Frank 67, 68
Sloan, Tom 89
Smithers, Charlie 221
Sparkles, Mr. 18
Spear, Bernard 42
Spear, Eric 39
Spicer, Dennis 89
Steele, Tommy 91
Stevenson, Albert 121
Stewart, Ed 224
Sting 74
Stock, Clive 171

Stokes, John 173
Stonehouse, Julie 23
Stringer, Ronnie 8, 79
Swain, Hal 117

Tango Trio, The 13
Tanner Sisters, The 63
Tarbuck, Jimmy 126, 131, 223
Terry-Thomas 86, 119, 134, 223
Thompson, Daley 201
Three Aberdonians, The 60
Thurber, James 202
Tiller Girls, The 56
Tiny Tim 145
Tonia & Rafael 105
Toomer, Pip 23
Trent, Bruce 218
Trinder, Tommy 1, 64, 163
Turner, Joan 163
Two Pirates, The 60
Tyler, Jean 104

Unwin, Stanley 110

Valentine, Dickie 92
Van Damm, Vivian 40, 41, 46, 48, 49, 52, 53, 86, 87
Vane, Denise 91
Varona, Olga 56
Vauncez, Sydney 192
Vaughan, Frankie 1, 125, 221
Villiers, Iris 99
Vinden, Alice 6, 8
Vinden, Bill 76
Vinden, Doris 6
Vinden, Edie 6
Vinden, George Jr. 6
Vinden, George Sr. 6
Vinden, Gertie 6
Vinden, Ivy 6
Vinden, Mary Ann 6

Vinden, Mike 193
Vinden, Queenie 6
Vinden, Stan 6, 9, 14, 22, 23
Viscount Slim, The 130
Volantes, The 63

Wade, John 145
Waldman, Ronald 55, 87
Walter's Comedy Dogs 60
Warris, Ben 117
Waterman, Dennis 179
Wayne, John 145
Weedon, Bert 173, 221
West, Mr. 11, 18
Western Brothers, The 8
Whittaker, Roger 134
Whelan, Albert 57
Wheel, Checker 60
Wheeler, Jimmy 57, 82
Williams, Bryn 172
Williams, Cissie 62, 88
Williams, Kenneth 84
Wilmott, Bertha 57
Wilton, Robb 1
Wings 179
Winters, Bernie 103, 119
Winters, Mike 103, 119
Wise, Ernie 3, 55, 119, 183
Wisdom, Norman 45, 67, 117, 145
Wong, Eva May 60
Wood, "Wee Georgie" 1, 117, 202
Woodward, Edward 2
Woodward, Milton 104
Wolfit, Sir Donald 125
Worth, Harry 144, 195
Wright, Billy 206, 207

Yardbirds, The 126
Young Brothers, The 105

Zio Angels Troupe, The 107

About the author

Mike Martin is a musician, performer, writer and lecturer.
He is a founder member of the comedy combo
The London Philharmonic Skiffle Orchestra
www.LPSO.co.uk

Other published works:
Noddies - The Film Extra's Guide (Arlon) ISBN 0-946273-22-7 and
From Crockett to Custer (Trafford) ISBN 1-4120-1878-1

POSTSCRIPT
Ray Martin became a Water Rat in 2012.
A new generation of Martin Brothers...